Praise for *Transitions at the Top*

"Without a doubt, corporations have raised their game on the use of various techniques to improve the likelihood that externally hired talent will succeed in their most business-critical roles. What many companies haven't done, however, is to spend the same amount of time on building a set of transition practices to further increase the probability these executives will thrive and prosper in their new roles and in their new companies. The cost of a failed transition is monumental, and comes in the form of missed market opportunities, a loss of business momentum, reputational damage, and potential damage to the credibility of the CEO and/or the company's board of directors. Fortunately, Dan Ciampa and David Dotlich outline a practical, compelling playbook that if properly executed, will substantially increase the chance of success in senior leadership transitions. A timely and important book on a very important subject."

L. Kevin Cox
Chief Human Resources Officer
American Express Company
Director - Kraft Foods Group
Director - Corporate Executive Board

"Senior transitions are seminal events but are often botched, at great cost to the company and its shareholders. Too often succession decisions are made by a board, with those crucial first months then left entirely to the new manager to navigate. This book takes a different vantage point and illuminates the critical role of the company, its board, and senior managers in making sure those vital successions work. Written in a straightforward, practical manner, a must read for all involved."

Ken Leibler
CEO Liberty Financial Companies and former President American Stock Exchange
Director - Northeast Utilities
Trustee - Putnam Investments Funds

"*Transitions at the Top* is a welcome, long-overdue addition to our thinking about leadership and transitions. Far too little attention has been paid to the dynamics and consequences of CEO succession, especially to the critical role the organization plays in driving success or failure. As Ciampa and Dotlich clearly demonstrate, the costs of botched succession processes are very high. And what it takes to make them work is not rocket science, nor is it overly costly or burdensome. It just takes discipline, clarity about roles, and unswerving commitment to the right principles and processes. Follow their advice and the result will be world-class succession planning and implementation. This is a book that every CEO, Board member and senior HR executive should read."

Michael Watkins
Author "First 90 Days"
Co-Founder Genesis Advisors

Transitions at the Top

Transitions at the Top

What Organizations Must Do to Make Sure New Leaders Succeed

Dan Ciampa and David L. Dotlich

WILEY

To Bruce Henderson, Chris Argyris, and Dick Beckhard. Friends who, over the years, took the time to react, challenge, and guide through my various transitions.

Dan Ciampa

CONTENTS

Preface   *xiii*

Acknowledgements   *xix*

Introduction   **1**

The Transition Challenge   3

The Roots of Failure   7

   Complexity   7

   Thinking Errors   8

   Execution Errors   9

   Roles for Success   11

      The Board's Role   11

      The CEO's Role   13

      The CHRO's Role   15

      The Senior Managers' Role   17

1 Complexity and Critical Crossroads   **21**

Complexity   25

   Individual Adjustments   25

      CEO   25

      Board   27

      CHRO   29

      Senior Managers   32

   Systemic Adjustments   34

      Strategic   34

      Operational   36

      Political   39

      Cultural   41

Summary   45

2 **Three Destructive Myths**   **47**

Myths Plaguing Transitions at the Top   56

*Myth 1: People Join Companies All the Time … It's No
Big Deal*   *58*

*Myth 2: Our Job Is Done When the One We Want Says
"Yes"*   *62*

Myth 3: We Know What He Can Do   *65*

How Transition Myths Bar Productive Thinking   71

Lack of Empathy   *71*

Lack of Learning   *73*

Lack of Questioning   *74*

Leaving Tough Questions Unanswered   76

Summary   79

3 **Errors of Execution**   **81**

Relationship between Incumbent and Successor   85

Preparing for Only One Transition   90

The Leader Who Departs   *90*

Derivative Defections   *93*

Mismanaging the Transition Process   96

*Not Organizing and Interpreting the Right
Information*   *96*

How Things Really Get Done   97

Culture and Power Structure   98

Power and Influence   104

Not Preparing Major Players for the Right Roles   *106*

Mishandling the Onboarding of the New Leader   *109*

Summary   114

4 **The Board's Role**   **117**

Directors as Major Players   121

Oversight for the Transition   127

Managing Relationships   134

Judging Performance 143
Expectations 146
Cultural and Political Attention 148
Summary 150

5 The CEO's Role 153
Controlling the Steps and Pace 157
Role 158
The Search and the Transition 162
Ensuring Other Players Do What They Must 166
Self-Management and Self-Awareness 171
Summary 177

6 The CHRO's Role 179
Great Senior Staffing Support 185
Help for the New Leader 192
What the New Leader Must Do 192
Learning 193
Visioning 194
Coalition Building 196
Methods and Mechanisms for Relationships 198
Connecting 201
Listening 203
Summary 210

7 The Senior Manager's Role 215
Shaping Organization Opinion 220
Delivering Support 227
Building Winning Relationships 234
Summary 241

8 Summary 245

Index 253

List of Figures

Figure I-1   Framework for Transition Success   19

Figure 1-1   The Way People Do Things Around Here   42

Figure 3-1   RASI Chart   107

Figure 3-2   First DraftThat the CHRO and CFO Reviewed with the
                  CEO to Begin the Process   110

Figure 4-1   The Board's Transition Role   127

Figure 5-1   The CEO's Transition Role   158

Figure 5-2   Transition Phases   163

Figure 6-1   The CHRO's Transition Role   184

Figure 6-2   Roles and Relationships   200

Figure 7-1   The SeniorManagers' Transition Role   220

List of Features

Transitions at the Top Fail Because   24

Transition Myths   58

The Transition is over When   62

Errors of Execution   84

PREFACE

It's never smooth or easy to transfer power from one leader to a successor. The incumbent may not be ready to leave because he believes there's more to do, but his board of directors insists. Or the board may not have the experience or patience to fulfill its accountability of ensuring leadership continuity. Or the search process may not be coordinated effectively by the human resources department, which may also fail to devise a useful, efficient onboarding program for the new leader. Or the organization may not be prepared for the changes that a leadership handoff brings, including the senior managers who may resist the new leader because one of them expected to be promoted or because a leadership change will threaten their power. For the new leader hired from the outside, especially one taking the chief executive officer (CEO) title for the first time, these gaps in thinking and execution by the company she is joining can cause her to fail. And the challenges become even more difficult to overcome when the leadership transition coincides with a change in strategic direction. In fact, changes in leadership are often made to seek changes in company strategy.

Before deciding to write this book, we asked ourselves whether the topic of transitions at the top deserved the effort that would have to go into it and whether another book on leadership was needed. We believe that most books do nothing more than repeat what has already been said and offer nothing novel to the question they pretend to answer. Indeed, most books should be articles. In the final analysis, our readers will be the judges of whether it adds something worthwhile. But, it is important to explain why we believe this book is needed.

We decided to write it (and to write a book rather than an article) because leadership transitions are complex, seminal events that herald a new era in the life of a company, and too many of them fail. As we'll show, when they fail, the costs are enormous—financially in lost revenue, strategically in misguided direction, operationally in loss of stability and predictability, culturally in damage to relationships and coalitions, and perhaps most tragic, personally in derailed careers. Transitions are big deals, and when they go wrong it is a setback for everyone involved.

Some failures happen because the new leader offered the top job was not ready for it yet and didn't have the help needed to overcome his shortcomings. But, we believe at least as often, the transition fails because the company doesn't do its part to ensure it succeeds.

Our experience suggests two core propositions. First, company missteps are a significant contributing factor to the high failure rate of executives at the top. They are as potent a reason for failure as what the incoming leader does or does not do. Second, the success rate of leadership transitions will not improve until CEOs who are preparing to pass the reins, boards that hire or promote successors and oversee the handoff, and the senior managers most involved in the hiring and assimilation of new leaders more fully understand what the hiring organization must do and avoid to improve the chances of success.

Right from the Start,[1] which Dan coauthored, was published in 1999 to introduce the topic of the new leader's role and responsibility in a transition at the top. It broke new ground as it offered a framework, examples of successes and failures, and advice to those hired as the number two expecting to succeed the CEO or those entering directly into the top position. In that book's conclusion, a section called "Implications for Future Research" suggested that the company's role be a topic that should be included in the responsibilities of the board, CEO, and the human resources department. The success of *Right from the Start* spawned other books on related topics, including principles of leadership succession, details of the transition process, and models and programs for senior-level onboarding. In 1999 there was no substantial onboarding market; today, it is a multibillion-dollar market for consultants worldwide. But, while these areas have been explored, there has been nothing written on the company's role in leadership transitions, at least from the literature searches we have done. So, we decided to write this book because it's time to explore this issue in a serious way. We also wrote this book because in our years of experience advising boards, CEOs, and senior teams, we continue to observe many implicit obstacles to the successful transfer of power, which are neither surfaced openly nor dealt with directly. Inherent in the pages that follow is our belief that even though companies state they want new leaders to succeed, they lack a working model of support, feedback, openness, and continuous improvement necessary for those new in a top position to succeed. Such a working model is required to counter an environment of competitiveness, silos, and more concern for enhancing one's own power than for what is good for the entire organization—conditions that characterize day-to-day life in most organizations and have the effect of rejecting the assimilation and contribution of new executives. We also recognize that, once embedded in the organization's culture, they are not easy to change. Indeed, in addition to years of advising others, we have experienced firsthand how difficult it is to change behavior and comfortable habits as members of boards of directors and as chairmen and CEOs. Our own attempts, frustrations, successes, and mistakes at getting top-level transitions right are embedded in the model we've proposed.

We hope this book sparks a host of new conversations among boards and executive teams about how to improve leadership transitions in their organizations. We hope also to add significantly and importantly to the literature so that the major players involved in a senior-level transition and those to whom they turn for help are better prepared. We do so first by detailing the problems associated with leadership transitions that lie within or are created by companies that hire or promote new leaders into the most senior position. Second, we define the roles and responsibilities of the key players involved and explore the interaction between them. Third, throughout the book we offer principles, guidelines, and specific actions that companies should employ to have the best chance for their leadership transitions to succeed.

As important as why we wrote this book is to point out that it is not a how-to manual for transitions. Neither all the potential hurdles that can block a successful handoff nor all the ways they can be overcome are provided here. It would be disingenuous for us to attempt such a thing because it would suggest that transitions at the top are simple. In fact, they are very complex in ways we explain in the chapters that follow.

This book concentrates on "planned transitions." By this we mean the handoffs that occur from an incumbent executive, usually the CEO, to a successor while both are on the job. We stress, however, that most of the issues confronting CEOs and successors during planned transitions emerge in similar form for other senior-level transitions, such as chief operating officer, division president, or executive or senior vice president. As a result, we hope to interest the broadest audience of readers who may be involved in various ways in the transitions of their organizations.

Our opinions are offered primarily to the following groups of readers:

- Members of boards of directors, especially lead directors, nonexecutive chairs, and heads of compensation and nomination and governance committees who must oversee and ultimately be accountable for top-level succession.

- CEOs and executive chairpersons, whose legacies in large part depend on the management of a successful transition.

- Chief human resources officers (CHROs) who are usually called on to manage the transition, coordinate its various parts, and provide the necessary in-house staffing and counsel.

- Senior managers who form the execution cadres that will make the agendas of new leaders in their organizations work and who must prepare the organization for the transition.

- New leaders who, in addition to how they must prepare on their own, need to know what they should expect from a well-run transition.

- Senior partners in private equity or venture capital firms who want to ensure the highest quality of execution by the individuals hired to lead businesses in which they invest and the boards that oversee them.

- Consultants and academics will find much of interest and relevance about the company's role in transitions and related issues of leadership, governance, business policy, strategy, organization culture, and human capital/talent management.

We hope we have provided the most authentic and seasoned portrayal possible of senior leader handoffs. In that we have seen successes and failures of many transitions from inside executive suites and boardrooms, including our own, we cite a host of actual examples to make our points. In a few cases we identify companies and executives by name. In most cases, however, we agreed not to identify individuals or their companies by name. We believe this approach permitted the leaders with whom we talked to describe their experiences and emotions, both positive and negative, with candor. Even so, none of the cases are fictional. Each example happened just as we have recorded it. One or the other of us participated in, witnessed, or discussed directly with key participants everything we have described.

Note

1. D. Ciampa and M. Watkins, *Right from the Start: Taking Charge in a New Leadership Role* (Harvard Business School Press, 1999), 3.

ACKNOWLEDGEMENTS

When something takes as long to be shaped as has this book, the list of people who contribute time, criticism, and ideas is long. First, of course, are the people whom we've had the opportunity to help and the privilege to work with over the courses of our careers. They turned to one of us to help during a time of great importance to their careers and organizations. Some were chairpersons or directors on boards that were in the midst of or were preparing for a top-level handoff; some were CEOs expecting to pass the baton to a successor; some were in charge of human resources functions, trying to add value for the CEO, the board, and the successor plus strengthen the culture of their organizations all at the same time; some were senior managers adapting to a change in leadership; and, some were the new leaders who hoped to move to the top spot or had taken over. Whatever their positions, we tried to give it our best information and counsel and help them face the problems that had to be solved and challenges that had to be met. As we worked together with them, we learned from them as much as they drew from us. The cases, propositions, and conclusions in *Transitions at the Top*, of course, could not have been developed otherwise; and for that, we are grateful.

Particular thanks from Dan go to: Matt Arnold (AstraZeneca), Brenda Barnes (Sara Lee), Dennis Berger (CDW), Tom Bergmann (Harley-Davidson), Joe Bonito (Bank of America), Celia Brown (Willis), Nick Brown (NAC Re), Lisa Buckley (Western Union), Cynthia Carroll (Alcan), Tony Coles (Onyx Pharmaceuticals), Susan Comparato (Syncora Guarantee), Kevin Cox (American Express),

Ken DiPietro (Biogen-Idec), Deborah Dunsire (Millennium Pharmaceuticals), Travis Engen (Alcan), Hugh Farrington (Hannaford Brothers), Jamie Fellowes (Fellowes), CJ Fraleigh (Shearer's), Stan Goldstein (Melville), Peter Greenleaf (AstraZeneca), Bob Haas (Levi-Strauss), John Johnson (ImClone), Bob Joy (Colgate), Julie Klapstein (Availity), Alan Lacy (Sears), Greg Lee (Whirlpool), Ken Leibler (Liberty Financial), Ken Love (Kimball Hill), Fiona Luck (XL Capital), Hank McKinnell (Pfizer), Mel Ming (Sesame Workshop), Brian O'Hara (XL Capital), Marc Oken (Bank of America), Michael Rice (Prudential), Bill Sigmund (GlaxoSmithKline), Tim Schwertfeger (Nuveen), Steve Tregay (FORMA Therapeutics), Mary Wadlinger (FORMA Therapeutics), and Andy Zopp (Exelon).

David would like to thank the following for their input, ideas, and support: Angela Lane, Tim Richmond, Kristen Weirick (AbbVie), Deanna Fidler (Aetna), Chris Blake, Sean Carroll, Martine DeFazio, Ahmed Fahour (Australia Post), Shari Ballard, Hubert Joly (Best Buy), Jean-Luc Duchemin (Carlson-Wagonlit Travel), Frank Appel, Roger Crook, Jürgen Gerdes, Rolf-Dirc Roitzheim, Larry Rosen, Ken Allen, Nicole Cipa, (Deutsche Post DHL), Bina Chaurasia, Selina Millstam, Arturo Poire, Hans Vestberg (Ericsson), Kevin Wilde (General Mills), Mindy Grossman (HSN), Matt Schuyler, Chris Nassettta (Hilton), Ken Meyers (Hospira), Tim Huval, Roger Cude (Humana), Sharon Brady (ITW), Jamie Dimon, Carlo Frappolli (JPMorgan Chase), Craig Buffie, Brian Fishel, Beth Mooney (KeyBank), Todd Fisher, Henry Kravis, Joan Lavin, Marc Lipschultz (KKR), Kate Guthrie, Ulf Bengtsson (Lloyd's), Lucien Alzari, Vincent Clerc, Ricardo Sookdeo (Maersk), Patty McPhee, Carol Surface, Matt Walter (Medtronic), Dottie Brienza (Merck), Vicki Lostetter (Microsoft), Annie Brown, Cameron Clyne, Louise Harvey-Wills, Anthony Healy, Rosemary Rogers, Andrew Thorburn (National Australia Bank), David Ayre, Monique Matheson, Mark Parker, Mike Tarbell (Nike), Carolynn Cameron, Peter Fasolo, Alex Gorsky, Mary Lauria, Mike Ullman,

Bill Weldon (JnN), Allan Church (Pepsi), Gordon Ballantyne, Tracey Gavegan, Catherine Livingstone, Katherine Paroz, Andy Penn, David Thodey (Telstra), Susan Chambers (Walmart), Paul Brown (Arby's), and Tad Walker (PartnerRe).

Some people who deserve special thanks took the time over the past couple of years to be sounding boards as we were refining our thoughts and trying to put years of experience in a readable form. For Dan, they are: Rick Anicetti, Greg Crecos, Mike Esposito, Gayl Mileszko, Jeff Miller, Colleen Reitan, Sally Sterling, and Liza Wright. For David, they are the outstanding team at Pivot Leadership, including Cade Cowan, Dennis Baltzley, Ron Meeks, Órla NicDomhnaill, Andrew Pek, Stacey Philpot, Derek Thompson, Alison Tisdall, Michael Van Impe, Albertina Vaughn, Rich Wetzler, all of the Pivot Principals and Associates, the Pivot Board of Advisers, Peter Cairo, David Miller, Jim Shanley, Janet Spencer; and our new colleagues from Korn Ferry: Gary Burnison, Kevin Cashman, Stu Crandell, RJ Heckman, Lewis Rusen, Brian Suh; and Dennis Casey with whom we are now teaming to better serve Boards, CEOs, and new leaders in the future. Candid feedback and support is always provided by Inger Buus, Mickey Connolly, Jill Connor, Barbara Elsberg, Richard Finn, Jackie Gittins, Neil Johnston, David Lange, Jim Motroni, Sonja Muller, Terry O'Connor, Adam Ortiz, Colin Pidd, Doug Ready, Steve Rhinesmith, and Antoine Tirard.

We also had the benefit of strong editorial support and administrative help. John Butman helped in preparing early materials for publisher proposals, and Bill Birchard helped us with shaping our case studies to emphasize the complexity of the transition process. Neda Talebzadeah and Anna Weiss provided important and useful research help. Luisa de Castro was always there when needed, as usual, and thanks to Kevin Tang for his help. Linda Zukauskas was indispensable in both researching and preparing the manuscript through many drafts. On the Pivot Leadership team, Anesu Mandisodza and

Joni Preece helped with the interviews and data analysis, and Brenda Fogelman has always been able to quietly and competently make things happen, from the beginning.

Dan Ciampa

Boston

David Dotlich

New York and Portland

INTRODUCTION

This is a book about transitions at the top of organizations. Like other books on this topic, it offers an answer to why the success rate is so low of those who have been hired or promoted into senior leadership positions and suggests ways to increase the probability of success. But, unlike others that have been published, this book deals with an aspect of transitions at the top that has been ignored. This will be, as far as we know, the first book to focus attention exclusively on the role of the organization and all of the key people involved with senior leader transitions, including the various individuals involved, systems, and processes. It delves deeply into what directors, the CEO, the head of human resources, and the other senior managers must do individually and collectively to best ensure the handoff from an incumbent leader to the one who will step in to replace her in a planned transition. In particular, it details:

- How the board should manage its accountability for overall continuity of leadership

- How the incumbent CEO should direct the entire sequence of activities that lead to a handoff of authority, ensure all pieces of the puzzle fit together, and ensure his successor has the best chance to succeed while handling the necessary task of his own exit

- How the chief human resources officer (CHRO) should coordinate the various steps of the search process and the transition process while also providing the staffing and counsel to the CEO

necessary for a smooth, successful handoff, all while navigating
the sometimes delicate position as the person in between the
relationship of the CEO and board

- How senior managers who report to the CEO (and will to his successor), can best prepare themselves and prepare their divisions or
functions for the changes that come from a transition at the top
while also providing important help to the new leader

We combine more than 80 years of experience in working with
and experiencing ourselves the planning and executing of senior-level
transitions and the organizational changes they cause. We have seen
firsthand the investment of effort, time, and money that companies
make in searching for a new CEO, assessing candidates, debating
choices, planning for various outcomes, making an offer, negotiating
terms, and finally securing the commitment of a new leader. But,
too often, once an offer is accepted, little else is done to ensure the
investment in search and selection yields a return. Those involved
believe the job is complete and return to their normal duties, leaving
the new leader and the organization she has taken over on their own,
unprepared to deal with the challenges of authority and organizational
change that any transition brings. There has been little research and
few books or articles about the steps that directors, CEOs, CHROs,
and other stakeholders should take to ensure the new leader has the
best chance of success. Most of what has been written has guided
new leaders rather than the organizations they join. Dan co-authored
a seminal book in this area (*Right from the Start*) and has advised
on successful transitions since managing his own succession in the
mid-1990s. He has the experience (rare in the advice business) of
having been a designated successor, and then, after being chairman
and CEO for a dozen years, hiring his successor and, over a planned
18-month transition, managing his own CEO handoff. David, a
former CHRO of Honeywell, is now chairman and CEO of Pivot
Leadership. He also works with boards and CEOs on talent and

development strategies, including succession. Pivot Leadership works with companies around the world to execute strategy, become aligned, and adapt to change, including onboarding new leaders through executive development programs.

The Transition Challenge

As we said in the Preface, we believe a book on the company's role in transitions is needed because failed transitions represent an urgent problem that has received too little attention and that must be solved. The costs of transition failure are very significant ... not only financially but also in career impact and company reputation. It is time to address this problem because the record of success of CEO transitions is dismal and it is getting worse.

According to one study, 15.3 percent of CEOs left the 2,500 largest global public companies in 2005, and 70 percent more than just a decade earlier.[1] The turnover range for chief executives of large North American corporations hovered around 10–11 percent in the mid-to-late 1990s, and then shot up to an average of 14 percent between 2000 and 2007.[2] Only 269 SEC-reported companies had to manage a CEO transition in 1999; in 2008, 1,484 companies managed a CEO transition.[3] In 2003, the Harvard Business School estimated a 40–60 percent failure rate of U.S. executives.[4]

Almost half of CEO departures are forced by the board (it was 46% in 2008, for example).[5] Not surprisingly, the number of CEOs forced to step down has affected the average tenure rate at this level. The majority of CEOs today have been in their positions for less than five years. When each of us became involved in this area, a CEO being fired was very rare, and most stayed in their positions for 10 or more years. The data also show that the first segment of a CEO's tenure is the most treacherous. A *Fortune* article in February 2012 estimated that 40 percent of executives who are hired into a job from outside or are promoted fail within the first 18 months. It reaffirms the 18-month rule that has been well known in the leadership advice area. It fact, this article notes that the failure rate has "stood at about 40% for at least fifteen years";[6] our experience affirms that it has been in effect much longer. In 2005, research from a management consulting firm found that about one-third of new managers and senior executives leave new positions within 18 months.[7]

CEOs who depart after 18 months on the job cost small-cap companies an estimated $12 million each. For large-cap companies, the figure is $52 million. Some research estimates that these departures add up to a minimum loss in the United States of $14 billion each year.[8] Other research shows that a failed leader transition can cost 10 to 20 times the executive's yearly compensation.[9]

And this represents only the obvious, visible costs. Even more damaging are the long-term effects on the company's ability to operate effectively and to innovate well enough to meet ever-changing customer needs and competitive challenges. When a new leader is hired, he inevitably redefines priorities, imports new ways of operating, and often is charged with an agenda to change strategic direction. But when he founders and is then replaced by the next leader who repeats the same drill, the resulting disruption and confusion risks pulling the company into a negative cycle that will be difficult to reverse.

Transition failure also levies a cost on the company's reputation externally in the eyes of customers, investors, and analysts, and importantly, internally in ways that affect employee motivation. The reputations of once-proud companies such as Hewlett-Packard have suffered greatly because of the transition mismanagement of their boards. Also, collateral damage of transition mistakes by the company includes injury to the careers of the talented, capable executives who fail after taking over the organization and the loss of key talent.

It is likely that the problem of higher turnover in senior positions won't go away any time soon, and that attention on it will increase.

New U.S. government regulations as well as rules of the New York Stock Exchange and NASDAQ require boards to develop a succession plan that is available to shareholders, who have become increasingly restive and demanding about CEO selection. But while the result has been more scrutiny by the media and shareholders on the selection of new CEOs, little or no attention is paid to the details of preparations made by the company, standards for getting ready for a new leader, or guidelines for the organization to maximize success once an offer has been accepted.

It is never a sure thing when someone takes on a job at the top. For one thing, the person chosen is often assuming more responsibility than he has ever had and facing strategic, operational, political, and personal challenges that are tougher and more complex than he has ever faced. And not only is this true of CEOs but also of the people selected as designated successors. Only about 25 percent of those next-in-line executives hired from the outside succeed in the CEO job, and only about 50 percent of those who have been promoted from within.[10]

Why are success rates not better? One answer is that people chosen as new leaders do not do a good enough job at preparing for and managing their entry into the top spot. Both experience with leadership transitions and research conducted at the Harvard Business School confirm that leaders who fail within a couple of years of assuming a top-level position make the same handful of mistakes:[11]

- They fail to use wisely the time between accepting the position and Day 1 in their jobs.
- They do not read the political situation well enough to understand the relationships, coalitions, and alliances most important to their success.
- They fail to understand the culture well enough or adequately manage it to follow their direction.

- They misread the capacity or willingness of the people they inherit to implement needed changes.

The net result of such missteps is that new leaders do not achieve notable successes within their all-important first 18 months. That in turn limits the commitment of a critical mass of people to support their agendas. Ultimately, the person at the top in this situation never attains the loyal followership needed for effective leadership.

We believe that the person assuming the senior spot can do much to succeed once in the top position if she moves quickly to avoid or resolve these common mistakes. But there is a second answer to the question of why more leaders do not succeed: that the organizations that have hired or promoted them have not done their part to ensure success. Until the company that hires or promotes leaders into its top positions does its part, the problem of transition failures will not be solved.

By "the company," we mean the major players who most determine its strategy, how it operates day-to-day, who is hired and who stays, how its various parts are expected to coordinate, and its culture. In particular, the players on the company's side of the transition equation who have the most significant roles in determining whether a transition at the top is successful are the board of directors, the CEO, the chief human resources officer, and the other key senior managers who report to the CEO.

When we refer to "leadership transition" we mean the process of maintaining strategic, operational, and cultural continuity as one leader passes the mantle of authority to a successor. That process spans the steps and events from before the winning candidate accepts the company's offer to the point that a critical mass of followers assign their loyalty to her as the established leader.

Because there are different paths to the top, there are various types of transitions. The CEO might be promoted from within after many years with the company, be hired directly from the outside into the CEO position, or come to the top position from the board of directors, either temporarily as a permanent leader is found or intending to stay. Also, the leader might become CEO through a *planned transition*, where he is hired into a high-level position (for example, as chief operating officer or division president) and moves up by way of a predetermined, managed process. While examples we use cover a range of possibilities, this book concentrates on planned transitions because they are more complex and include steps that are necessary in other types of handoffs.

Thinking through what that process should be for any particular transition situation should include a thorough understanding of why so many handoffs at the top fail.

The Roots of Failure

It may seem at first glance that the challenge of a transition is simple: Lay out the capabilities needed in the new leader, manage the search well, find the best person possible, and the rest will take care of itself. "After all," as one CEO put it, "we've done all we can." Sixteen months later, that same person said, "How could we have gotten it so wrong?" The answer is that he and his transition team did not do all that they could have. The fact is that the transition of the leader is a complex cascade of steps and events that last for many months and are affected by strong emotions.

Complexity

Chapter 1 explains that a leadership transition is not a simple transaction but rather is a process that has many moving parts that exist through a string of interdependent steps. If decisions involving each are made on the basis of the wrong logic or too carelessly or for the wrong reasons, it can cause the whole process to go off track.

Not only does the new leader need to make adjustments but each of the major players also must adjust. The directors must ensure that the process is off on the right foot without trying to do the work that management should be doing. Also they must adjust to the reality that they are hiring someone who will be key to meeting the financial needs of today, and at the same time must be mindful that they are hiring the person who will create the company's future.

The CEO must adjust as she walks the line between continuing to run the business that has her stamp on it and laying the groundwork for her successor to take over, ensuring that thoughts of her legacy do not impinge on either.

The CHRO must adjust as he carries out the coordinating responsibility of the person in the middle. He must be helpful to the new leader in preparing and onboarding, to the CEO as he directs the process, and to the senior leaders as they prepare the organization for the transition and the operational changes it will bring.

The senior managers must adjust to the entry of a new person who will be their new boss. In doing so, they will no doubt have to adjust the operational plans for which they have carefully geared their departments' processes, systems, and people.

Each major player must be ready to adjust and adapt to the changing demands of this dynamic process that touches on the strategic, operational, political, cultural, and personal realms of any company. Denying its complexity is the surest way to open the door that leads to errors. These errors fall into two categories: errors in thinking and errors in execution.

Thinking Errors

In the same way that major players ignore or remain unaware of the complexity they face in a top-level transition, they commit errors in how they perceive the task ahead in ways that block them from the goal of a successful handoff. Chapter 2 describes a number of these think-ing errors and the underlining attitudes that cause them. They are most apparent in the form of three myths that commonly appear in organi-zations where transitions at the top fail.

The first myth is typified by the statement from a CEO, who said, "People join companies all the time; it's nothing to get all excited about." The attitude behind this was that a top-level transition does not warrant special attention or planning but can be handled as a routine event.

The second myth, this time described by a lead director, is "Our job is done when the one we want says 'Yes.'" The underlying attitude here is that the board can relax and back off once the candidate it wants has agreed to an offer. Directors who assume the CEO will take it from there are ignorant of their special responsibilities, ones that they alone must fulfill.

The third myth, "We *know* what he can do," was uttered by the head of human resources of a large corporation that had just rehired an executive who had left several years before. It masks the attitude that past experience or familiarity can predict a new leader's performance in a job he has never done under conditions he has never faced.

Thinking errors are particularly destructive when committed by people in positions of authority who express them with certainty even though they may not have been thought through carefully. When fol-lowers fail to question or raise concerns, the collusion leads to errors in the execution of the transition.

Execution Errors

Chapter 3 reviews common errors that major players make as they execute the steps of the transition process. The first major execution error is one of omission as the directors and CEO simply ignore the need for ensuring that the demands of the transition are handled.

Either from ignorance, organizational dysfunction, or laziness, a surprising percentage of companies make no effort to smooth the way for a new leader.

The second common execution error is when the directors either miss or ignore warning signs in the relationship between the CEO and the designated successor. Problems in this relationship pose the most serious block to transition success because of the need for trust between the incumbent and the person who is preparing to take over.

It is the board's responsibility to monitor the quality of the relationship and make sure that both parties are doing whatever is necessary for the relationship to be a factor that facilitates success rather than one that enables failure. Also, the CHRO has an important role to play here. It is he who should be close enough to the CEO and to the new leader to see the signs of trouble, and should be the one of all the major players with the training to recognize such problems early enough that they can be avoided.

The third execution error is when the company is affected by a type of tunnel vision that brings into focus only the new leader coming aboard but ignores the fact that for every new leader elevated to the top position in a planned transition, there is another transition as the incumbent leaves, and often there are other "derivative defections" when senior managers leave because of disappointment at not being awarded the top job or because their influence will decline with a new leader. As we stress throughout this book, the organization is a general system where when changes happen to one part, other parts will be affected in some way. The wise board and CEO will recognize this system-wide interdependence in how they plan for and carry out their transition duties.

The final common execution error is mismanaging the process of steps and events that make up the transition. Of course, every transition is different because each one happens in a unique organization culture with people who have unique personalities, strengths, and weaknesses. But, while each approach must be tailored to the particular conditions and demands of the situation, every top-level transition should be designed and implemented on the basis of a primary guiding principle: Transitions at the most senior level must be treated as special events because they are unlike transitions at any other level. What is good enough in the case of a new functional vice president or general manager will be insufficient for a CEO handoff.

Lack of appreciation of this principle contributes to three missteps that are described in Chapter 3: not organizing and interpreting the information that is most important to the new leader's success, particularly cultural and political information; inadequate preparation of people for the roles they must perform in order for the transition to be a success; and mishandling the part of the transition process that has to do with onboarding the new leader. Poorly designed programs to assimilate the new leader commonly detract from a smooth transition, especially when the new leader is coming into a culture and political structure that are unlike what he has experienced before.

Roles for Success

Errors of thinking and of execution can be minimized if the major players do their parts. Chapters 4 through 7 detail the role, the most impactful contributions, and the key success factors for each of the major players: the board, the CEO, the CHRO, and the senior managers.

The Board's Role   Directors must assume overall accountability for the transition's success. Chapter 4 highlights why and how the directors who are most involved must be engaged, informed participants. At the same time they must be careful to not be so active that the CEO's role is compromised. When that happens, not far behind is confusion or, worse, divided loyalties of the CHRO, senior managers, and also the new leader. Finding and maintaining this right balance is a key success factor not only for the board's role but also for the entire handoff.

In addition to accepting accountability, the board must manage relationships adroitly with both the incumbent leader and the new leader. With the existing CEO, the relationship must be that of a partner in making the transition a success. That requires the board to agree with the CEO on the rules by which they will work together, and to be as open to his point of view about how the transition should be managed as the CEO should be to the board's point of view. A partnership relationship also allows for input and advice from directors to the CEO, and vice versa. For advice to work, especially for a leader from his board, it must be given in an effective way by directors and also must be taken well by the leader. Chapter 4 explores this sometimes delicate interaction and the part the board and the CEO play to make the most of it during a handoff.

True partnerships are not common between a board and CEO. This chapter explores how new rules and regulations governing the makeup of boards and the relationship with the CEO have affected the potential for the board–CEO partnership. But we also suggest a more important reason for the lack of partnerships at this level: Boards and CEOs have not made it a high-enough priority. Even though new regulations may force boards and their CEOs to have a more arm's-length relationship, they require nothing that prevents a partnership relationship. It is a matter of having it as an important goal and putting in the effort to make it happen.

In Chapter 4 we also examine the formation of the relationship between the board and the new leader. Starting in the first interview, both parties share responsibility to shape a relationship that is positive and constructive, with the CEO playing a pivotal role. In addition, we look closely at the impact on that relationship of how the board intends to judge the new leader's performance and how it sets expectations for the new leader to eventually become CEO.

The two parts of the board's role in a top-level transition, then, are to be accountable for the transition and to adroitly manage the relationships with the CEO and the new leader. That role depends on three imperatives. The first imperative to ensure both parts of this role is to provide oversight that is both wise and useful for the transition. That often comes down to finding the right balance between backing off too much to avoid intruding on the CEO's responsibilities and being too involved.

The second imperative necessary for the board to fulfill its role is to enable the CEO to exit gracefully and at the right time while also enabling the new leader to master what she must in order to meet the company's emerging challenges as well as the political reality of her entry.

The third imperative is to pay particular attention to the culture and its political dynamics as the transition goes through its various steps. This chapter identifies specific actions that boards can take to do so that enable them to stay within their role while still being actively engaged.

The CEO's Role   Chapter 5 concentrates on the role of the CEO in a leadership transition. This role has two major parts: to direct the design and implementation of the transition's various steps, and to ensure that the CEO's successor assimilates effectively into the organization and, ultimately, moves up to the top position.

The first part requires that certain standard elements be in place that are important to any handoff, such as expectations and roles being clear, the right amount of communication, ways to measure progress, and ensuring that the transition is on the agenda of each major player. The key here is an organized, efficient process. The second part requires the CEO to believe that the success of the person who next steps into the CEO position is the final, important objective on his watch. We explore how CEOs fulfill this priority.

Of course, the way the CEO performs each is always tailored to the situation and personalities involved. We describe two cases where each CEO took a different path toward the same objective of a successor successfully taking hold. One CEO took on the role of *counselor* to his successor, coaching him actively and throughout the transition. The other CEO became an *instructor*, ensuring the new leader grasped what she had to and that she had the help needed to shape the relationships that were going to be most important, especially ones with managers who would end up reporting to her. These were different approaches with each fitting the situation that existed in each company, and that fit the personalities and abilities of each CEO.

Three imperatives must be handled well by the CEO in order for this role to be fulfilled and the transition to be directed effectively as the new leader moves up. The first is that the CEO control the steps and pace of the transition process. This starts with choosing the entry point and position in the organization for the new leader. The next step is the CEO clarifying his mental image of the optimal person to be his successor, of how they will interact once she is aboard, and what the handoff should be like if it works smoothly and effectively. The next element necessary to control steps and pace is for the search process to be juxtaposed and to overlap effectively with the process for the transition. This chapter explores each in detail and describes the points of overlap as well as potential tensions and problems.

The second imperative for the CEO is to ensure the other major players do what they must for the transition's success. We explore how the CEO can do so in ways ranging from the bully pulpit of his office to his personal persuasiveness to various ways to involve and educate. We also see why it is particularly important to involve in the transition the senior managers (that is, the CEO's direct reports) who will eventually report to the new leader.

The third imperative is the CEO's own self-management and self-awareness as she passes the mantle of authority to her successor.

The CEO must manage her own emotions during this time, one that can be quite stressful for any leader. She must also sharpen her awareness of her impact on others as the handoff proceeds. The degree that the CEO can do both effectively will go a long way to determining how well she hands over authority to her successor. It will also in large part determine the state of mind in which she leaves the organization as well as how employees will view her as she walks away. While it is difficult to move into the top spot for a new leader, it can be just as hard to leave it. For the CEO who has devoted significant time and energy to leading the company, departing raises important questions of what has been accomplished, what is being left behind, and what is next for the CEO. Chapter 5 looks in detail at ways the CEO can address these crucial questions.

The CHRO's Role   Chapter 6 looks at the role of the chief human resources officer (CHRO) in a transition at the top. While the board is accountable and the CEO must direct the transition, the CHRO's role in a top-level transition is divided into two parts. First, he is the one who should ensure each step operates as it should, that they all fit together in the right way, and that there is the appropriate degree of coordination with related activities such as the search process. It is also to the CHRO that falls the responsibility for the new leader's assimilation into the organization and also communication to the organization about the transition. This includes ensuring each transition step operates as it must; that the various parts of the process fit together to form a general system where one part interacts appropriately with others; and that the execution of the major tasks is smooth, efficient, and effective.

The second part of the CHRO's role is to be an internal advisor to the CEO on the transition. This includes four major areas. First is being the CEO's sounding board on key issues of thinking and execution. As the search moves to completion and thoughts turn to the transition, if the CEO sees the signs of potential problems in thinking about the transition or in its execution, the CHRO should be the person the CEO calls. Being helpful on this requires a complete understanding of the nature of a transition and a clear mental picture of the optimal one for that particular organization.

The second area where the CHRO should be a useful advisor is the nature of the company's political system. As we point out in several chapters, the structure of relationships, coalitions, and alliances has a significant impact on the transition. The CHRO should be the person among the CEO's direct reports who understands this political structure best and has the skills to prevent political problems from affecting the transition.

Third is to ensure that the CEO's objectives and directives are clearly communicated to the major players and, where necessary, the organization as a whole. Also, the CHRO should be the person who performs a similar function for the board in its communication with the CEO.

The final part of the CHRO's advisory role is to be the confidant and connector of the major players. In this part, the CHRO should be the one to whom each of the other players confide and communicate. As a result, it is he who is best able to, for example, describe the mood of the senior managers to the board or to answer questions of the senior managers about the succession process. In this regard, the CHRO is the person in the middle, a position that requires judgment, wisdom, and political skill (without coming across as being political). This chapter explores this fine line.

There are three imperatives that the CHRO must master to fulfill this role. First, he must have the skills and temperament to provide great senior staffing support to the CEO. In this regard, he plays the same role for the CEO that, for example, a chief of staff plays for a U.S. president. We describe these abilities in this chapter. The second imperative is to ensure the new leader has the help needed to make a smooth, effective entry and then to proceed through the portion of the transition that follows Day 1 on the job. The third imperative is to provide the structure for and formulate ways to enhance the relationships that are necessary for the transition's success. The most important ones are between the CEO and the board, between the CEO and the new leader, and between the new leader and the board. This chapter gets into detail on the methods and mechanisms that can help the CHRO in this most important area.

The Senior Managers' Role Chapter 7 covers the role of the senior managers. Even though being a senior manager on the executive leadership team is one of the most complex positions in any organization, senior managers usually are not as involved as they should be in companywide, strategically important issues such as a transition to the next CEO. But the role is an important one for at least three reasons. First, the senior managers must communicate to their divisions or functions regarding a new strategic direction and the reasons for the transition that brings the new leader aboard. Second, they must make sure that the day-to-day operations continue to produce near-term results in spite of any interruption caused by the transition or related organizational changes. And, third, it is to this group that falls the problem of adapting plans, systems, and processes when strategic and operational requirements change.

The senior managers' role in the transition is to prepare the organization for the handoff and to make sure both they and their functions or departments adapt to a new leadership style and, possibly, to new strategic and operational priorities. Preparing the organization includes communicating to the departments or functions at the right cadence and levels of specificity, making sure that both communication as well as any changes necessary are in sync with those of peers.

Being ready to adapt to a new leadership style and priorities starts with a thorough understanding of the new leader and of the new direction she represents, including what knowledge, skills, and behavior are necessary for the organization to thrive as it heads in a new direction. It also requires that the senior managers build the capability of their organizations to be able to do what is required. Finally, it means that the senior managers must have the skills and the opportunity to inform the new leader of the organization's strengths and shortcomings in an insightful, useful way.

There are three imperatives necessary to fulfill this role. First is to shape organizational opinion so that the various parts of the organization line up in support of the transition and its objectives. This requires the senior managers to think through what the pending change means for the parts of the organization they control and to coordinate with their peers so that each works not only downward (communicating and directing to the departments or functions that report to them) but also sideways (working with and supporting their peers). Sometimes this requires senior managers to take initiative. Chapter 7 looks at the experience of one senior manager who took the initiative to discover the implications of the CEO transition in her organization. As a result, she became a leader among her peers as they shaped the opinions of the organization.

The second imperative is a step beyond shaping opinion: to deliver the support of employees who report to the senior managers and also those who are loyal to them wherever in the organization they may be located. That requires that the senior managers accept that the change agenda as well as the new leader is best for the organization and best for the senior managers themselves. Often, that requires new behavior and a willingness to share power. In this chapter, we look at one case where a powerful senior manager went through just such a process of behavior change and power sharing. The overall task in achieving this imperative is to understand the organizational, political, and personal dynamics that surround any group of senior managers. It also means ensuring that these organizational, political, and personal dynamics are utilized in a positive way to achieve the changes that are necessary rather than allowing them to become barriers to progress. This chapter describes ways senior managers can achieve that.

The third imperative is for the senior managers to construct solid working relationships with the new leader and in the process, with one another so that the entire senior manager group is headed in the same direction. Sometimes achieving that end requires the CEO, as he is passing the baton to the new leader, to put extraordinary time and effort into ensuring that the senior managers are prepared. Chapter 7 looks carefully at several examples where CEOs did just that.

Figure I.1 depicts schematically the core reasons for failure of top-level transitions and the roles necessary for success on the company side of the transition equation.

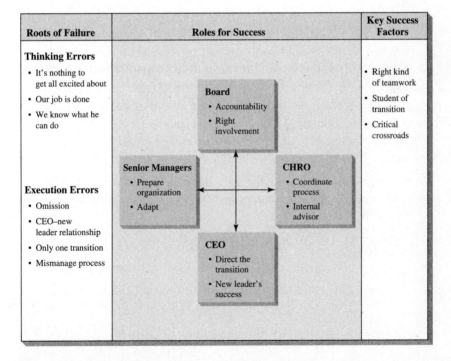

Figure I.1   Framework for Transition Success

Notes

1. C. Lucier, P. Kocourek, and R. Habbell, "CEO Succession 2005: The Crest of the Wave," Strategy+Business, May 30, 2006, accessed November 13, 2014, http://www.strategy-business.com/article/06210?pg=all

2. N. Stoddard and C. Wycoff, "The Cost of CEO Failure," *Chief Executive, December 12, 2008, accessed January 13, 2015,* http://chiefexecutive.net/the -costs-of-ceo-failure

3. J.C. Wilcox, J. Eichbaum, and M. Tonello, "The Role of the Board in Turbulent Times: CEO Succession Planning," The Conference Board, August 2009, accessed January 13, 2015, https://www.conference-board.org/publications/ publicationdetail.cfm?publicationid=1681

4. Ray B. Williams, "CEO Failures: How On-Boarding Can Help," *Psychology Today*, May 2, 2010, accessed January 13, 2015, http://www.psychologytoday .com/blog/wired-success/201005/ceo-failures-how-boarding-can-help

5. Tonello et al., "The Role of the Board." p. 4.

6. Anne Fisher, "New job? Get a Head Start Now," *Fortune*, February 17, 2012, accessed January 13, 2015, http://fortune.com/2012/02/17/new-job-get-a -head-start-now/

7. Ray B. Williams, "CEO Failures: How On-Boarding Can Help," *Psychology Today*, May 2, 2010, accessed January 13, 2015, http://www.psychologytoday .com/blog/wired-success/201005/ceo-failures-how-boarding-can-help

8. N. Stoddard and C. Wycoff, "Pick a CEO Who Truly Fits the Company," Forbes.com (April 9, 2009, accessed January 13, 2015, http://www .forbes.com/2009/04/09/ceo-succession-planning-leadership-governance-fit .html

9. C. Dierickx and J. McGill, "The Dark Side of CEO Succession," *Chief Executive* (May 11, 2007, accessed January 13, 2015, http://chiefexecutive.net/the -dark-side-of-ceo-succession

10. D. Ciampa and M. Watkins, *Right from the Start* (Harvard Business School Press, 1999), 3.

11. Ibid.

1 Complexity and Critical Crossroads

A lot is at stake during the transition of one top executive to the next, especially at the CEO level. Emotions often run high and can cause an otherwise simple event to take on outsized importance. Consider the case of Dave, a 62-year-old CEO who had taken over a midsized technology company. As he edged toward retirement, the board was committed to finding an executive to replace him and lead the company into a new era of management.

Dave had been brought on five years earlier by private-equity investors who had taken the company private to fix problems that had come from costs that were too high and the lack of discipline or an infrastructure to support rapid growth. In getting the company back into shape, Dave had turned it into the second largest in the industry in revenue and the leader in profits. It had grown rapidly, not only financially but organizationally, and had gone from being just a high-potential company when Dave took over to a large, successful corporation.

In discussions with the board, Dave agreed to manage a planned transition. The company had become too big and complex for any one of the existing senior managers to lead when Dave left. The plan was to conduct a search for an executive to be hired into a new position as executive vice president that combined marketing, sales, new product development, and business development. If that worked well in the first year or two, the executive vice president would move to chief operating officer and then, a year later and upon Dave's retirement, to CEO.

Dave had enlisted his chief human resources officer, Wes, to run the details of the search and find the best executive search firm. The two met weekly to review progress. One of those meetings included a conference call with the search firm's senior partner, who mentioned that one candidate, whom we will call Jim, had been "enthusiastically endorsed" by the most influential director, Harvey, who had worked with Jim in another company.

When Dave learned of Harvey's endorsement, he became visibly upset. "Why did it take all this time before I knew this guy is Harvey's favorite?" he asked Wes after the call. "Is this a setup? If they know each other well, how can I trust this new guy? Will he go around me to Harvey? If Harvey wants to find out what's going on, will Jim be able to say, 'No, go to Dave'? I need to get on this with [the lead director] right away." And, testily to Wes, "Did you know about this?"

Wes said had not been aware of it. "Dave, I understand how upset you are," said Wes, "but let's find out exactly what happened. Before you call [the lead director], let me handle this."

Without revealing Dave's suspicions, Wes talked separately to the lead director and to Harvey. It turned out that the first mention of Jim's name was by the search firm rather than Harvey and that Harvey had merely said he knew Jim and had always been impressed with him, stopping well short of an "enthusiastic endorsement."

Dave's worry that former connections would disrupt the special CEO–board relationship was largely put to rest. While Dave's concerns were valid about the potential problem of his backup and a key board member being longtime acquaintances, there was no evidence that it should stand in the way of Jim being a candidate.

But, it provided a reminder to Wes of how important absolute trust was to the formation of this relationship.

From Dave's perspective the relationship with his designated successor was hardly a trivial matter. The worst-case scenario would be if comments from a subordinate to a director were taken out of context and, as Dave put it, that he would "get blindsided at a board meeting."

Wanting to avoid a potential blindsiding may seem an issue leaders should not worry about at a major turning point in the leadership of a company. But in fact, faulty communication can lead to inaccurate assumptions that in turn can evolve into relationship problems that, if not handled in just the right way, can cause a transition to fail. Indeed, a series of such small errors often explain why a high percentage of new leaders fail to reach their two-year anniversaries.

Because of skillful transition management by Dave, Wes, and the board, however, Jim was not one of them. His interviews with directors and with Dave went better than expected. The board and Dave agreed that to attract Jim to the company, the job had to be expanded from executive vice president for marketing and sales to chief operating officer. Jim was impressive enough that all believed that he was ready for that job. Indeed, Jim rose to the occasion, and three years later he became CEO as Dave retired on schedule.

As with any leadership situation as complex as a CEO succession, there were many reasons this one was a success. While they will be detailed throughout this chapter, there were two that should be emphasized:

- Dave was mature enough to understand his first suspicious reaction as just that—a first reaction. He wisely pushed the pause button and waited for facts to be gathered before making any accusations. He and Wes agreed that, while Dave's concerns were valid about the potential problem of his backup and a key board member being longtime acquaintances, no evidence existed that it should stand in the way of Jim being a candidate.

- Wes, the CHRO, operated in a model way. His decision to in effect step in between his boss and a potential conflict with the board, which could have turned into a crisis, gave the chance for Dave to reflect rather than react and for someone who was more objective to gather the facts. Wes realized that the relationship of Jim and a director could be a hurdle that Jim would have to overcome later unless his relationship with Dave became a positive, trusting one.

The success of Dave, Wes, and Jim in the management of a transition provides a helpful example for how transitions can and should be handled. It is an exception, however. In too many cases, when major players in a transition come to these crossroads, they react in ways that derail the transition. Throughout this book, we describe success stories but also many such problematic handoffs and the reasons for them. We chose to begin with a successful one to make a key point: Leadership handoffs can and will turn out well if the major players react appropriately at critically important crossroads. They don't need to succumb to inappropriate reactions that can easily cause negative results.

It is our position that most transition failures take place because the major players are unprepared for the critical crossroads they encounter, and in particular because they underestimate or ignore the complexity of the process. The transition is a general system made up of individual, interrelated steps where reaction to one step affects the nature of those that follow. The success rate of leadership transitions will not improve until the major players become students of this dynamic transition system and its complexity.

Transitions at the top fail because major players are unprepared for critical crossroads ... often, because they underestimate or ignore the complexity of the transition process.

Complexity

What makes leadership transitions complex? It is a combination of two factors:

- The adjustments required by the individual major players involved on the company side of the equation and the interactions between them (the sitting CEO, the board, the CHRO, and the senior managers)
- The systemic adjustments in the organization that accompany the transition (strategically, operationally, politically, and culturally)

Individual Adjustments

On the individual front, each of the major players must become a student of transitions because each has something valuable to gain in managing the complexity and making the transition go well.

CEO   The sitting CEO's primary responsibility, of course, is leading the organization so that its various stakeholders receive what has been promised. The stakeholders each look to the CEO to ensure delivery. Investors expect the collective efforts of employees will produce a return on their investments. Customers expect value, quality, and reliability. Suppliers want predictability, consistency, and accurate forecasts. Employees want a place where they can feel valued, be challenged, contribute, and be compensated fairly. And communities want a good corporate citizen. It is a big enough job during normal, stable times to steer the organization so these varied and often-conflicting needs are satisfied. But when something happens that upends the normal course of events, the CEO's job becomes tougher. The bigger the change, the more complexity is added to the mix.

A change that qualifies as major is when the strategy is recast to the point that the way the company operates must change in a fundamental way. Another change that qualifies as major is a CEO transition. And it is not infrequent that they coincide.

That was the case with Dave. As we said, Dave had been CEO for five years, and during that time he brought order, stability, and discipline needed for the business to grow profitably. He was working on a new strategy in the months prior to agreeing with the board that he would find a successor. The strategy he had taken over when he had joined as CEO had worked well, but he believed the company was coming to the end of one era and was poised to begin another. He led his senior managers through a process to envision a company in five years that was larger and more efficient, dominated the industry in market share, and was its leading innovator. The board endorsed the effort and encouraged Dave to formulate a detailed strategic plan. It was in process when the decision was made to look for a successor.

At a time of his own leadership transition and also a significant shift in strategy, the sitting CEO has his hands full. He must perform the normal CEO tasks of representing the company to outside stakeholders, being the beacon of the company's mission and values inside, and keep the business running day-to-day to profitably deliver quarterly revenue. In addition, he must take on two other tasks that are not only significant but are also the type that become even more complex if not done right the first time. The first is assimilating a successor and deftly managing the handoff. The second is to actively fulfill his role as chief visionary and chief strategist: chief visionary so his people believe in the direction in which he is headed and chief strategist so there is a realistic plan to move the whole company forward.

These items take up much of the CEO's efforts and schedule. But they occupy only one part of his mind. In addition, his thoughts are taken up with what the handoff means to him personally and to the legacy he will leave behind. We will discuss this personal aspect in detail in Chapter 5 and in various parts of other chapters, as described by the three dozen CEOs with whom we talked. For now, the point is that when added to a strategy upgrade, running the day-to-day business, and being the chief visionary, managing one's own transition with its organizational and personal implications adds a great deal for any CEO to an already complex role.

Board The board also faces a great deal of complexity in handling a transition. In cases where directors, and not the CEO, are primarily responsible for managing the transition, the board must devote significant time on top of its regular duties. And, of course, as it does so, it must marshal the resources of the company and utilize them well. Even in cases where the CEO manages the process, the board must organize for and devote time to overseeing the overall effort by ensuring the process is well designed and managed and that directors are available at critical junctures. Perhaps what brings complexity for the board as much as anything else is managing relationships, including with the CEO as he prepares to depart.

In one case, the board and CEO/chairman (who was also the company's founder) agreed on a retirement date. The CEO was in his early seventies and had devoted the majority of his career to starting and building the company into the leader in its industry. He was fêted regularly as an industry visionary, and his company regarded him as an employer of choice.

These were the best of times for him, the reward for a life of taking risks and working 18-hour days. He was in good health and seemed to be finally closing in on an acquisition he had been pursuing for several years, one that would bring a product line and a geographic market that would increase his company's global reach. Even though he had said yes to the board about retiring, he thought he could put off the directors and leave on his own terms and when he was ready. He had decided that when he did leave, he would remain as chairman and his longtime COO would become CEO. "After all I've done for this place, [the board] will do what I want them to do," he boasted to an advisor.

But the board had different ideas. The lead director held several informal discussions with the independent directors without the CEO's knowledge; they all agreed that it was the right time for the CEO to give up both titles and to leave the board. As the lead director put it later, "What tipped the scales for many of us was him pushing his choice on us. None of us believed that [the COO] could lead the company, and that [the CEO] intended to stay on as chairman said to us it was his way of staying in control. All of us knew that this was a recipe for the company to go backward rather than forward."

The board ran the search entirely on its own with the lead director and chair of the compensation committee teaming up to spend significant time. The only company employee involved at all was the head of human resources, and she only as the compensation committee and final candidate were negotiating a package.

When the board takes on such a role, whether in a case like this or when the CEO is no longer in the company, it moves to the high end of the complexity scale. For one thing, by taking over, the board forfeits the chance to share the choice, and the responsibility, with the CEO. Another level of complexity for the board is added once the new leader accepts the board's offer.

In this case, the board made the mistake of deciding that its job was done when the candidate it wanted accepted its offer. It told the chief financial officer (CFO) and head of human resources to arrange for the appropriate onboarding. But because neither had been involved in the drama that led up to the new CEO joining, and since the CEO/founder was still in place completing his final days in the company, they were unprepared to fill in the new leader appropriately. As a result, briefings were incomplete. Fortunately, the new leader is a talented and mature executive who was able to overcome these oversights and make sure they didn't turn into setbacks. But, the cost of not preparing for the handoff once the new leader said yes was that it took longer for him to get to know the culture, and in particular for him to judge who remained loyal to the former CEO and whom to trust.

Complexity for the board increases the more it becomes involved in a CEO transition. By design, directors are not intimately familiar with how the organization operates day to day, and most do not get to know well the culture or power structure. When they are pulled into a role that demands knowledge in these areas, they scramble and ultimately do what needs to be done with much effort, or they flounder and leave behind problems that the new leader and his managers must solve. This case fell into the do-what's-needed category. While the scramble to make everything go well all worked out, a good deal of luck was involved. At the top the stakes are too high to depend on luck.

CHRO A transition at the top demands that others besides the CEO do a hefty part of the execution-related work necessary for a smooth handoff. The reason is not that the CEO has a big workload but that it is usually best for him to be in a position to make decisions based on options posed by someone closer to the details. We'll explore this in greater detail in Chapters 5 and 6.

Execution-related work includes finding the right search firm, making sure it has the necessary expertise and network, and then managing the relationship so that the firm delivers the service needed. It also means keeping the CEO informed without dragging her into too much detail, but all the while ensuring that the search reflects the CEO's and the board's objectives. Playing that role often requires conducting shuttle diplomacy between directors and the CEO. It also means paying attention to the impact of the transition on the climate, on the ability of the executive team to make decisions and solve problems, and especially on the attitudes and motivations of senior managers.

Execution-related work also includes being the primary contact for the new leader, acting as a safe sounding board who helps in the onboarding stage as well as with the broader demands of the transition. We described these sorts of tasks in the Introduction by suggesting that the CHRO should take on this role. In completing the research for this book, we interviewed 25 CHROs from companies such as American Express, CDW, Walmart, Aetna, ITW, Humana, Best Buy, Telstra, Biogen-Idec, and Johnson & Johnson. The results are included as case studies, some disguised, as well as in shaping the CHRO's role in planned transitions.

In Chapter 6, we will get into more detail on why the CHRO should be the one best equipped to fulfill this role. The question here concerns the complexity faced by that person during a transition.

Wes, the CHRO in the earlier case, offers an example. He had been hired from a larger corporation known as one of the best in the world at human resources and a training ground for many human resources executives who moved on to CHRO positions in other companies. He had moved through labor relations, compensation and benefits, executive compensation, and management and organization development, and had been a generalist in a large division. He was well prepared to be CHRO when recruited seven years earlier. He inherited a function that provided only the most basic services and was staffed with people who had never worked in a company with a top-notch human-resources function. His first couple of years were taken up with importing people with more experience and establishing the systems that, as he put it, would make sure "the trains ran on time."

Wes was pleased when Dave was hired because of the sophistication and experience the new CEO brought to the company. The two men hit it off right away. Because Wes was reminded of the executives he had worked with in his previous company, he understood the standards that Dave had for performance and knew what he expected from his direct reports. The one thing that Wes had not done in his career was work on a CEO transition. But because of Dave's capabilities and their relationship, he looked forward to taking on the challenge.

Wes soon discovered that his general role of coordinator of both the search and the transition processes was a bit more complicated than he had expected. Ensuring execution of each event and step required him to wear a few hats. One was the role of *communicator*, the person who ensured the various players were informed about that which they needed to know and when they needed to know it. Second was his role as the *interpreter* who could ensure that what the major players expected of one another was clearly understood. The subtlety of these two parts of his role was that they were not intended to substitute for but rather to facilitate communication between Dave and the board and between Dave and the senior managers. And, finally, Wes was the *sounding board* for Dave and the senior managers. It was Wes to whom Dave turned to finalize the job expectations of Jim as well as the final compensation package, and with whom he talked through the pluses and minuses of Jim entering as COO. And, when the senior managers wondered how Jim's role would affect them and how they should prepare, they turned to Wes.

Complexity during a transition can come in many forms. For the CHRO, it comes in the form of the paradoxes inherent in the behavior needed to do well when wearing each hat. The three roles of coordinator require the CHRO to be organized but also flexible, to assertively employ sharp influence skills but also be aware of the limits of his authority, to work closely with the board but be always mindful that he works for the CEO, and to counsel the new leader in developing a relationship with the CEO but also help the CEO judge the new leader's performance. The result of having to manage these paradoxes is that the CHRO is very much the person in the middle, as was Wes in his work with Dave and the board.

Wes became especially active at the point in the search process that calls for detailed specifications of the position to be filled and the optimal profile of the person who best meets them. Because the detailing of specifications sets the tone for all that follows, it is one of the search's most important steps. Some boards or CEOs make the mistake of outsourcing the definition of specifications to search firms, but Dave did not fall into that trap. He instructed Wes to draft specifications and then discuss them with the lead director, then with whomever else on the board the lead director suggested, and then meet with the search firm to finalize them.

Wes wanted to do more than just pass a draft of specifications past a few board members. He asked for Dave's approval to discuss with the lead director a way to lay out clearly the roles that the board and Dave would play in each step of both the search and the transition. Dave agreed because he trusted both the lead director and Wes to handle this task. Clarifying the CEO and board roles had the added benefit of clarifying expectations for Wes's role. Wes's navigation between these strong-willed executives resulted in a "responsibility chart" that laid out for each major step in the process the person or group who had responsibility, who had ultimate authority, and who needed to be informed. The process passed the first test by resulting in specifications that all were involved with defining and to which all agreed.

Senior Managers   Once the transition moves through the step of the new leader saying yes to the company's offer, two elements of complexity are added to the mix. One is that the attention of, and the emotions of, the senior managers increases. The other is that preparation of the organization moves into high gear, something that each senior manager is responsible for in the units he or she runs.

Preparing the organization includes not only letting one's department know that someone new is about to join the company but also what it will mean to the routine of the department and its ability to meet its annual targets. It will require more preparation if the new leader comes in as boss rather than as a peer. In that case, the senior managers must be ready for presentations to justify strategies, annual plans, and budgets as well as reviews of the talent and potential of direct reports. Chapter 7 offers a case of such a situation.

As explained in the Introduction, by "senior managers" we mean the managers who direct business units, divisions, and functions, usually as direct reports to the CEO. The reporting relationship to the new leader depends on whether he was hired: (1) as the number-two person in the organization (for example, as COO or president) with people reporting to him who had been reporting directly to the CEO or (2) into a position as part of the CEO's senior leadership team and as a peer of those who report to the CEO.

Jim's case is an example. As mentioned, Dave and the board first defined the job for a successor as executive vice president of sales and marketing. The idea was for the new person to enter as a peer to the people who reported to Dave and move up to chief operating officer after proving his capabilities. While it would have meant a reorganization at the level below the top team (the sales, marketing, and business-development functions reported separately to the CEO), upheaval at the top management level would have been avoided. Also, a gradual ascent would have afforded time for the new person to win over Dave's direct reports.

But as sometimes happens, Jim emerged through the search as someone who exceeded the specifications for an executive vice president, and he made it clear he would only join the company as COO. The directors and Dave were sufficiently impressed that they rethought their original plan and offered him the COO spot. One result was that the upheaval at the senior team level—which Dave had expected to avoid by Jim taking hold gradually—had to be faced before Jim came aboard.

From the point of view of the senior managers, the entry of a new leader means disruption of routine regardless of whether she enters as a peer or boss. The managers have to adapt to the new leader's communication and management style, and often to new information requirements if the new leader comes in with a mandate to change what she has taken over. More important than routine can be the need to build a relationship with the new leader, something that depends on the position at which the new leader enters.

If the new leader joins as a peer, the senior manager has to develop a relationship with someone who could be a competitor for the CEO position and/or an eventual boss. If she enters as the senior managers' new boss, they have to prepare for and then navigate a new situation as they report to someone new. Complexity for senior managers, then, comes from the need to prepare their organization for a new key player or boss. This requires either justifying or recasting the plans they are following, as well as shaping a new relationship with someone whose position not only impacts the way their unit operates but could impact their career aspirations.

Systemic Adjustments

In addition to the individual adjustments required of the major players during a transition at the top, adjustments are also required for the total system. To start with, a transition often heralds changes to the strategy. This requires changes in the systems that propel day-to-day operations. Changes to the strategy and operations in turn cause changes in the political structure as relationships are reshaped and eventually to the culture as a whole as one era ends and another begins.

Strategic   Sometimes, a transition at the top ushers in a change in strategic direction when the board hires the new leader with the primary mission of charting a new strategic path once aboard, as was the case with Lou Gerstner when he took the helm at IBM in 1993, or more recently, with Meg Whitman at Hewlett Packard in 2011 or Marissa Mayer at Yahoo in 2012. But a transition can also happen after the decision to chart a new strategic path and as a major step in that direction. That was the case with Dave and Jim.

Once the search for his successor was under way, Dave and his team prepared for a special meeting of the board to have a detailed review of the current strategy, something that had been planned well before and independently of the decision about CEO succession. Dave had convinced the board that, while the current strategy had done its job in guiding the company to its current point, it would be inadequate going forward. He set about formulating a new one.

Every good leader has a personal master plan that he usually does not reveal publically but that guides the achievement of the strategy he has promised to deliver. Dave's was based on three beliefs, and each had attached to it a significant risk.

- He believed a new strategy must strike a balance between, on one hand, learning to act like a large, mature organization that could control its growth, and on the other hand, retaining its informality and entrepreneurial spirit that provided for the experimentation and fast decision making that had been its hallmarks. Such a balance, difficult in the best of circumstances, was made even more so by his two other beliefs.

- He believed that to meet growth expectations there would have to be a broadening of products and services, something that could only be done through a significant acquisition. The risk was that the managers in his company had their hands full with the demands he currently was putting on them and would have a hard time also assimilating a new organization.

- He believed he had to get the culture prepared for the board's primary objective of the company once again going public, a change that would be significant since it had operated for five years hidden from the bright-light scrutiny of the financial markets. There was no way of predicting just when the time was right for a public offering, but when it was, he had to make sure the company was ready.

To be successful, the strategy based on these beliefs required the company's day-to-day operations to be predictable and efficient. Forecasts had to be accurate, commitments made had to be met, there had to be fewer unpredictable interruptions, and all that had to be done in a way that costs came down rather than increased. In addition, the plan to ensure these objectives were fulfilled had to be communicated in a way that motivated the company's managers to make changes to the habits and routines with which they had become comfortable. Given the way the company operated currently, there was a lot of work to do on the operational front.

Operational   The operational infrastructure of a company comprises systems and processes. Three systems form the backbone of that infrastructure: information, measurement, and rewards. The processes, both formal and informal, that the leader depends upon to solve problems and make decisions are fueled by these three core systems. A transition at the top affects both systems and processes in three ways:

- **If the strategy changes, new processes will be needed to support it.**

  If, for example, a company depended on organic growth and the new plan called for growth through acquisition, there would have to be a merging of information systems with the company acquired, as well as a merging or conversion of measurement and rewards systems. This would in turn require adjustments to the processes on which the leaders of the acquired organization depend to understand the climate and the concerns of employees. In a planned transition, as the tenures of the sitting CEO and her successor overlap, both must be involved in ensuring changes are made.

- **If the new leader reorganizes because he has a different interpretation of how to best respond to the marketplace, or simply because the inherited structure does not fit how he intends to lead, systems and processes are sure to be changed.**

Jim made such a change six months after joining as COO. Sales and marketing had been run by two vice presidents reporting directly to Dave. Dave had managed the company through an organizational structure that was fairly flat with wide spans of control. When Jim was hired as COO, the senior staff functions of finance, legal, and human resources remained reporting to Dave while marketing, sales, service, business development, new product development, and two business units moved under Jim. The person who was head of sales left the company soon after Jim joined for a new, larger position at a competitor. Jim took advantage of this, and to become more familiar with field operations and be in close contact with customers, he became the de facto head of sales. He left the job open on the organization chart, however, implying that he would eventually name someone else.

After using his first six months assessing what he had inherited and becoming clear about his priorities for the next couple years, Jim decided he should concentrate on the service, business development, and new product development areas. As a result, he made three organization structure changes that had a profound impact on operations: (1) The two business units were combined under one general manager; (2) all of sales was placed under a single vice president; and (3) the information technology department (which had been reporting to the CFO) moved to report directly to Jim under a new vice president of information technology hired from outside. A more strategic approach was necessary for information system design and management, including redesigning how information from the field was disseminated and used. By combining the two divisions, planning and control functions could also be simplified.

- **The leader must assess how information comes to his or her office, how it is dealt with once there, and how decisions are communicated.**

Every leader is supported by an administrative structure of some sort. Most, managed by an executive assistant, adequately support the leader during normal, stable times so that he is prepared and on time. The structure coordinates his schedule, communication to the organization, and preparation for staff meetings or special events such as board meetings. But as useful as they are during times of stability, normal administrative systems do not offer enough for the new leader during times of change. For one thing, the systems were designed for his predecessor, and for another, as in the case of Jim, for a different organization structure.

For the new leader implementing fundamental changes, the administrative system that supports her must be proactive and anticipatory, something not usually done by one's executive assistant. It must look for the most useful research trends on issues that are important to the leader, make sure decisions on those issues come to the leader's attention neither too early nor too late, ensure coordination and communication between the CEO and her senior managers and with the board, and find formal and informal ways for the leader to understand the mood of the organization as changes are being implemented and also where there are pockets of resistance. Structuring a system giving these benefits takes a familiarity with the strategy, a keen sense of the political structure, and an accurate diagnosis of the leaders' decision-making style. These are tasks best taken on by someone in the role of a senior staff aide. We look at this role in more detail in Chapter 6.

Political   The political facet of organization life is made up of the alliances and coalitions that determine how key decisions are made, whose opinion has the most weight, who influences whom, and why. It determines whose ideas and decisions are supported as much as or often more than any other factor. The rational, financial case for a particular change in strategy, for example, is understood if it lays out the long-term benefits to the company's current and future well-being. Similarly, a change in a key operational system will be grasped if it is made clear how it will better enable employees to achieve what is expected of them and what they expect of themselves. But understanding of a new idea is quite different than commitment to do what it requires, especially when that requirement means behaving differently.

When done well, the rational, financial case will move minds, but it rarely will move hearts. To change behavior, both hearts and minds must be affected. For that to happen, much more is required of the leader than merely laying out the rational case for change. He must know who is aligned with whom, understand what the most influential people want, and grasp the source of the power they have over the ideas and opinions of others.

How does all this apply to transitions at the top? In at least two ways:

- As we have pointed out, the transition cannot be called a success until the loyalty of influential managers has been won by the new leader. Only then will they follow his lead and will there be the sort of leadership continuity that can ensure continuous financial success. For that to happen, the new leader must win at least as much followership as his predecessor. That requires him to figure out who has the most influence among the supportive senior managers and also among the managers under them. Why did they follow his predecessor? What motivates them and why? What did he do to win their support? Who resisted? Why? Now that there will be a handoff to someone else, what will be required to win the support of people who have been loyal to the predecessor? Can others be convinced to support the new leader?

- The new leader will arrive at the point where he knows what to concentrate on and the changes that are necessary to put his stamp on the organization and make it his. As pointed out before, in Jim's case that point came at about the six-month mark. By then, he had decided what had to be kept but strengthened and what had to be changed. But the changes meant that the roles of some influential managers would be altered in ways they would not be happy about. In the months when he ran the sales force directly, Jim wisely used market tours, customer visits, and sales meetings not only to direct the day-to-day business but also to judge who had the most sway. As he was learning that, he also discovered who in sales support, finance, information technology, marketing, and the business units were influenced the most by the senior sales managers.

It became apparent to him that two regional sales managers had outsized influence compared to their peers. Jim made sure he got to know both. He decided that one would support the changes he wanted to make while the other would resist. Jim spent more time in the region of the supportive manager and learned that she had been trying for some time to convince the CFO and sales support to change the way they measured progress on the sales plan. She wanted her sales group to be more incentivized to sell new products that were more attractive in her markets but also had higher long-term margin potential. Jim agreed with her idea and set out to discover why it had met resistance.

He found out that her hard-charging style was off-putting to the CFO, and that because she hadn't made the case persuasively enough that this new measurement approach would benefit the business overall, her arguments came across as self-serving. As the CFO put it,

"She just wants an easier way for her to make her numbers because these products are more attractive [to customers in her region]."

Jim made her cause his own and arranged for her to have help to make the case differently, including counsel to adjust her style as well as advice on preparing a cost–benefit business case for the change. The change in measurement of revenue was incorporated in the reorganization package Jim announced. Meanwhile, the regional manager who resisted Jim's changes announced his retirement (having been given no choice by Jim), and the new regional manager who had been pushing the new measurement system was promoted to run the entire sales force.

Strategic, operational, and political are three important categories of adjustments required during a top-level transition that affect the whole system and add to the complexity that comes with a handoff. The final category that is systemic in nature comes from the company's culture.

Cultural Grasping the culture of an organization that is new to a person hired into a top spot is more difficult than any of the other three systemic elements because it involves delving into several layers and being able to interpret inferential data. Especially when coming from outside, it will only be after six months or so that a new leader can fully answer what should be one of her most important questions: How are things done around here? She will first notice patterns of behavior that determine how information is communicated, problems are identified, and decisions made. To understand them, she must dig deeper. She will find that those behavior patterns are supported by policies that are in turn a function of expectations reflected in systems that determine how performance is measured and managed. Those systems are shaped to reinforce certain rituals and traditions that have evolved over time. At the base of this cultural pyramid are the core beliefs, unique in each organization, that after a while aren't questioned but are reflected in

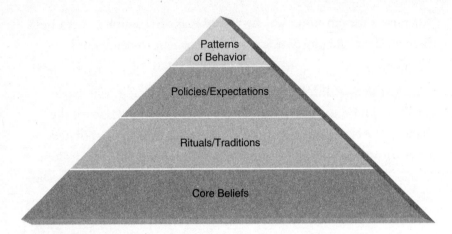

Figure 1.1   The Way People Do Things Around Here

each of the layers above it and are just accepted as "the way people do things around here" (Figure 1.1).

Before joining and settling in, it is difficult to grasp these layers of behavior, politics, expectations, rituals, traditions, and beliefs. They're rarely explained to the new leader by the major players because they themselves do not recognize them well enough to articulate a description. But although invisible, they are always there, combining to shape the culture.

In Jim's case, Dave put the how-we-do-things-around-here question front and center by scheduling Jim to meet with the CFO and general counsel in his first-round interview, as well as two managers one level below the executive team in the second round. Few people being courted as designated successors expect to meet with people who would be peers and might be competitors for the top job. Even fewer expect to meet with likely subordinates. By making this part of the interview process, the unspoken message from Dave was that an important element of the culture was inclusiveness.

Dave had been CEO long enough and his impact on the organization had been forceful enough that he had caused the culture to change; this practice of inclusiveness was just one example of the culture he had shaped. Understanding Dave's leadership philosophy would be necessary in order for Jim to fully grasp the culture, and that in turn would be necessary to his winning the followership required to become the next CEO. Dave understood this and provided Jim the chance to understand the culture before he was hired through the interview schedule and also later through an important step during Jim's onboarding.

Dave had quickly come to the decision that Jim was the best candidate to help him take the company to its next level. As a result, it was he who recommended to the board that, in order to get Jim, the job offered should be chief operating officer rather than executive vice president. He also sensed that Jim and he had quite different leadership styles, and that could make it difficult for Jim to fit into the company's culture.

An assessment of Jim's style had been done as part of the search process. One of its conclusions was that he made decisions in a "one-alone way," gathering information but not revealing what he was thinking, and then deciding on the path he was going to take on his own. In this regard, his approach was the opposite of Dave's, who became clear about the issues he faced and options for handling them by engaging people, testing ideas, and gauging the reactions of others.

Dave's way of getting clear about decisions was a function of not only Dave's learning style but also his leadership philosophy. He believed it vital that the people who were to be involved in implementing an important decision be involved as much as possible in every stage of its evolution. He was convinced that this approach was at the core of the trust that he believed necessary among members of his senior team.

As Dave began to get to know the person who he and the board expected to be the next CEO, he wondered how such a fundamental difference would affect their ability to work together. Typical of how

Dave would approach such a question, he wandered into Wes's office to talk about it.

Wes suggested that Dave and Jim meet to talk about their styles of decision making and leadership. He followed up with a memo to Dave laying out a day-long agenda to do so. Then, with Dave's knowledge, Wes talked to Jim. Wes, perhaps sensitive to Jim's reactions about the aspects of the company's culture that were unfamiliar to him, sensed that Jim was a bit surprised about this idea as well. It took several questions from Wes to get Jim to admit he was more concerned than surprised. Did it mean that Dave was having second thoughts? Had he seen something that worried him?

Wes took advantage of the opportunity to describe Dave's style and what he had sensed so far about Jim's, and went on to explain what he believed Dave envisioned about the type of culture the company needed to continue to grow and be successful as a public company. It was at this point that Wes discovered that Jim had felt awkward at the requirement to interview with a diverse group of people. Wes explained that inclusiveness was an important part of Dave's leadership philosophy, something Jim needed to understand to get a sense of the culture of the company. He pointed out that Dave wanting to discuss style and philosophy was not a sign of second-guessing his decision. If Dave didn't believe that Jim was the best choice to be COO, Jim wouldn't have gotten an offer. Even though it had been the board's decision, it would have chosen Jim only if Dave was squarely behind him as the choice.

Wes suggested Jim consider the session with Dave as an opportunity that few people in his position get early in their tenures and that, if it went well, would ensure that the relationship between him and Dave started on the right note. If that happened, the whole company would line up behind both of them. In the end, the meeting between Dave and Jim took place and, among other things, gave each an understanding of the styles of the other executive and also resulted in an agreement of respective roles of CEO and COO that enabled each to leverage what he did well.

Summary

There were three objectives for this chapter:

- Describe a top-level succession that went well.
- Emphasize the complexity inherent in a succession of this type.
- Suggest that what makes the difference between a successful and unsuccessful transition is the recognition of and management of its complexity.

Even a successful transition encounters stumbling blocks because of complexity, but skilled executives and directors can take steps to overcome them. The complexity stems not just from challenges facing each of the four key players—directors, CEO, CHRO, and senior managers—but also from the strategic, operational, political, and cultural systems in which they work. The surest step to success, one taken by Dave and Jim, is an understanding of the complexity caused by the interaction of these forces. Once the major players gain that understanding, they position themselves to overcome stumbling blocks and turn challenges into opportunities that benefit all.

2 Three Destructive Myths

Why is it that otherwise-competent leaders and senior managers who do a good job of their strategic, financial, and operational duties fail to win at the transition game? Many are capable players at their positions, work diligently, put in the time required, and have earned the admiration inside and outside their teams and of their followers. When it comes to this challenge, though, they strike out much of the time, despite exceptions like Dave and Jim in the previous chapter.

The answer is a lack of clear thinking by directors, CEOs, and their direct reports. Let's explore this idea with the case of Barbara, who started her career working at a company as an intern while still an MBA student. She felt at home almost immediately in the company because of the discipline with which it went about its day-to-day operations. It had invested heavily and over a long period in process improvement and was a frequent benchmark for other companies because of its predictable, efficient operations. Its insistence on measuring progress enabled Barbara to, as she put it, "understand where things stood. There was no mystery. I hate ambiguity."

Barbara did her second-year thesis on the company's enterprise resource planning system (ERP), and she accepted its job offer before taking any other interviews. She entered as a senior analyst in the strategic planning department. After two years, she was promoted to manager, and after a third, to director. The next several years were spent in senior financial planning and control positions in the controller's office. Then she was promoted again to the CFO spot in one of the company's larger operating divisions based in Europe. She spent the next four years there dealing with the strategic, financial, and information needs of the company's major international markets. In particular, she co-led the team that opened new markets in China and Southeast Asia.

She was then moved back to corporate finance, but this time as the number-two person for the company's treasurer. This opened up new areas for Barbara, broadening her view of corporate management and deepening her experience in financing operations and expansion. Then, after two years, she was promoted to corporate controller, essentially the second in command in the finance department.

Five years later, Barbara took stock of her career. She'd been at the company for almost 25 years, was in her late 40s, and had excelled in each of her positions. By that time, her experience was broad and deep. It included operations; strategy; acquisitions and integration; management of IT, ERP, and supply chain; international; the control as well as the treasury sides of corporate finance; and broad management responsibility for a large controllership function.

Up to that point, Barbara had assumed she'd stay at the company for her entire career. It was large enough that there was little chance of a lack of interesting challenges, she had built an impressive reputation, and could look forward to a handsome payout from the long-term incentive plan. Then, a call came from a recruiter. She had received a number of such calls but none that struck her as intriguing enough to leave. But this one was different.

Four months later, Barbara had accepted a position as CFO of a successful, midsize corporation that was poised to become larger and more complex. Its board had just hired a CEO who wanted to put together a new team to take the company into its next era. While in a different industry from the one where she had spent her career up to that point, it was facing many problems with which she was familiar. It had just begun to penetrate foreign markets and to launch its international push, starting in China and Southeast Asia. It had experimented with continuous improvement, Six Sigma, and Lean approaches, but had not spent as much time or gotten as deeply into them as Barbara's company. And while not as large as what Barbara was used to, it was substantial enough to have the mass and complexity she enjoyed and in many ways greater growth potential than her company had.

The CEO told her that the finance organization was competent for what had been needed, but not sophisticated enough to provide the discipline and structure necessary for the growth he had promised. Because the strategy would mean the company doing things it hadn't experienced before, he said he needed the finance function to establish a new foundation by driving the strategy process, instilling financial discipline, and keeping a tight rein on costs. She was pleased to hear that she'd have regular interaction with the board and attend all of its meetings. When he agreed to move IT and the supply chain under her and to give her responsibility for the Six Sigma/Lean program he intended to introduce, she agreed to take the job.

Barbara had worked for her whole career in a large, sophisticated corporation and had gotten used to its financial and technological resources. As she put it, "I knew I'd been spoiled ... and I'd probably never have [resources like that] again." But she had also never worked in another organization's culture. She had always felt proud to be an employee because of the way her company hired and trained people and approached talent needs, its standards for how objectives and plans were established, its insistence on measurement of progress and holding people accountable, and the way it balanced needs for efficiency and productivity with a drive to do things as professionally and as well as possible. At one level, she understood that these sorts of things would not exist in her new company, but she assumed they could be put in place and that their absence would not affect her ability to do what was expected.

Barbara worked hard to make sure that what she left behind was helpful to whoever would assume her duties. She documented in-process programs and laid out implications for implementing them. She also met with each of her direct reports as well as the people at lower levels in whose careers she had taken particular interest.

As a result, she had little time to think about her new company, and because after her years there and the relationships she had formed, her departure was more emotional than she had anticipated, she was exhausted. She informed the head of human resources in her new company that she would like to take an often-delayed vacation. He told her that would not be a problem. She returned the week before she agreed to start her new job.

As all this was going on in Barbara's life, what was her new company doing to make sure that her entry would be as smooth and effective as possible? To answer that, let's step back to understand its expectations for a new CFO.

The company had been started 25 years before by managers who left the industry leader because they believed it had become complacent, bureaucratic, and slow. Frustrated that gains in the marketplace and new product introductions were subjected to endless review and that concern about cost had trumped innovation, they vowed that in their new company there would be a minimum of rules dictating behavior and a minimum of structure, whether decision making or organizational.

Within a few years after the company went public, all the founders had left. The management team was made up of people promoted from within, with the exception of the financial and legal vice presidents, who had been hired because of their public-company experience. Over the next dozen years, the company became larger but experienced significant growing pains. Not surprisingly, it struggled the most when it required coordination between units and control of costs. These faults brought regular pressure from analysts and institutional investors to increase systems and controls.

The new CEO was hired to bring financial and operational discipline that the board told him was overdue. The directors were impressed by his track record of having done so in his previous two companies and in his description of the superstructure necessary for such a task. He believed an early step was to hire a CFO who could take charge of this task. Because it would be his first new hire and one he believed was vital for both the company's and his own success, he decided to manage the search himself and to bring in a search firm he had worked with rather than the one the CHRO suggested.

He wanted someone who had hands-on experience in a high-performing, efficient company, who was tough-minded and analytical, and who was hungry to show his or her capabilities. Barbara was only the second candidate he talked with, but when he met her he knew he had found the right person. He told that to his search consultant and began immediately to convince the chairman and the heads of the finance and the compensation committees.

While it was known in the company that the search was in progress, the CEO instructed his executive team to not reveal its status or that Barbara was the top candidate. When the CHRO pointed out that it was a practice in the company for a candidate to talk with people who would be direct reports, the CEO dismissed the idea. As a result, Barbara's appointment was unexpected, and what stood out most in the announcement was the name of the corporation where she had spent her career, one most saw as too structured, overly control oriented, bureaucratic, and especially to younger employees, somewhat old-fashioned.

The net effect of all this was that planning for Barbara's transition was less effective and less helpful than it should have been. There were several reasons.

- *The CHRO didn't make it a priority.* He was still sizing up the CEO and determining the best way to build a relationship with him. When the CEO decided on a recruiter other than the one who had worked for the company on several searches, the CHRO surmised the CEO wanted to do things his way. He offered to help by being the main contact for the search firm and also arranging for Barbara to go through a style and personality assessment process. But when the CEO showed little interest in either, he backed off rather than risking the relationship. Also, it was a mistake to endorse Barbara's decision to take a vacation, leaving her no time to be ready to take hold.

- *The CEO didn't devote the time necessary* to making sure Barbara's transition would pave the way for her early success in a role she had never had. By taking personal charge of the search he underlined its importance, but once the offer was accepted, the objective was ignored of getting Barbara ready and paving the way for her to take hold in a powerful, visible position. They had met twice for interviews, and after she accepted, they met for a dinner that included the CEO's wife with little chance to talk about the business. She had many questions and sensed that there were others she hadn't thought of. She had spent the most time with the CHRO, who had helped on compensation issues and administrative details of joining the company, but who wasn't well versed on the strategic or operational issues or on explaining the CEO's style.

- *The organization was not prepared.* It was not a surprise to anyone that a new CFO would be hired soon, and all of the senior executives agreed that more operational and financial discipline was needed; and, they were ready to follow the lead of the person hired. But that goodwill was squandered by the lack of planning and preparation. For one thing, the functions that the CEO moved under Barbara came as a shock to the people who were responsible for them. IT had been reporting to the CFO and the supply chain to the executive vice president of operations, who had also thought that the Six Sigma/Lean effort the CEO had talked about would report to him.

- *There was also a poor job done of preparing what would be Barbara's new organization.* The CEO was correct when he characterized the finance organization as "technically solid." It was made up of competent people whose abilities had helped the company succeed. But it was also true that it had neither the breadth nor depth to support going much further. The problem was that no one had made that clear to the people in the department.

  The person who had been CFO was a longtime employee and fiercely proud of what it had taken to construct systems and staff in a new, fast-growing company. Under him, people were recruited who fit the entrepreneurial culture rather than what the company would need as it expanded. Even though part of the responsibility was planning and control, the finance people believed that too much of either was anathema to the culture of the company.

Barbara's tenure in the company lasted just over a year. She had worked harder than she ever had before and, at least functionally, had much to show for it. She had created more useful and accurate financial and information systems, established a more reliable, predictable strategic planning process, and built financial and IT staffs that were more experienced. The board and analysts reacted very well to her.

She had proven that she had the functional capability to be a CFO of a corporation of substantial size. Inadequate functional skill was not the reason she failed. The most obvious reason Barbara failed was that her style was a mismatch for this company. More precisely, she failed because the company never perceived that as a problem and did very little to solve it.

When faced with an important decision, she asked for more analysis, frustrating those involved. When she launched the Six Sigma/Lean effort, she ran into resistance to its size and centralized structure, and because she didn't handle it well, the resistance stiffened. When final plans for a joint venture in China were set by Barbara and a small group of her strategy people, marketing managers complained loudly that they had not been adequately involved. They believed the finance department was dictating terms of engagement in a market for which they would be responsible.

After she left and had time to reflect on the previous year, Barbara put her experience in perspective. "The change in culture was too great. After over 20 years of operating in one way, I didn't adjust as well as I should have to an entrepreneurial company. I think I could have if I'd realized the things that should have been different." Unsaid by Barbara was that while she could have done more to better ensure her success, most of the "things that should have been different" were in control of the company that hired her.

For example, she didn't see the announcement of her appointment until the day she started her new job and only then discovered that it emphasized her former company instead of her excitement about joining the new one. It was also not until then that she wished she'd sent a personal message to her coworkers and that she had met or at least telephoned her direct reports. In reflecting back on her first weeks, Barbara recalled, "I didn't have a playbook on the important stuff. I'd never done this before, and it wasn't until I started the steps I could have taken occurred to me."

The first days in a new environment are always hectic, but Barbara's were even more so because she had been away on vacation. Along with the poor execution of her position announcement, the human resources department had designed an onboarding program that laid out financial, planning, and organizational information and included meetings with key people. "But," said Barbara, "What I realized later was that I knew very little about how the place really operated, who had the most influence, how decisions got made ... that sort of thing. I knew little about the culture before I joined."

In the finance department, she found a greater gap than she had imagined between what the CEO wanted of her function and what the people who reported to her believed to be their mission and priorities. Rather than a team devoted to control, risk assessment, and monitoring, she found one that responded to what the operating divisions asked for.

> My people took pride in responding fast to what marketing or the plants needed ... not in finding something that they had missed or shouldn't be doing in the first place. That was the most difficult part of my job, reorienting people's mindset right within finance. It surprised me how much of that I needed to do. And I couldn't just fire everyone and start from scratch.

The company seemed as ignorant about Barbara's needs and style as she was about the culture. A management style assessment might have helped, or simply asking some more questions to determine the match of her style to how the company operated. A better onboarding program would also have helped. Because the CEO had shown little interest in it and the CHRO didn't push it, preparation provided by human resources was nothing more than an orientation program. Better communication would have helped as well. Both she and others were put at a disadvantage by the lack of communication before she started. That was the time for her to have in-depth conversations about the people and culture so that at least she might have had a plan to understand the political environment. Such conversations could have provided information on pockets of resistance or support, and they would have allowed for her department to be

briefed on expectations and why Barbara's background had been
so attractive.

We have been part of, observed, and analyzed hundreds of these
situations, and seen many people like Barbara struggle more than
necessary because the companies that hired or promoted them didn't
do their part to ensure a successful transition into a new position.
Once again, we believe that one primary reason for the high percentage
of failures is that the responsibilities of the four key players on the
company's side of the equation (the board, the CEO, CHRO, and
senior managers) have never been laid out with enough detail or
clarity. One of the reasons these responsibilities have not been laid out
is that people believe in a trio of myths related to transitions at the top.
These myths are described in what follows to illustrate why so many
sitting directors, CEOs, CHROs, and senior managers get behind the
curve in transition management. And as the next chapter shows, these
failures in thinking then lead to failures in execution.

Myths Plaguing Transitions at the Top

The major players in successful transitions tend to exhibit two kinds
of awareness that are not found with people in companies where
leadership handoffs are not successful. They're more aware of what a
new leader will experience and are, therefore, more empathetic when
it comes to the challenges of taking hold in a top position for the first
time and/or in an unfamiliar organization. They also tend to be more
aware of the impact of the culture, relationships, and political realities
of their own organization.

As an example, consider the foresight of a CEO speaking of the
successor he had just hired:

> He's very strategic, very bright, and with his financial background
> will zero in on the economic drivers he needs to know. We talked a
> lot about them [during the recruiting process] and I'm not worried

about those things. But, we have to realize that he's coming from a place that does things much differently [from the way we operate here]. We are more of a process-oriented place than [where he came from] and relationships are more important here. We didn't talk as much about this and we have to help him out to make sure he gets it. If he doesn't, even as smart as he is, he's going to have trouble here.

This CEO realized that while a complete recruiting process is important to hiring the best person, it cannot prepare leaders for the taking-hold challenges they face. Instead, the major players must make a special effort to grasp the needs of new leaders and engage in constructive transition thinking. In organizations where it is recognized that even the most accomplished people need some help, and there are deliberate efforts to provide it, leadership handoffs have a much greater chance of success.

All the companies we talked with in researching this book stated that they recognized the need to be more aware of the barriers to transition success in theory, but that in practice, that awareness is often sacrificed to the urge to move forward quickly to hire an attractive candidate. Some noted that they have instituted what might be called "breakwaters" to slow down the process and ensure careful deliberation. Aetna, for example, after several unsuccessful efforts to import executives, invests in considerable discussion at its executive committee to define the cultural attributes that should be displayed by a successful candidate. Humana makes sure that interviews focus on values and underlying motivations of new hires to ensure their skills, behavior, and attitude align with the company's strategy. American Express conducts formal style and personality assessments of every senior manager candidate to match against the analysis and perception of internal managers.

But the high failure rate of senior-level transitions suggests that awareness and attempts to put it into practice are not common. In too many organizations, the lack of awareness represents inadequate transition thinking—thinking that is not constructive and leads to behavior that contributes to the failure of people who could otherwise succeed. Indeed, it is our observation that inadequate transition thinking has a greater impact on the handoff failing than constructive thinking has on its success.

Inadequate thinking reveals itself through the negative assumptions, or "transition myths," represented in comments made to us by directors or senior officers before or during transitions in their companies. One effect of these myths is to suggest that the transition is not as complex as it actually is and requires little preparation. By denying the gravity of the transition challenge, the myths can be especially destructive.

Transition Myths

- People join companies all the time … it's no big deal.
- Our job is done when the one we want says "Yes."
- We know what he can do.

Myth 1: People Join Companies All the Time … It's No Big Deal

This first myth suggests that coming into a senior-level position can be handled as a routine event that requires no special preparation or management. Sometimes, that belief takes hold because of the assumption that if someone is bright and accomplished enough to get to a top-level position, she does not need help. As one board chairman put it, "She's come from a tough, high-performance company and did a heck of job there. She's very bright and really knows her stuff. She'll figure it out."

Other times the belief that a transition does not require special attention is because of the context that the leader enters. As an example, consider the case of a CEO leading his company through a major transformation that required centralizing all information, sourcing, and technology under a new chief technology officer (CTO), a powerful position that required a significant reorganization and triggered complaints from senior managers. Worried at the resistance the new executive would face, the CHRO suggested a taking-hold plan to ensure a smooth entry. The CEO, however, who was frustrated with the pace of change, replied that the adjustment necessary was not for the new CTO but for the company's managers.

"They have to get used to some new realities of this marketplace we're in," said the CEO. "They're the ones who have to change … [The CTO] is coming in to bring us something we don't have now. He's the key to us getting to the next level. We need our guys to get with the program … Give me a plan for that."

Regardless of why a director or CEO believes it, assuming entry into a new culture does not have to be planned carefully is naïve, short-sighted, and as we'll see in some of the cases that follow, ultimately damaging to the business. In this case, the CEO was impatient to improve performance and became angry at resistance to change. The creation of the CTO position was an important part of his change agenda, and just one reason he should have been more active personally in managing its introduction. He knew there would be negative reactions and, therefore, resistance to the person hired. But he did nothing to ease the new executive's entry.

To add to the list of what the company should have done, the CHRO failed to help in three ways. First, he failed at one of his primary responsibilities: to ensure a climate of cooperation, especially for programs as strategically important as information, sourcing, and technology. A second failure was not ensuring a smooth entry for the CTO so that early successes would be easier. Third, it is to the CHRO that falls the task of counseling the CEO on managing the culture, including feedback on what the CEO is doing to hinder progress on what he wants. But this CHRO stayed silent. Later he explained, "I didn't want to get him even more angry."

The behavior of the CEO and the CHRO also meant that groundwork with the other senior executives was not laid before the CTO entered and he was unprepared for what he encountered. As a result it was difficult for him to gather information needed to assess improvement opportunities and initiatives that had been attempted or to gain the support of his peers during his first few months. That in turn made the positive impact that the CTO eventually brought to the company take much longer than it should have.

This was a time for this company to improve how it operated as quickly as possible to stop a decline in market share and an erosion of operating income. Each month that went by without action was digging a deeper hole. It was, of course, not that the CEO and CHRO intended to make entry more difficult or to extend how long it would take to see the benefit of needed change. Rather, the problem was that they did not appreciate the situation from the new CTO's point of view and as a result failed to anticipate blocks he would encounter.

The same lack of CEO and CHRO planning applies to the case of Barbara, who could also have used some help with style and political issues. At her previous company, her performance reviews had been exemplary, always with the highest rating in quality of work and results achieved. She was rated at less than the top score, however, in two categories that should have been a warning to her new company. One was in developing talent: because she set such a high bar and was so demanding, turnover was higher compared to departments run by most of her peers. Another was building deep relationships with coworkers: her 360-degree appraisal results revealed a general belief that Barbara was "remote," "not easy to get to know as a person," and "tends to not show a lot of interest in coworkers as people, only what they can contribute to what's important to her."

Once at her new company, Barbara, like any executive coming from the outside, proved to have a mix of strengths and weaknesses when it came to tackling the requirements of her new job. Her strengths and weaknesses were not new; they were the same she had in her previous company. But because the culture required a different mix, they revealed themselves more prominently. She needed help adapting to the new environment, but she had no one to turn to for feedback or to provide air cover.

The suggestion of the CHRO of a style assessment might have helped. Asking more questions in the interview process to compare her style to how the company operated certainly would have helped. But both she and others were put at a disadvantage by a lack of curiousness regarding these issues as she moved through the interview process, which was the right moment for in-depth conversations regarding people, culture, and political reality as well as functional capability and background.

Before Barbara was hired, the IT chief reported directly to the CEO and the executive vice president of operations was responsible for the supply chain and, he thought, the new Six Sigma/Lean effort. When the CEO agreed to assign these responsibilities to Barbara, he probably did consider that these executives would not react favorably, but did not consider how their reactions would affect Barbara's early days on the job.

No matter how bright or experienced, leaders cannot succeed as newly hired senior executives entirely on their own. They need help in different forms and, ideally, through a network balanced with several types of advisors who play unique roles.[1] Especially in the early stages of a transition, each source of help is not necessarily of equal weight. As we see in this case, help that the CEO can provide through being aware of the challenges of getting started sets a tone that can get a transition off to the wrong start. The CHRO can meanwhile provide important help if aware of the need to interpret culture and political reality.

But having acted on the mythical belief that "people join companies all the time … it's no big deal," the players in Barbara's transition triggered destructive behavior that led to her undoing.

Myth 2: Our Job Is Done When the One We Want Says "Yes"

As damaging to a successful transition as underestimating the effects on a new leader is the belief that underlies this quote. It was said by a lead director of a company that had hired a new chief operating officer with the expectation that he would be the designated successor to the CEO. The director was responding to the question of what role the board would play in the transition. He continued, "Well, we just found out he said 'Yes.' Now, [the CEO] has to deal with those transition questions. That's his job, not the board's. And if the [COO] has problems adapting, that's what HR is there for."

The assumption this director made is too common in companies hiring a new senior executive. In fact, the board's accountability doesn't end when an offer is accepted but could last for months after she joins. It must remain involved in the transition through the point it is clear that there will be leadership continuity, that is, until the new leader is established, has completed taking hold of new responsibilities, and has earned credibility from early successes. It is only then that the transition has been successfully completed.

The transition is over when it is apparent that there will be leadership continuity, that is, when the new leader

- Is established
- Has taken hold of new responsibilities
- Has earned credibility from early successes

Everyone loses if the transition process is compromised because of relationship problems between major players. In this case, such problems caused the board to pull back and not be adequately involved in the transition.

The CEO had struggled with the board for some time over the degree of influence each would have on important questions. When the board demanded that the CEO have a backup, he insisted that he be in charge of the search. Several board members objected, which led to heated arguments, some of in front of the company's senior executives. Tempers cooled and the directors decided to let the CEO handle the search, since, as one director pointed out, "He has to make this relationship work—the [COO] job reports to him. Of course, he has to be the one in charge of it."

But there was another reason, more complicated. The longtime outside counsel who was present at most board meetings explained,

> The feelings between some of the directors and [the CEO] were never great. He's a good executive, very strong in some of the things that the company needed when he took over. It was a tough time. We were not doing well, and this guy was willing to face up to some things that had been allowed to fester for a long time. He cleaned things up, so the board gave him a lot of room. But he used that freedom in a way that the board didn't like. They'd argue a lot. All of them are pretty strong-willed and stubborn, that's why we're where we are today.

When the CEO won the right to manage the search for his successor, some directors, as the outside counsel put it, "wanted to use this as a way to stick it to him in case it got screwed up. They'd let him run the search and get out on a limb, then watch to see if he was going to stumble. But they weren't going to help him."

The COO did not know of the tension that existed before he joined. While he was a talented operations executive, he didn't have much experience with boards or in political situations like the one he entered. As company results improved, the CEO became more assertive about decisions he believed should be his alone, often not letting the board know that he had made them. The relationship between the CEO and board became more strained and confrontations increased. Seven months later, the board fired the CEO and replaced him with the COO.

The new CEO took hold and performed well, but his transition was more prolonged than it should have been. "I was convinced that I could eventually be the best CEO for this company but I needed some time to settle in, get some experience with things I never did before like [managing relationships with the board] and dealing with [analysts, investors, and the media]." The political drama between the CEO and directors made for a tense environment and hindered a relationship with the board from forming when the CEO was COO. At a time when directors could have counseled him and explained what they expected, "Relationships with the board were pretty strained so there was not a lot of communication. It would have helped if I had more access to them."

The board had disengaged just when he needed its support. "All of a sudden, I was there," he said of the situation he was thrust into. "It worked eventually, but we wasted a lot of time."

The board and CEO share responsibilities as shepherds of the transition. Together they must pay particular attention to events that can either accelerate or hinder progress. It's a mistake for directors not to stay involved with the transition process as it unfolds. When that happens, the board is guilty of not becoming a student of the phases transitions go through. They are unaware what makes a great one and do not understand what must exist in the company's culture for the handoff to go well. The outcomes of these errors are having unrealistic expectations about the duration of a successful handoff and not understanding what the new leader is experiencing. The result is the lack of help on the issues that can make the difference between success and failure.

The new leader's early successes will be much more difficult and it will take longer to become established, take hold of new responsibilities, and earn credibility if the people on the company side of the equation withdraw from the transition. That is what happened to Barbara. Not only did the major players largely fail to prepare for her entry, they also did not act as a positive force for her transition once she arrived.

CEOs and boards have different roles to play, and as we've seen, it's important that one not intrude too much on the tasks for which the other is best equipped. But in the end, each must do its part; if not, the transition will be defeated by passive insiders who offer insufficient help. This can then trigger a downward spiral: withholding help leads to inactivity, inactivity leads to wrong assumptions, wrong assumptions lead to unhelpful actions, unhelpful actions lead to miscommunication, miscommunication leads to relationship problems, and relationship problems lead to transition failure.

In the case just described, the spiral was interrupted by the board's action to fire the CEO and elevate the COO, eliminating what was becoming a poisonous atmosphere. If that had not happened, the spiral would have continued. The point is that the downward spiral is hard to stop when people do not, from the start, reject the myth that implies they can become disengaged from the new leader before the transition is complete.

Myth 3: We Know What He Can Do

The wording of this myth comes from a CHRO who put the emphasis on the word *know*. He and the CEO had made a series of assumptions about the readiness of someone they knew to assume a senior post that would in large part determine the success of the whole corporation for years to come. In reality, they did not know the gaps in what was an impressive menu of this executive's skills and did not know how those skills would hold up in a different mix of strategic, operational, political, personal, and cultural factors in their organization.

The CHRO was referring to an executive, whom we'll call Jack, who was returning after four and a half years of being president of a smaller company. The corporation Jack was returning to was different from the one he'd left and was reorganizing to streamline and gain efficiency. Of its dozen divisions, half were large but aging, operating in markets where growth had slowed considerably. The rest were smaller but had higher growth and profit potential. An outside strategy study had pointed out that the traditional businesses were too expensive to operate separately given their slower-growth prospects. It recommended selling two and merging the rest into one mega-division. The assumption was that the mass achieved by combining divisions would offer several advantages no competitor could match.

The consultant's financial analysis claimed that if the company could quickly reach certain revenue targets and economies of scale, the return provided would generate the capital needed to accelerate growth of the smaller divisions. It also recommended that since the older divisions consumed most of the services of procurement, supply chain, and human resources, that those services move from corporate to the mega-division, thereby absorbing most of the shared-services costs.

When the company's top team was finalizing plans for the reorganization, one of them commented that Jack would be the ideal person to run the mega-division, and he had heard that Jack might be interested. In truth, Jack was eager to find a way to exit the company he was running. It faced a raft of quality and safety problems, turnover was high, and revenue had declined, leaving fewer resources for problem-solving. Jack was prepared to jump at the chance to return to the security of the larger, more stable corporation.

As the group discussed the idea, it became more appealing to the CEO based on three assumptions. One was that Jack would need no orientation because he was familiar with the company. Another was that he would know how to handle an organization with a standalone structure of operating and administrative units where all staff functions were reporting to him. A third was that he was familiar with running a business with revenue and headcount similar to the company he was running as president.

These assumptions contributed to the statement, and myth, uttered by the CHRO. Indeed, everyone assumed Jack was ideally suited for this challenge, including Jack himself. But he was facing some personal issues. He was drained after several years in the top spot. His confidence was damaged because things had not turned out as he had hoped. He concluded it would be best for him career-wise and emotionally to return to his former company. After all, he had done well there, had maintained many friends, and remembered it as a climate where the pace was more steady, where he had had more resources, and where he had always felt comfortable. The second assumption he made was that the consultants' analysis and conclusions were valid and realistic.

But the company's optimistic assumptions glossed over realities that should have raised questions of whether Jack was a good match, and that resulted in the company's wrongheaded thinking. One example was that the structure and the people in its key spots were put in place with no consideration of who would run the new organization. Ignored were the political and relationship realities that become apparent when matching styles and compensating for shortcomings. The structure should have been tentative so that Jack could adjust it. Because it wasn't, it became a political, relationship problem, one that contributed to the failure of this transition.

The main antagonist in this story, whom we'll call Nick, had competed aggressively for the top job. After Jack accepted the offer to be president, Nick was made an executive vice president. He had been hired five years before as a division marketing vice president just as

Jack was leaving. His impressive performance won him a promotion quickly and he soon took over sales as well. Then he became general manager of one of the divisions. He opened new markets, often finding ones that competitors had ignored. Before the competition was aware of it, Nick had taken control of high-growth niches. He was adept at exploiting his competitors' weak spots.

Because Nick was a talent the company did not want to lose, when Jack was named as division president, Nick was given a retention bonus. He was also told to be patient, that if he kept performing well, he would get the next division president job that was available. But Nick was bitterly disappointed. He told colleagues he should not be made to wait for a job running a major division. He had earned the chance to become division president right away, and he boasted that he was the best person to run the mega-division.

All of that, of course, set the stage for competition between Jack and Nick. Eventually, the rivalry drew everyone on the division's top team into the conflict. Loyalties were split and sides were drawn. Integration of former divisions slowed as people could not agree on positioning and pricing in shared markets. Service to customers suffered. Competitors saw fresh opportunities to gain an edge. Midlevel managers saw the conflict and became confused about policies and direction. The result was slow decision making and mixed messages at a time when success depended on decisiveness and coordination.

A year after Jack started, the new division was behind its revenue and cost targets and had failed to gain market share. Jack, who had inherited the first year's financial plan, presented an annual operating plan for the subsequent year. After reviewing the division's performance, detailing its strengths and weaknesses compared to competitors, and specifying the most promising growth opportunities, he argued that expectations had been unrealistically high when the division was started. The task of merging units that had operated in different ways was more difficult than anyone had imagined.

Jack promised that he would eventually deliver on the mission and its strategy and, through them, the corporation's resurgence. But he said it was going to take more time. He laid out a 24-month plan that would provide for a modest revenue increase in the next year while integration continued and new systems were put in place. He projected growth in Year 2 at the rate that the plan he had inherited had called for in the current year. "Is everyone on your team behind this plan?," the CEO asked. Jack admitted that there had been "vigorous debate ... but, this is our plan."

Jack was not aware that Nick had gone to the CEO in advance to say he disagreed with the plan Jack would be presenting and believed a more aggressive plan was both needed and achievable. After hearing Jack's plan the next day, the CEO wasn't sure what he was more disappointed in—Jack's conclusion that it would be another two years before he would see the returns he wanted or that Jack hadn't anticipated that Nick would do an end run and try to take advantage of Jack's predicament.

A week later, the CEO asked to see Jack and said, "It's not working. I've decided to go in another direction in terms of leadership of the division." He explained that Nick would be promoted to the top spot. "You've done the job in getting this started and I appreciate all the hard work it took. The base is there for growth now, but I can't wait another two years to get to where we should be now." It was then that Jack had learned that Nick had gone to the CEO with an alternative plan.

At this writing, it is not yet clear whether Jack's plan was the right one. It may well be the optimal path for the business rather than the more aggressive one the CEO favored. But it is clear that the major players knew far less than they should have about Jack, the need for a successful transition, and the political, cultural, and personal blocks to a successful handoff.

On a personal level, they didn't know enough about how anxious Jack was to leave the company he ran. No one had checked into why it was experiencing difficulties. Had they done so they would have learned that, although he was smart and solid financially and operationally, he was neither aggressive nor entrepreneurial. The CEO had not thought to talk to the people Jack had formerly reported to in his own corporation, people who could have confirmed that Jack's cautious decision-making style was unsuited for the pace the CEO demanded and for the strategy the company had adopted. Taking risks, bold visions, and driving people under stressful conditions were not what Jack enjoyed; he was not an effective leader for the situation he was in.

On the political front, the company did nothing to prepare for the political environment Jack walked into, an environment that signaled a cultural shift in the company. The compensation system had changed from collective sharing of profits to rewarding individual effort. There was competition and backstabbing where in the past there had been an all-in-it-together attitude. The culture had changed with the retirement of managers who had maintained the corporation's traditional values. One symbol of that change was that the CEO rewarded Nick for going around his boss and being disloyal.

The case of Jack is a tale of failure because of assumptions all along the way. The strategy consultants assumed that a mega-division would capture market share more quickly than was realistic, and that the cultural impediments were unimportant. Jack assumed that if he went back to where he had felt better about himself, he would do well again. The CEO assumed that, because Jack had spent much of his career at the corporation, he would view the current challenges as the CEO did; and because he had been president of a company, he was equipped to handle the mega-division's challenges in the way that the CEO wanted them handled.

Over the past decade, more companies are investing in detailed, external assessments of a candidate's style and personality as part of the vetting process before making a formal offer. If done well, these attempts at learning more about a candidate can shed light on under-lying motivations, likely reactions to stress, or cultural fit, which could derail what on the surface appears to be a good match. We believe more companies should take such a step before a final decision on a new leader; but even then it is important to consider it just one more piece of data. Nothing can predict with a high degree of accuracy whether a newcomer will be successful, even, as was the case with Jack, with the benefit of past experience and familiarity. Credentials, experience, and even formal assessments can predict only so much. One never knows the degree to which a new leader will master culture, the politics, and a changing environment until he has joined the company. This is all the more reason for the major players to remain involved well beyond the new leader's first day on the job. Boards, CEOs, CHROs, and senior managers must be aware of the myths they often, by default, take as articles of faith.

How Transition Myths Bar Productive Thinking

The three myths prevent the major players from understanding the complex realities of the transition, and they also prevent deeper thinking needed to manage those realities. Specifically, they hinder: (1) empathy for the new leader, (2) learning about the transition process; and (3) questioning that can bring about constant improvement. Empathy, learning, and questioning—when they are obstructed, the transition process will not be managed to the greatest benefit of the new leader or the organization.

Lack of Empathy

A major hindrance that stems from the three transition myths is a lack of empathy. Do the major players understand and share the thoughts, feelings, and challenges of the new leader? When executives come in from the outside, they enter unknown and often inhospitable territory.

Usually, they have no political support initially, are unsure whom to trust, and must find their own way. And if they are implementing a change agenda, they are under pressure to make quick progress. Success may be doubly hard to achieve because it depends on making good on a predecessor's promises and plans, as well as an organization that may not be best to achieve the inherited strategy.

When major players default to passivity it is often because they have not put in the effort necessary to fully appreciate the difficulties the new leader faces or the situation from her point of view. The new leader faces the challenges of winning the loyalty of subordinates she has not selected and who may resist needed changes, of forging relationships with senior managers she does not know and who may be competitors but whose cooperation is essential, and of doing all this while leaving behind a support system and familiar practices in her former company. In her new environment, with much to learn about the business and culture, the new leader can fall behind if her new boss or peers fail to help, which is much more likely if they don't understand her feelings and how she views the difficulties she faces.

Barbara is an example. Because people in her new company largely embraced the three transition myths, she was left without an empathetic transition team. Empathy would have suggested she needed help adjusting the expectations of people in the finance department, who, for the sake of growing the business, had to migrate from division support staff to corporate watchdogs. Empathy would have highlighted how she needed help handling colleagues who bristled at having been made her subordinates. And it would have revealed a host of personal style changes she would have to make to transition successfully into a less formal, less disciplined company. But transition thinking stuck in neutral meant that the needed empathy was not forthcoming.

The people who thrived in Barbara's new company were bright and creative but chafed at the idea of an ordered, process-oriented culture. Since the era of the founders, they had been encouraged to work remotely if they chose and come to the office at any hour, practices rare at the time. A few of them, given unusual latitude to pursue new ideas, created products and services that were very successful. As revenue grew, more like-minded people were attracted to the company, fueling more creativity and innovation. The company stayed true to the founders' intent for many years and discouraged process infrastructure or systems. When Barbara tried to introduce control and coordination across department and unit boundaries, she did so because the company needed them in order to change, but she had little help because no one tried to put themselves in her spot.

Lack of Learning

A second big mistake that stems from transition myths is that boards, CEOs, CHROs, and senior managers do not become students of leadership transitions. Lulled into thinking the transition task is easy, they do not take necessary steps that can help ensure success.

One step to kick-start learning might be asking CEOs and directors in other companies about their transition experiences and what they would change if given the chance to conduct the transition again. Another could be studying summaries of the most relevant literature. From such steps, guidelines can become clear for transition planning.

While these basic steps can be useful, in those cases, the major players need to go further. They need to adopt habits of the transition student. If not, the benefit of initial learning will be elusive. For example, they may appreciate the impact of culture in general, but unless they go further they won't identify the specific elements of their own culture that have the most impact on the handoff's success. One no-cost way to discover them is through the simple step that few companies take: senior executives talking with people who have recently joined and left about why they stay or go. Another is to analyze employee surveys in a way that not only catalogues their opinions about issues and problems of importance but also provides an accurate, vivid picture of what it is like to work in the company and the barriers to both performance and satisfaction. Lack of such knowledge lulls the major players (directors in particular) into believing that things are different than they are, which in turn blocks what is needed for transition success.

Some learning should come from initiative taken by the CEO and directors, such as seeking out people they know in other companies. Other ways to learn, such as identifying relevant literature, finding companies to benchmark, and preparing briefings on relevant topics, might be best suited for a senior staff aide, perhaps in a chief-of-staff position or from a strategic planning unit. CHROs are best equipped to survey the culture and translate requirements to other major players and new leaders as well as to recruiters. Many of the people interviewed said they conduct reviews of transitions that fail in order to better understand what went wrong and why. Some of them maximized the learning that can result by doing so in depth and in an organized way. For example, Aetna's executive committee devoted an entire meeting to the question of why a transition failed and what the company should have done differently. If done well, and allowed to delve into the actual reasons for failure, even if they expose mistakes of powerful executives, such a discussion can reveal important insight about how decisions are made, gaps in communication, and the weaknesses of the decision-making process.

Lack of Questioning

The third hindrance that stems from transition myths is that boards, CEOs, CHROs, and senior managers do not question enough or deeply enough to identify what else can be done. They need to take into account, on one hand, the combination of the new leader's strengths and weaknesses, and on the other, the strategic and operational needs of the company, its culture, and its political environment.

A good example is the CEO who insisted that his top managers change when his CHRO asked him to endorse a taking-hold plan for his new CTO. Had the CHRO asked the right questions, he would have learned that he was mistaken. The CEO had in fact thought quite deeply about the taking-hold needs of the new executive and would have welcomed a well-thought-through plan. The CHRO read the CEO's reaction as dismissing the concern, but the reaction actually signaled nothing more than the frustration of the CEO over the slow pace with which his organization was adapting to market changes and its general resistance to change.

If the CHRO had persevered, he might have realized that the general resistance to change was a problem that his department should have analyzed and recommended steps to improve. But without the right questioning, his conclusion was that his boss was angry and had made up his mind that the senior managers were the ones on which to concentrate. Instead of asking questions to understand what was at the root of the CEO's comment, the CHRO backed off, trapped by the myths of transition. The same was true in the cases of the people responsible for the transitions of Jack and of Barbara.

In Barbara's case, the CHRO, a veteran of the company, avoided in several ways putting more effort into questioning. One tactic he could have used was to have Barbara interview with her future direct reports. Another was to arrange for her to go through a style assessment. A third was to use a search firm familiar with the company culture. All of these tactics should have resulted in flagging a mismatch of Barbara's style with the way her new company operated.

The CHRO had wanted to be the main contact for the search so that he could better monitor the process. The CEO, however, made the mistake of insisting on running the hiring process himself. The CHRO was complicit in this fault by his lack of finding a way to engage the CEO. He should have done so by asking questions of what the CEO wanted to achieve in running the process himself. If he had, he might have discovered that the CEO wanted to make sure the CFO who was hired was disciplined and tough enough to make the changes that were necessary. If he had continued to question the CEO, he might have also found out his biggest concern: even though the CEO believed he had to drive the search for his signature new hire himself, he was worried that he did not have enough hours in the day to do that plus what was currently on his to-do list.

If the dialog had gone in that direction, the CHRO might have asked, "How can I help you solve that problem?" He could have then followed up with a plan for taking on the more time-consuming steps of the search, thereby conserving the CEO's time while allowing him to still be in control of the hiring. The lack of deep questioning and dialogue left many questions neither raised nor addressed.

This fault is particularly common if a company, by virtue of its culture, fails to operate on the belief that problems, mistakes, and failures should be as openly discussed as successes. Open questioning has the benefit of increasing the self-awareness of the people in the company as to what motivates and causes them to act as they do. It is in this way that questioning is a significant factor for transition success.

Leaving Tough Questions Unanswered

In the end, the most harmful effect of transition myths is that they prevent serious discussion about the most important transition issues. If the major players succumb to these myths, they will less readily bring up tough questions or answer them.

One such tough question comes from the strategic realm: How can the new leader best graft a new strategy onto the one the organization is currently pursuing in a way that the organization does not reject it?

If the knowledge, skills, and behaviors of most managers and those who report to them are geared for the existing strategy, how can a leader new to her job and still establishing her own credibility manage the change to one that requires different knowledge, skills, and behaviors? As Barbara found out, even the right strategy can be rejected if it collides with an accepted culture and people's comfortable habits.

The next tough question is from the operational realm: How can we maintain operational momentum for short-term results while implementing processes and systems necessary both for the new leader to achieve his objectives and also for a new strategy? How does a leadership transition happening while there is a change of strategy affect our ability to continue to operate in a cost-effective, predicable, high-quality way? Once again, the question came up for Barbara and a good answer was not apparent to anyone, certainly not when contrasted with the open communication and relationship building of Dave and Jim in the previous chapter.

A tough question from the political realm is this: How can we help new leaders understand our company's political structure while also ensuring they adapt it to meet the strategic and operational objectives they were hired to implement? In the previous chapter, we saw how Dave helped Jim with this question by giving him a guided tour through the ranks of his top team and explaining the company's power structure. Who had influence? Who had power? Why? Who was allied with whom? What were the political hindering and facilitating factors for Jim to build relationships? In contrast, this chapter describes how Barbara and Jack never received adequate help to explicitly address this question. How would things have turned out had more serious transition thinking been done?

A fourth tough question comes from the personal realm: How can a new leader best take control and establish himself assertively and with confidence while also pausing to understand the needs and motivations of the people he has inherited? How can we help him push (his agenda on the organization) and pull (from people their needs) at the same time? Also, what must be added to the new leader's abilities to fulfill his own expectations as well as the expectations of those who hired him and those in the organization who depend on his leadership? This was a balance that was not managed well in Barbara's case.

Finally, consider a tough question from the cultural realm: How can we help the new leader understand the company's cultural norms so that she can make the culture work for her to achieve what she was hired to do? Certainly, Barbara desperately needed to address this question, but could not do so on her own without the CEO and senior managers. That conversation never took place. Once she had accepted the offer and before her first day on the job, they could have asked: What norms will most affect Barbara's success? Which ones might have to change given what we have asked her to do? Do the people she will inherit have the capacity and willingness to change? If not, how can we help her?

And so we see the destructive nature of these three pernicious myths. They can be like suffocating fog, depriving the major players of the light necessary to gain a clear grasp of the transition's inherent complexity. They can lock them into passivity when it comes to thinking about their roles and can block the open atmosphere necessary for productive and frank conversation about the most important questions that are tough to answer even under the best of circumstances.

Sadly, these myths lure smart people into the kind of unskillful thinking that leads new leaders like Barbara to fail. The lesson is obvious yet commonly missed: The clearer the thinking done by new leaders and people responsible for their transitions, the better the chances of success for everyone. If people on the receiving end of a new leader are uttering or perpetuating myths, they are putting their companies at enormous risk.

Summary

The intent of this chapter was to describe the errors in how transitions at the top are perceived. While these thinking errors present themselves in a variety of ways, at their root is a set of basic assumptions about the transfer of power and the challenges of assuming authority at the very top of an organization.

The case of Barbara showed their effects on a talented executive trying to take hold in an unfamiliar culture. That case introduced three myths that commonly appear in organizations that experience failed handoffs. The first myth suggests that taking on supreme authority should be a routine event. On the contrary, as we have shown, it is anything but routine, especially in cases where the successor enters from outside the organization and is expected to implement a change agenda.

The second myth has to do with the point at which success can be declared. Some transitions fail when the board or CEO back away too quickly, leaving the new leader without sufficient guidance or help. We offered a definition for completed, successful transitions: one can declare the transition over when there is true leadership continuity as measured by the new leader being established, having taken hold of necessary new responsibilities, and, most of all, having earned credibility as a result of the tangible successes she has achieved or, even better, enabled others to achieve.

The third myth can be seen as the arrogance of assumed knowledge. We recounted a case of a talented senior manager who returned to the company where he began his career.

(continued)

(continued)

His transition failed because of faulty logic, wishful thinking, and laziness in planning and preparation, problems shared by all of the players involved. The combination opened the door to politically toxic behavior that had negative consequences to both managers involved as well as to the culture.

This chapter also showed how faulty core assumptions lead to behavior that blocks transition success. The lack of empathy displayed, lack of learning from successes or mistakes, and inadequate questioning contribute to preventing serious discussion about the most crucial transition issues. The convergence of faulty thinking about transitions at the top leads to errors of execution.

Note

1. D. Ciampa, *Taking Advice: How Leaders Get Good Counsel and Use It Wisely* (Harvard Business School Press, 2006).

3 Errors of Execution

A lan was the longtime chairman/CEO of a company where he had worked for most of his career, moving up through the accounting and financial management paths to become CFO, and then into the top job. He was fiercely proud of the company's traditions and heritage and described himself as a "conservative traditionalist." He believed that a reliable, well-designed product would attract customers on its own, that brand management and advertising were much less important areas in which to invest, that small, safe steps were better than large, bold strategic moves, and that keeping costs low, even if cost-reduction might jeopardize innovation, was one of the most important tasks of a CEO. He abhorred taking risks. It was, therefore, surprising that Alan would hire Wayne as his designated successor.

Wayne had spent most of his career in a large consumer-packaged goods corporation. Trained as an engineer and with an MBA, he entered that company in its operations and logistics area. Soon, his competitiveness, self-confidence, motivational style, and presentation skills enabled him to move to brand management. Once there, he climbed the company's organizational ladder, ending up running one of the largest business units. He had done well, but given the quality of talent he was competing with, Wayne realized that the chances were low of his ever running the corporation.

What attracted Wayne to Alan's company was the chance to be CEO in a few years. The offer was to join as the head of its largest operating division, reporting to Alan. If things went well, in a couple of years he would become chief operating officer and then CEO, at which point Alan would retire.

Although it meant moving from a place where he had established himself into a new industry and a company with a very different culture, the excitement of a change and challenge of mastering a new business were very attractive. He'd always been a risk taker, and through his style, hard work, and intelligence he had always achieved what he had set out to do. He was sure he would do the same in his new company.

A few years later, after he had become CEO, Wayne had achieved most of what the board had asked. Revenue had improved, and a new product had been launched that was not only at a premium price with high margins but had changed the company's image, especially appealing to younger customers who were not drawn to the company's traditional products. He had revitalized new product development, creating a pipeline of exciting projects for the future. He had also expanded the corporation's reach with a joint venture agreement in China that was starting to open up that huge market for its products and brought the promise of lower-cost suppliers.

On the organizational front, Wayne had attracted a group of impressive designers, engineers, and marketing managers to the company and was building an international team to expand market reach and create a worldwide supply chain. Externally, Wayne had developed solid relationships with customers and was a favorite of institutional investors and analysts who had been used to a very different approach from the company. He had changed the company's traditional approach in which it provided little information beyond what was required and generally treated analysts as necessary irritants.

After Wayne had served a year and a half as CEO, the various stakeholders had good things to say about him. They liked that the company was seen as innovative, a reputation that had slipped in the years before Wayne arrived. Even longtime employees who had been skeptical of his ideas and approach were impressed with the results of the changes he had implemented, including the effects on their retirement plans from the increase in the stock price.

It was, then, all the more surprising to many people that, less than two years after he had been elevated to the top spot, Wayne was forced out of the company by the board. The stock, marketplace, new product, and revenue gains that resulted from his leadership weren't enough to save his job. The one goal that remained elusive was profit. It had stayed stubbornly low, largely due to the investments Wayne had made. He stressed to the board that the infrastructure, systems, and talent in international, marketing, and new products would all pay off. The board initially assured him it was solidly in support, but over time that support eroded.

Wayne's story is not the only one where a leader leaves the top spot unexpectedly without a crisis or without due cause. What goes wrong in these cases?

There are a combination of factors. Usually there are one or two root causes. Sometimes it comes down to the organization the new leader has inherited not being able to stay up with his ambitious change agenda. That was one of the root causes in Wayne's case. But even that would not have the impact it did without another, more seminal root cause that fed and exacerbated the problem—the fragileness of the CEO/designated successor relationship. The relationship between Wayne and Alan never gelled—in fact, it fell apart before coming together fully, indicating a failure in transition management of the major players.

Part of the fault in cases such as these can be found in the thinking errors covered in the previous chapter. In the case of Wayne, one of the most important was the assumption by the board that the relationship between Alan and Wayne needed little of their attention. The directors didn't wrestle enough with the tough questions that need to be answered to achieve success in these situations: How does a new leader with a change agenda best grasp the culture of the organization he is taking over so that its limitations to achieve that agenda are clear?

How much and how quickly can an organization be pushed to change? What are the likely traps for a new leader who reports to a predecessor with a different style and approach to the business? What are the responsibilities of the incumbent leader to ensure the success of the person who follows? How can the powerful needs for recognition and respect of the predecessor be balanced with the equally strong needs for recognition and respect of the successor?

These questions are tough ones to answer in a general way because every situation is different with unique pressures from strategic, operational, political, and cultural forces. They are especially tough because of the complexities on the personal front where the needs of each individual for achievement, affiliation, and power are strong. How carefully the major players think about such questions is one part of the formula for a transition's success. The more important part, of course, is what they do about them. That's where errors of execution come in.

Errors of Execution

- Not preparing for or attempting to manage the transition

- Missing or ignoring problems in the relationship between the incumbent and successor

- Preparing for only one transition

  The departing leader
  Derivative defections

- Mismanaging the transition process

  Miscalculating information needed
  Failure of major players to prepare
  Poorly handling onboarding

The most egregious error is not even attempting to manage a hand-off in any planned or formal way. In a survey by executive search firm Heidrick & Struggles and the Rock Center for Corporate Governance at Stanford University, half the companies reported provided no formal transition plan for the new leader.[1]

Beyond the failure to prepare and have a plan for a top-level transition, there are three other categories of execution errors. One is missing or ignoring problems in the relationship between the incumbent and successor.

The next error category is when the major players prepare only for one transition, the most apparent one where the incumbent hands power to her successor, but ignore the other, derivative transitions that inevitably take place as a result of the primary one.

The final one is mismanaging the transition process by miscalculating the information that will be most relevant to the major players to adequately prepare for their roles, and doing a poor job of handling the onboarding of the new leader.

Relationship between Incumbent and Successor

The error that most seriously confounds transitions is when the four players ignore, miss, or underestimate problems in the relationship between the new leader and the one being replaced. Even though, after the handoff, this relationship is often seen as having been important to success, it is commonly ignored beforehand. Boards of directors, in particular, are frequently surprised by its complexity and struggle with its difficulty. In the case of Wayne and Alan, the directors should have been prepared to help over an extended period because the potential for problems was apparent before the succession search started.

The first sign, months earlier, came when John, the lead director, concluded that it was time to start the conversation with Alan about stepping aside. Approaching Alan on this subject was not easy for John, who had joined the board shortly after Alan had been promoted to chairman and CEO. That was 10 years earlier, and they had hit it off right away. Both had similar backgrounds and had come up the ladders of their careers in the finance function. John appreciated that Alan had lobbied the directors for him to be named lead director.

But in spite of his personal feelings, John believed he had a responsibility to address some worrisome signs. He had seen the company's once-admired reputation for innovation stagnate and its once-celebrated customer service erode. The senior management group was made up of people who had been in the company for many years, and was not at all diverse. In fact, it had been a while since anyone new had been hired at that level. John also noticed that, over the previous year, presentations at board meetings lacked thorough thinking and offered few new conclusions. Many of the senior managers who spoke at the meetings seemed unsure of details. Although John didn't see any disasters-in-the-making, he worried about complacency at a time when the economy was growing and competitors were trying aggressively to grab market share.

The conversation with Alan didn't go well. Alan argued that the company's balance sheet remained strong and when the often-delayed new product was released, the company's reputation for innovation as well as its revenue flow would be restored. Even more worrisome to John was Alan's defensiveness as they talked. At one point, becoming emotional when speaking of all he had done for the company, Alan said, "and instead of criticism from directors who are on the board because of me, I should get a 'thank-you,' and even though you think I'm not doing the right things, I know the rest of the board supports me."

It was now clear to John that the state of the company was prob-ably worse than he had thought. If Alan had reacted that way to a director raising questions, he was unlikely to listen to the concerns of his managers when they pointed to problems.

A month later, it wasn't a surprise to John when he learned that Alan was actively lining up support among directors closest to him. It did not take long for the board to fracture into two camps, one supporting John and the other Alan. Discussions became increasingly tense as the board insisted that Alan understand it was intent on an orderly transition. Under pressure, Alan agreed to step aside as CEO and remain chairman if a longtime vice president became CEO. The board rejected that idea, firm in the belief that new blood was needed. In the end, Alan agreed to an outside search for a designated successor.

Wayne joined the company six months later. Within two and half years, he became CEO, the first outsider in the company's history to be named to the job. Alan retained the chairman title and would fully retire shortly after the business seemed to be doing better, with the new product line leading the way.

The board was relieved that the tension was left behind and the handoff to Wayne had been successful. Alan continued to maneuver behind the scenes, however. Although no longer a director, he mounted a campaign to discredit his successor. He convinced a majority of the board that Wayne's strategy was inherently flawed because it had not produced enough early profit growth along with top-line increases. The board remained divided, but within two years, it forced Wayne out of the company and eventually reinstated Alan as CEO. John resigned as director when the board chose Alan over Wayne, chagrined when he discovered Alan's scheme. Several years later, the company had failed to boost profitability by only cutting costs and was sold to one of its competitors at a price most analysts considered a bargain.

This failed transition was not caused by a board that was unconcerned or uninvolved. The directors devoted a significant amount of time to the succession. Nor was it due to directors avoiding responsibility. John, who was committed to executing his duty as a board member, sacrificed a friendship as well as a board seat to raise questions about Alan's fitness to continue as CEO.

Instead, this transition failed for two interrelated reasons. The first was the inability of Alan and Wayne to forge a positive working relationship. Had they been able to do so, the results would have been positive as they could have concentrated on taking advantage of the complementary abilities each had to address the company's challenges.

Alan's deep knowledge of the company's capabilities and his financial background should have meshed well with Wayne's leadership capabilities and marketing skills. Had it, they might well have decided on the correct approach for the company going forward at a point in between Wayne's risk-taking and Alan's conservatism. In addition, each man had a compelling reason for the company to thrive. Alan had spent his whole career there and as his legacy wanted to see it become more successful before retiring. Wayne knew that the ticket to the CEO spot was profitable, sustainable growth, which meant significant changes to an organization that was more loyal to Alan than to Wayne. Having Alan on his side would have made his job of changing the culture much easier.

The key to making the most of this potential win-win outcome for both executives was a collaborative relationship, and the key to that was the behavior of each executive. Because they did not agree, it was more important than ever that each would listen carefully to the other's point of view, be willing to negotiate, think through differences, and strive to find common ground. Doing these sorts of things requires trust, something that could not be developed without the board's active engagement and help under the pressure of an underperforming business with two people with very different personalities who did not know each other.

The second reason for the failure was within the company itself and the inability of the board to address it. The strategy had become muddled even before Wayne was hired, but the board was not close enough to the business to recognize what had to change or what a better strategy might be. As John discovered, Alan was not prepared to answer those questions because he wanted the company to remain on its former strategic path and in his control. That control, however, was not producing the results that it once had. What had been a disciplined, efficient organization had become much less so. Decisions were left unmade and problems unresolved. Meanwhile, a lack of investment in development and hiring of people with new skills and ideas hurt innovation.

Other than John's attempt, the board never engaged Alan in a serious conversation about what needed to change for the company's ongoing success strategically, operationally, or culturally. Instead, it hired Wayne, who had very different ideas about the right strategic path and how the company should operate. It hoped that he would solve the problems that the board should have identified and made progress on before the transition began.

Instead of actively engaging so that these two leaders and their different visions could be combined, the board left Alan and Wayne in the ring to fight it out. It could have established the rules of engagement and refereed a process for a complete review of the company's strategy and of its ability to operate in an effective way going forward. It might have directed Alan and Wayne to do a deep, complete strategic and operational review and come back with a path both could endorse. If, after such a review, the two men could not agree, the board could have interceded and mediated, or told them to try harder, and if they could not agree, they both had to leave the company and another search would produce a new CEO.

Instead, these two strong-willed executives were allowed to follow separate strategic paths, each convinced it was the correct one for the company. The result was confusion among managers regarding the direction of the business, which in turn led to more uncertainty on important decisions. As serious, the culture was damaged as managers were forced to choose sides and assign their loyalty to either Alan or Wayne, just as the board had been.

Preparing for Only One Transition

The second category of execution errors stems from the assumption that the only transition to be concerned about is the one in which the new leader is brought in to assume responsibility from a predecessor. It is understandable that the major players on the company side would tend to devote all their attention to the new leader. For one thing, the fortunes of the company and its various stakeholders depend on his success. Since the head of human resources and other senior managers will work for the new person, or at least alongside as a peer, they may also be anxious to build a relationship. But while it is important for all concerned to prepare for the new leader's successful entry, doing so without also paying attention to the leader who is stepping aside, as well as to other managers who may depart, is a path of risk for both the successor and the organization.

The Leader Who Departs

The idealized handoff is one where the sitting CEO leaves the company he has run having met many challenges, planned a next step that is attractive enough to pull him away willingly, and feeling satisfied that he has left the company in a stronger state than when he took over. Sometimes the sitting CEO is capable enough to make that happen, as Dave was upon the arrival of Jim in Chapter 1. Dave may have wanted more control of the transition, but in the end, he left satisfied that the company was in much better shape than when he had joined, in fact, than it had ever been.

Dave could leave willingly because he had arranged activities to attract him to his next life phase. He had been a director of another company for several years and looked forward to becoming even more involved. He had agreed to be on another corporate board in a different industry, a healthcare company doing research on a disease that had left its mark on his family. And he had been asked by the university where he had received his graduate degree to chair its fundraising campaign and was welcome any time he wanted to be a guest lecturer. In other words, Dave had accomplished what he had set out to do, had done the best job he could, and was looking forward to new challenges.

Contrast that with Alan, whose resistance to the change attempts of the board masked his personal fear of leaving the job that had defined him. The first sign of a problem was Alan's insistence that his loyal, longtime subordinate be his replacement and that he remain as chairman. That would have meant that nothing would change except who held the CEO title. Alan was on no outside boards, or involved in any not-for-profit activities. He had toiled long and hard at the company, doggedly weathering the ups and downs of business cycles and internal politics to get to the top spot. There were few other employees who were as associated emotionally with the company or were as proud of it. All this meant that when the lead director talked about a new strategic direction, the need for change in the way the company operated, and an outsider as his successor, it was a difficult pill for Alan to swallow.

The results of these two cases, polar opposites, pivoted on four elements, which played out differently in each situation: planning, business conditions, personality, and help. In Dave and Wes's case, planning was front of mind. The two men made sure there was an explicit plan for Dave to exit the company, developed as the preparation for Jim's entry was being finalized. There was no such effort at exit planning for Alan.

As for business conditions, the pressure of declining revenue and missed new product introductions complicated Alan's departure even more than his emotional connection to the company. Because of what his position as head of the company represented to him, Alan desperately wanted to see the company in good financial shape before he left. Dave's company, on the other hand, had come through a tough patch early in his tenure and under his leadership had become stronger in the years before the transition.

As for personality, Alan said once, "I dislike conversation." He described himself as much more comfortable, "alone, going over the numbers" than engaging with other people. He had few friends; even longtime associates and colleagues knew little about his background before he joined the company or family history. In fact, all of this became a part of the problem in forming a relationship with Wayne, whose personality was much more like Dave's. Dave was gregarious, social, and communicative. He enjoyed people, relished interacting in conversations, and had always been active in whichever community he had lived and worked.

There is not an optimal model of the type of planning, state of the business, or leader personality that leads to the smoothest exit of the incumbent. The point, rather, is that these conditions should be taken into account. There should be an exit plan, the conditions under which the business operates at the time of the handoff are important to factor in, and the personality of the CEO will in large part determine her reaction to the pressures of leaving. The CEO herself should be aware of these issues and willing to explore them, but just as important, the board must as well and must not shrink from including the incumbent's exit plan as part of its overall responsibilities.

The final difference in exit situations of these two executives was help available, and more precisely, how it was used. Wes was in place as CHRO when Dave joined and the two worked closely until Dave left. In fact, they maintained a social relationship afterward.

Dave was a sophisticated enough manager to know what to ask of human resources and the role it should play, and also realized that the more Wes was involved in the strategy and operations of the business, the more benefit the human resources department would provide. He also involved Wes in each board meeting and allowed him to have an independent relationship with the chairman of the compensation committee. By the time of the transition, Dave and Wes had formed the sort of trust-based relationship that allowed Wes to step in assertively when he thought Dave needed feedback. Also, Dave sought out Wes as a sounding board as he mapped out his post-CEO plans.

By contrast, the head of human resources in Alan's company did not report to the CEO and was not on the senior executive group. She reported to the general counsel as part of a general administrative department. She had begun at the company as a secretary and worked her way up to director of personnel administration, a unit whose name was changed to human resources only shortly before Wayne was hired. She did not attend board meetings and had rarely talked with a director.

Dave had learned through the years the importance of advice from people in the organizations he had been a part of, from his mentors, and from objective outsiders. He did not shy away from asking for it when he needed help or from listening when it was offered with the right motives. Had Alan learned this important leadership ability, things would have turned out differently for everyone involved.[2]

Derivative Defections

Along with errors in helping the incumbent leader depart are those related to departures of various senior managers triggered by the CEO handoff. Some of these departures come from managers who, upon learning the agenda or experiencing the style of the new leader, decide that the changes to come are ones they either do not want to experience or do not want to convince their people to support. As these top people walk out the door, they take with them institutional knowledge, customer relationships, and valuable experience. Even when they have agreed not to recruit colleagues, others loyal to them often follow on their own. As this "derivative defection syndrome" takes hold, directors, the CEO, the CHRO, and senior managers can fumble the effort to minimize its impact unless they are prepared to take action.

Another way the derivative defection syndrome can cause damage after a transition is when senior managers leave because they either were not considered for the top job or were considered and were not chosen. The major consequence when this happens, as with any of the upper-level managers who leave, is the loss of experience and knowledge. The higher the level of manager, the greater the impact.

There are cases where such senior level departures are expected, even encouraged. When Jack Welch was replaced by Jeff Immelt at General Electric, two of the executives who had reported to Welch left. James McNerney became CEO of 3M and Robert Nardelli took the job of CEO at The Home Depot. Welch knew the ones who did not get promoted would leave. He wanted Immelt to choose his own team of people loyal to him as the new CEO. He also knew that there was a strong pipeline of people qualified to be at that level. In addition, Welch took pride in the fact that GE could boast of being a "net exporter of talent" by providing CEOs for other companies. By being known in that way, GE could attract even better talent to the corporation. Importantly, what made this situation work for all concerned was GE's celebrated management development process and the skill of the line managers to grow talent over the 20 years of Welch's tenure.

When that foundation is not in place, the impact of derivative defection syndrome can be quite damaging. The seeds of this damage are sown before the actual transition if the company gives too little attention to performance management and talent development. With the right systems, the board and CEO understand the capabilities and potential of all senior managers. That knowledge should answer some key questions: Who might leave when the CEO does? Who has the capabilities for filling the positions that might go vacant? How is promoting one executive going to affect the motivation of others? How will executives on the senior team react to an outsider being their boss? CEOs, CHROs, and boards unable to respond to such questions have failed to prepare for the inevitable transition by making sure there is a pipeline of talent.

Typically, the possibility of derivative defections is not described during the transition planning process. As a result, managers are encouraged to view themselves as potential successors; but, once that line is crossed, it is difficult for them to settle for a lesser position. Or, then they perceive they are in direct competition with peers, causing interpersonal and teamwork problems. If either perception is allowed to fester for an extended period, a zero-sum, winners-or-losers situation is inevitable, making the restoration of trust all but impossible.

Even in companies that have not prepared for derivative defections, it is possible to avoid their more serious consequences. In one company, after the departure of two senior managers, the CEO took advantage by reorganizing and hiring several new top executives right away to acquire the skills needed for its new direction. The CHRO commented, "Some of the managers in the level below had aspired to those roles and were disappointed." The CEO and CHRO patiently explained the skills and experiences the new people brought. "We tackled [derivative defections] head on by explaining why we needed new talent, that we were going into new areas and these people had the experience we needed to help us all."

In addition to explaining the rationale for hiring new executives, the company wisely revamped its management development efforts.

The CHRO continued, "We told them that we were going to help them develop the skills and get the experiences they needed so that the next time there were openings, they'd be ready. If we had not done these two things [patiently explaining the rationale and revamping talent development], we would have been in trouble."

Mismanaging the Transition Process

The third category that execution errors fall into is mismanaging the transition process. While the particular conditions and demands that shape the details of the process vary, all transitions should be designed and implemented based on one guiding principle: transitions at the most senior level are unlike those of any other in the organization. What works in the case of a new vice president or general manager will not be sufficient for the entry of a designated successor to the CEO.

Often, the lack of understanding of the nature of transitions at the most senior level leads to three missteps: first, not organizing and interpreting the type of information most important to the incoming leader's success; second, not adequately preparing people inside the company for the roles they should play in the transition; and third, mishandling the onboarding process.

Not Organizing and Interpreting the Right Information

Usually, four kinds of information are gathered for new leaders: financial (such as financial results and forecasts), planning (such as strategic plans and annual operating plans), organizational (such as organization structure and backgrounds of key people), and reputational (such as analysts' reports and consulting studies). Although this information is useful, most of it is publicly available and probably surfaced during the new leader's due diligence and preparation for interviews. An official packet supplied to the incoming leader adds confidential information and may confirm hypotheses, but even this has limited value for the issues of most importance to the transition.

Much of the time, the information provided to new leaders before they officially take hold lacks enough insight into the areas that are most likely to cause them to fail. More analysis of the financials or deeper understanding of the strategy are not on the list of reasons new leaders at the top have unsuccessful transitions. Rather, the factors that pose the biggest danger lie in the two areas that are rarely addressed before starting or during onboarding: how things really get done internally as well as externally and the nature of the culture and power structure.

How Things Really Get Done   To achieve early wins, the new leader must learn how the company operates day to day as it responds to changes of the ecosystem in which it exists. Before joining, he is limited to what is described in interviews, which may not be objective or well-informed. The hiring organization doesn't provide enough insight or detail if it only goes as far as organization charts that show formal lines of communication and theoretical paths for promotion. More useful would be descriptions of the company's processes, which lie at the core of how things actually get done. Examples of such processes are planning and budgeting, acquisition and integration, innovation and new product introduction, manufacturing and distribution, the supply chain, and talent acquisition and development.

Which processes are most critical to the company varies depending on strategy, industry, and culture. But they combine to form the organization's central nervous system through which passes vital information and determine how and how efficiently decisions are made. It is by understanding core processes that the new leader can pinpoint wasted effort, what barriers employees face to meeting their goals and contributing to the organization, the efficiency and accuracy of information, the sources of innovation, and how problems are solved that cross department lines. It is in processes that lay the opportunities for improvement that the skilled new leader can attack for early successes. Much of the time, though, such understanding doesn't come until weeks or months after the first day on the job. The earlier the new leader can grasp where opportunities lie, the better the chance for a winning transition.

In addition to internal processes are external forces that exert great pressure on the organization and which the new leader must appreciate, such as regulatory agencies and product or service interest groups. Also important is the collection of opinions and critiques on social media from disgruntled customers or current and former employees. Much of the information on such sources is either in the experiences of particular people in the company, or increasingly, from media sites such as Glass Door. The wise new leader will take advantage of both sources to gain a sense of how things really get done.

The period after accepting an offer and prior to the official start is the time to begin the study of the most important processes. The task for the CEO, CHRO, and senior managers is to depict how things really get done in a way that can be explained clearly to the new leader. The task for the new leader is to ask for such a description. When individuals on either side of the transition equation do their parts, the new leader will enter an organization ready to utilize him.

Culture and Power Structure   Related to understanding how things get done, and in some ways even more important to understand, is the organization's culture, including its power structure. But while grasping the rhythm and nuance of day-to-day operations is not always easy, it is even more difficult with the culture and the influence pattern that affects behavior. To explain why, it is important to offer some background.

It has not always been the case that culture (in the form of beliefs, habits, practices, and behavior of people in the company) has been recognized as a separate and vital topic for the leader to be concerned with. The application in industry can be traced back to the projects done by Elton Mayo of the Harvard Business School at Western Electric's Hawthorne, Illinois, plants in 1927. The research's insights about worker behavior were groundbreaking, but they largely remained topics of academic research until experiments conducted by a few pioneering manufacturing companies starting in the mid-1950s. That was followed by some organization development consultants applying them in the 1960s.[3] Their first step was to define the term and attempt to measure it.

While surveys of employees' attitudes were common, measuring the work environment, or culture, was not attempted seriously before the late 1960s. The research of George Litwin at the Harvard Business School fueled the vanguard of thinking about organization climate.[4] It was first used by one of the pioneering research and consulting firms in this area (The Behavioral Science Center of Sterling Institute, later McBer & Co.) as it conducted some of the earliest culture surveys.

As consultants were learning how to measure culture, the topic of how to manage it was entering management education. Programs to train leaders to better manage the motivation of subordinates and to improve problem-solving ability in groups began to include ways to better understand the often obscure forces of organizational culture. Interest in this topic was beginning to grow slowly. Then, in the late 1970s and early 1980s, something unrelated happened that, more than anything else up to that point, put this topic on the agenda of corporate America: the threat from Japanese corporations that were making substantial inroads in markets traditionally dominated by U.S. companies.

The first substantive analysis of this push was done by George Stalk and Jim Abegglen of the Boston Consulting Group in the 1970s.[5] In parallel came the development of Total Quality and Just-in-Time (JIT) programs, which brought new, more effective ways to improve quality, speed, and efficiency in product design, manufacturing, and distribution. Common assumptions about this era are that these techniques were imported via Japanese production systems. In fact, of the discrete techniques in the JIT process, only one (*Kanban*) had not been developed in the United States. Another common assumption about this era is that automation and advanced production systems gave Japan's companies the edge. Here again, most were invented in the United States and in use in U.S. companies.

The reason Japanese companies outperformed competitors was not that they invented new, proprietary production techniques or automated systems. Rather, it was how they employed ones that had already been developed. To the Americans who first witnessed Japanese production systems in action, the most noticeable differences were that people across departments cooperated when there was a problem that affected only one, that workers at the lowest levels had the license to push through changes and even stop a production line, and that, while goals were as clear as they were in U.S. plants, in Japanese ones, feedback on progress was everywhere. Little was hidden. Further, components such as these were wrapped in a drumbeat of continuous improvement that all workers and managers were expected to believe in and were supported by constant training and education programs (at a time when U.S. companies cut such programs to pare costs). In other words, the difference lay in the organizational cultures of companies in Japan that were different from those of their American competitors.

This realization that culture impacted company performance caused leaders to pay attention to it. The more that connection became apparent, the more consultants and other advisors added to cultural theories and practices; and the more they competed with one another for air time and credit, the sharper became the theories and the more practical the tools to apply them for their clients. To complete the cycle, the consultants and clients informed business schools of these new practices and what worked and what did not in factories, warehouses, labs, and offices. This enabled professors to make their research and teaching more relevant and practical. It was in this way that a generation of managers grew professionally over the last three decades with *organization culture* on their list of things that needed to be mastered.

Today, it is common to find the term in the popular media as a primary reason for leaders leaving companies prematurely because of a mismatch between their styles and the cultures of their companies. It is also now on the list of most boards for CEO selection.

For a new leader, in addition to its importance in selection, the organization culture is one of the most important areas to understand after agreeing to an offer. For one thing, the culture is a window into how people behave. Especially if she enters with a change agenda and regardless of the particular nature of what must be changed, the new leader must be as clear as possible in her own mind about the behavior necessary of managers and those who report to them to bring about new and different results.

Most companies suffer from a gap between the culture that is optimal for their strategies and the actual one that exists. To attract the best candidate, the optimal culture is usually the one that is described and it is only after the new leader is aboard that the gap becomes apparent. There are some exceptions. One is at Best Buy, where CEO Hubert Joly and CHRO Shari Ballard spend time with recruiters in the early stages of a search to clarify the actual culture. Also, during interviews as well as once hired, discussions are held to ensure new leaders understand the de facto environment.

Take the example of one of the primary objectives Wayne took on—increasing innovation. Wayne recognized that the company's ability to introduce innovative products had slipped over the previous 10 years, and to achieve his objective of being a successful CEO, he had to restore it. First, he had to discover why it had been lost.

Before starting, while reviewing detailed operating reports, he learned that spending on new equipment and design systems had not declined. Turnover reports showed that, while there had been some retirements, no evidence existed of any significant loss of engineering talent. He realized that the answer could be found in cultural rather than financial or technical causes. Since there were no formal employee surveys, he did not discover those reasons until he had been aboard for a couple of months.

He made a point of spending time in the design labs and talking with all of the engineers. He did the same in prototype and preproduction manufacturing as well as in marketing. He discovered there had been three changes, each made for a good reason, but taken together they had probably contributed quite a bit to this problem.

First, the longtime head of engineering had retired, replaced by a subordinate who brought less experience to the job and had neither the longstanding relationships nor the collaborative style of his predecessor. Second, the retired executive had chaired a steering committee of people from the departments involved in new product development that had served as a vehicle for idea generation, joint problem solving, and team building. After a layoff and to save time for those who remained, department heads stopped the meetings. Third, while at higher levels there had been much talk about the dip in innovation, Wayne discovered that none of the senior executives had talked to the engineers, production supervisors, or marketing managers about what they believed was behind it or what to do about it.

In general, what Wayne had found was that morale was low because the people closest to the activities to produce innovative products thought their opinions did not matter to upper management, that cooperation between departments was less than needed because there was no longer a forum for communication, and that the manager promoted into the top engineering job was over his head in being able to direct and control but also motivate.

Wayne took five steps: (1) He reinstituted the steering committee and chaired it himself to underline its importance; (2) he regularly visited the departments, often unannounced, and made a practice of having an informal lunch with each department's people once a month; (3) he instituted a reward and recognition system tied to innovative activity; (4) he arranged for research projects for the company from the engineering school he had attended, including an internship program to recruit new, younger talent; and (5) he replaced the head of engineering with a more experienced industry veteran, recruited from a competitor. The steps that Wayne took are an example of how a leader can begin to change the culture of the organization he has taken over.

Wayne realized that signs of the organization's culture include the amount of communication that takes place that employees believe to be accurate and useful, the degree they feel involved in decisions affecting them, and whether there is a general willingness to cooperate and help one another. Cultures reveal themselves through the accumulation of such signs over time, resulting in habits and practices that become so common and natural that people don't think about them. It is for this reason that Marvin Bower, the former CEO of McKinsey & Co., famously defined culture as, "just the way we do things around here." As habits and practices prove to be important to the work that must be done, they are rewarded and translated into standards for new hires and promotion, thereby reinforcing them even more deeply. These in turn accumulate over time, evolving into widespread norms that define the accepted ways of behaving.

Communication, involvement, and cooperation are the three determinants of company norms and people's behavior that Wayne managed quite well. It was in this way that he planted the first seeds to change the culture. His actions represented an approach to leading that differed sharply from the norms in the company. In his five years as a senior officer and then CEO, he repeated and reinforced this approach in dealing with other challenges. In each case, he generally achieved what he set out to do and the accumulated successes began to change the culture of the company. One of the primary reasons he did not remain CEO, however, was due to another facet of the culture that was even more entrenched and powerful, which he did not manage as well.

Power and Influence   Who controls opinions and exerts influence on the most important issues? Who follows whom? Why? Which constituencies are most important to the company's strategy and long-term success? Are the same ones most important to operations effectiveness and short-term successes? Which alliances can be used to support the new leader's agenda? Which ones pose significant blocks? Who stands to gain from the new leader's success and who will benefit from his agenda? Who will not benefit and/or be threatened? Of the people affected, which ones are the more influential?

These sorts of questions represent the markers of that part of "the way things are done" that has to do with power and influence in the actual culture. Answering them will indicate for the new leader where there is likely support, where there may be resistance, whom to depend on, and who is likely to become loyal. If the people who control constituencies have much to gain from the leader's agenda and approach, the chance of his success is enhanced; and, of course, if they stand to lose or are threatened by what the leader wants to accomplish, his success will be jeopardized. Whichever way the answer points, that knowledge is important for someone who is taking hold. It was an analysis of these power dynamics that Wayne did not do as complete a job on as he did on the other cultural signs of communication, involvement, and cooperation.

In spite of the success of many of Wayne's initiatives and the benefit they could provide for many people in the company, a significant cohort resisted the changes that came along with these benefits. The resistors were threatened by a more collaborative environment because they might have to sacrifice their influence. They were also used to an environment where they could hold information and use its dissemination to enhance their department's or their own influence. They were worried that, if Wayne's style prevailed, they would also lose the power of wielding information as they liked. Further, the more senior managers found it difficult to involve their people in decision making, so they were afraid of being embarrassed and losing face.

These were understandable reactions as many managers had only worked in the culture into which Wayne came. They were at the core of the resistance to change that Wayne had to overcome to create the sort of behavior needed for the company to be on a more promising track. Weakening this resistance was a difficult challenge, especially under the time pressure and high expectations of a transition.

Even this challenge was not what caused this handoff to fail in the end. Rather, it was another manifestation of power and influence—this one having to do not with the organization Wayne had control over, but with Alan and the board. Through a combination of not reading accurately enough the power and influence structure of the board and also underestimating both Alan's political skills and his determination to get his way, Wayne allowed Alan the space and time to undermine him. The result was that Wayne lost the support of the majority of directors.

There are three messages from Wayne's story that are vital for any new leader, especially one with a change agenda. First, the new leader will succeed to the degree that he adeptly and carefully understands and manages the culture of the organization he enters, relying on multiple data points to gain a complete view and adjusting his approach as he learns more. Second, he must take nothing for granted and study the culture, how it became what it is, and why it has adopted the habits, practices, and norms that characterize it. Third, and most important at the CEO level, the new leader must understand the coalitions and alliances that make up the power structure of the organization and, also, who stands to gain or lose from his success.

For the major players there are also three messages. First, these cultural factors are important ingredients for the new leader's success. Second, the major players must be prepared to explain the culture clearly and in a practical way to the new leader. Third, such a step should be taken when any manager is hired, but one difference with handoffs at the top is that the power and influence aspect of the culture is the most important for the new leader to understand.

Not Preparing Major Players for the Right Roles

A second way a transition process can be mismanaged is to not take the steps necessary to ensure the major players are prepared to do their part or to create a network among them for coordination of actions as the search and transition processes play out. This can happen when the roles, responsibilities, and expectations of each player are inadequately defined, when the areas of overlap are not clear enough to each player, and when there are insufficient forums for sharing information that needs to be known.

There is no one standard way to be clear about roles, responsibilities, and expectations that is best for every situation. But there is a technique that can be helpful, called "responsibility charting." The product of that technique is a *RASI chart* (for *responsibility, authority, support, inform*) as shown in Figure 3.1. It was used by Wes, the CHRO in the company where Dave and Jim were involved in a CEO handoff.

Responsibility charting is a technique that dates to the 1960s when the U.S. State Department funded development programs in Africa. In one of them, done for the Western Nigeria Civil Service, a role negotiation exercise was designed that combined the teamwork and management concepts the American trainers thought necessary with African standards of authority and ethnic and tribal traditions. The primary trainer in that program was Dick Beckhard.[6] As he went on to teach and advise corporations in teamwork and organization

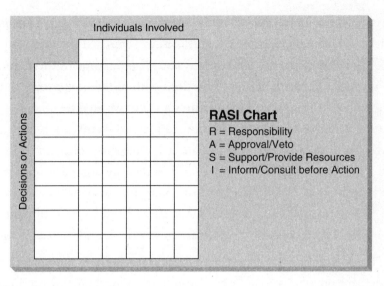

Figure 3.1 RASI Chart

development, he sharpened the technique and used it in situations where people had to come together to accomplish complicated tasks. It became known simply as "RASI charting."

It was adopted by the manufacturing research, consulting, and software firm Rath & Strong, starting in the 1970s for use with companies in aerospace, semiconductor, and high-tech manufacturing where matrix organization structures became common and that often developed products through cross-functional design and development teams of people drawn from various departments. These ad-hoc groups would, for example, get to the point of developing and testing a prototype product, and when ready for scaled-up production, would hand it to the line organization and disband.

Of course, because each project was under intense time pressure, there was a premium on quickly identifying and lessening any hurdles to getting the job done. Since most projects involved product designs or applications that hadn't been tried before, many of those hurdles were technical in nature and unique, one-at-a-time events specific to each product and industry. But there was usually another type of hurdle, this one not technical but related to people and relationships. This type often presented in two ways: (1) People came to these teams from various departments and functions with different approaches and beliefs about the task, and many times had not worked together before; as a result, there were often communication and teamwork problems that slowed the project's progress; and (2) once the group did its job and a prototype was done, the handoff to the line organization was often problematic because decision-making authority or how support was to be provided had not been made clear. These two coordination and culture issues contributed to missed schedules and increased costs.

Responsibility charting proved helpful in clarifying and gaining agreement on who should be responsible for crucial tasks, who should support them, and so forth. This technique has been widely used since by many global corporations in a variety of situations where people from different functions must come together and collaborate to achieve a common goal, such as in CEO transitions.

In one CEO transition, the RASI chart was produced in five steps.

- The tasks necessary for the transition were laid out in sequence.

- A chart was constructed with those tasks listed on the vertical axis and the names of each player on the horizontal axis.

- Each player completed the chart, indicating who should have primary responsibility for each task, who should have ultimate authority or veto power, who must provide material support to ensure the task is completed, and who must be informed about the step as it is being completed.

- The individual charts with R, A, S, or I designations were analyzed and a summary prepared indicating agreements and differences.

- The major players met to discuss each step and agree on optimal coverage of each task, something that took several meetings.

This process led to three results. The first was a written chart that defined the role of each player, which resulted from negotiation and open dialog. From that dialog, a second result was that expectations of each person by the others became clearer. And third, each player had the same document to refer to and to use as a guide as they continued to work together through the steps of the transition.

In another company that hired the eventual designated successor to the CEO, who entered as an executive vice president, the RASI chart laid out 17 steps that covered the period before the new leader accepted the company's offer and the period between acceptance and the new leader's first day on the job. There were four people most involved in these steps: the CEO, the director who was chair of the nomination/governance committee, the CHRO, and the CFO. To start the process, the CHRO and CFO worked together to draft the chart, then reviewed it with the CEO (Figure 3.2). The three of them then met with the director. Discussions followed and the CEO, CHRO, and CFO regularly revised and honed the chart while staying with the general framework.

Mishandling the Onboarding of the New Leader

The third type of common execution error is doing a poor job of the administration of new leader onboarding programs. Sometimes, it is because they become too complex. One seen recently was at a company hiring a senior-level executive who would be among three possible successors to the CEO. It was described through a presentation of 49 slides. It included 61 steps and called for the involvement of dozens of managers throughout the company. The new leader was to be assigned a "peer coach" and also a "mentor" in addition to an outside coach. Included were details of suggested "learning programs" as well as a six-month personal development project. When it was shown to the new leader, he remarked that this sounded like a full-time

		CEO	Director	CHRO	CFO
Pre-Yes	Draft of Transition Steps	A	I	R	S
	Review with Director	R		S	S
	Review Impact of New Hire on Strategic Initiative Underway	A		S	R
	Review Impact on Organization Change in Process	A		R	S
	Meet on Assessments of Final two Candidates	R	A	R	I
	Decide on Final Compensation Package	R	A	R	S
	Draft Onboarding (First 30 Days)	A	I	R	S
Yes	Finalize Transition Plan	A	I	R	S
	Offsite Meeting with New Leader	R	I	S	I
	Review Decision and Plan with Executive Leadership Team	R		S	S
	Contact Significant Stakeholders	R	A	S	S
	Announcement to Organization	A	I	R	S
	Press Release	A	I	R	S
	Preparation Meeting with New Leader	I		R	S
	Offsite CEO and New Leader	R	I	I	I
	Finalize Week 1 Meetings Plan	I		R	S
Day 1	Executive Leadership Team Meeting/Introductions	R	I	S	S

Figure 3.2   First Draft That the CHRO and CFO Reviewed with the CEO to Begin the Process

job and, "If I follow this plan, I won't have any time left for what I was hired for."

This was a case of a program that was constructed with the best of intentions, and that much sincere effort was devoted to, but that badly missed the mark. How could that have happened?

The CEO came up with the plan of three positions under her from which an eventual successor would come. She was confident that two of her direct reports should have the chance for her job when she retired, but she was not so confident in their abilities that she did not want another option. She discussed the search with her CHRO, stressing the need for someone who had the potential to move to CEO.

Because it was time to take a fresh look at the future of the industry and chart a new strategy for the company that would only begin under her tenure, she created a new position combining strategy, information technology, and business development. She reasoned that if she found the right person to work closely with on the future of the company, he or she might be the best one to lead it as it pursued that new path.

Five months later, Michael joined. He had been recruited from a different industry and was younger than any of the people who would be his peers reporting to the CEO. He knew he had much to learn about the dynamics of the industry, life cycles of the company's products and services, and the most promising acquisition targets. When he was told that the company had spent much time on a plan to get him up to speed quickly, he was pleased and anxious to get started. It was, then, all the more disappointing, when Alice, the chief learning officer (CLO) who reported to the CHRO, described the onboarding plan that she and her staff had developed.

Alice was a bit younger than Michael and had worked at the company for five years. After college and two years serving as a Teach for America volunteer, she had earned a doctorate in organization studies and then worked for a management training and consulting firm for three years. The work had been doing style and personality assessments and delivering management training programs for not-for-profit organizations and small- to medium-sized businesses. She joined the company in its management development unit, and when human resources reorganized and created the CLO spot a year before, she had won the job.

She had created a few onboarding programs for midlevel managers but had not done one for a senior executive and looked forward to the challenge. It had seemed to Alice that direct contact with the CEO and involvement in the search would have been necessary steps for the best onboarding program, but it was apparent to her that the CHRO preferred that he be the only person talking with the CEO. As a result,

Alice had no contact with the CEO as she designed the onboarding program; in fact, while she had given presentations to the senior staff and had been in meetings with the CEO, Alice had not met with her one-on-one.

The CHRO was the person from the department who directed the search. The person who ran recruiting had been in contact with the search firm and the manager of compensation and benefits had worked with the company's advisors to shape the financial package, but all contact with the CEO and Michael had been through the CHRO.

Michael ended up as CEO a few years later, having helped reorient the business. He forced the CHRO into early retirement within his first year as CEO as part of a general renewal of talent at the top. One of the objectives he gave to the new CHRO was to figure out the best way to ensure that the people he was hiring had the right sort of help as they took hold, and before that, as they prepared, how to best enter the company. "My onboarding experience was just not helpful on the things that I most needed. It wasn't horrible or even difficult. [Rather] it was sort of useless. I didn't pay any attention to it and figured out on my own what I needed. I know a lot of work went into it, but it was work that was wasted."

He went on to say that the right program would have been quite helpful. "I was staring at zero in terms of real understanding of the things I needed to know and I needed help from people here who knew them. I eventually got it, but it could have been a lot easier and happened a lot faster."

There were two reasons that Michael's onboarding effort was not helpful. Chief among them was that Alice was not equipped to be the sole author of the plan. She did not have enough experience; in particular, there was little in her background that enabled her to grasp the pressures and needs of executives coming from outside into a top position. Also, she was ignorant of the context of why Michael had been hired. By not having direct access to the CEO, she did not grasp why someone like him would have been hired or the CEO's expectations of what Michael would produce.

The CHRO bears the primarily responsibility for this execution error. He coveted the relationships with the CEO and Michael and kept his people from having any direct contact with them. But more damaging, he left Alice out on a limb and gave her no help. Even though he did not allow her direct access to the two principal actors, he let her go to center stage on her own. She was the one who explained the plan to Michael, and around the same time, presented a summary of it to the CEO.

The positive result of all this was explained by Michael. While his experience had not been particularly helpful, it did not sour him on the potential benefit of onboarding. "My [experience] just makes it more important to me that we get this right this time. It can be a very useful tool, but it's got to be done in the right way."

The sad irony of wasted opportunities due to mismanaging the onboarding of senior-level people is that it happens even in companies where other activities are best-in-class and benchmark-worthy. These companies have honed systems to identify and mitigate virtually all types of risks by being aware of their financial consequences. But ensuring the early productivity of new senior executives, or more importantly, ways to avoid their failure, has largely been ignored. Given the large number of executives who change jobs every year, it leaves these organizations vulnerable to expensive disruption. Executives in typical Fortune 500 companies change jobs often: 35 percent in total with 22 percent changing jobs within the company and about 13 percent hired from outside.[7]

But, when it is done well, the right effort by the company will pay off. One study showed that when following a systematic process geared to the strategic and operational objectives of the business as well as to the onboarding needs of individuals, there was about a 40 percent improvement in performance in early days and a 1,400 percent return on investment.[8]

Michael Watkins, in his groundbreaking research in this area, identifies a handful of reasons for onboarding errors. He points out that these programs are inadequate when cultural fit is not sufficiently taken into account, when support for the executive joining is inadequate, when the key stakeholders are not made apparent to the new leader and help is not provided to develop relationships with them, when help that is provided does not conform to the evolving needs of the transition or get delivered in a just-in-time way, when there is an absence of what Watkins calls action-forcing events that are planned versus serendipitous, and when the process is structured by the hiring organization rather than its pace being set by the new leader.

Onboarding programs, as we know the term today, have become ubiquitous. In many companies, they are automatically expected when new leaders are hired. But if the programs are mismanaged, they will hinder rather than help their success.

Summary

Because of the difficulty of executing a transition successfully, in the next four chapters we give guidelines for success. These guidelines stem from our experience as CEOs ourselves and as advisors to boards with transitioning CEOs. We start in the next chapter with guidelines for the board. That is followed by guidelines for the sitting CEO—the most critical player on the company side of the transition—and then guidelines for responsibilities of the CHRO and senior managers. The focus is kept on CEO-level transitions, but most of the principles apply to other top-level transitions.

The case of Alan and Wayne shows well how boards, CEOs, CHROs, and senior managers ignore these guidelines at their peril. As the case of Dave and Jim showed in Chapter 1, boards, CEOs, CHROs, and senior managers can outperform peer companies in transitions by adopting specific time-tested tactics. In spite of the complex system in which transitions take place, informed and conscientious transition teams can avoid errors in execution and benefit from a smooth transition.

Notes

1. Rock Center for Corporate Governance, "New CEO and Board Research from Heidrick & Struggles and Stanford's Rock Center Reveals Serious Gaps in CEO Succession Planning," Stanford University, June 16, 2010, accessed November 19, 2014, https://rockcenter.law.stanford.edu/2010/06/16/new-ceo-and-board -research-from-heidrick-struggles-and-stanford%E2%80%99s-rock-center -reveals-serious-gaps-in-ceo-succession-planning/

2. A framework for leaders to master the challenge of taking advice is described in D. Ciampa, *Taking Advice: How Leaders Get Good Counsel and Use It Wisely* (Harvard Business School Press, 2006), 6.

3. There were two manufacturing companies that provide examples. One was Red Jacket Manufacturing Company, a pump manufacturer in Davenport, Iowa, whose CEO, Jim Richard, was one of the early leaders to experiment with what he called "democratic management" in the 1950s. The gains in productivity and employee loyalty attracted the attention of larger companies. One was Polaroid, whose founder, Ed Land, recruited Richard as the company's first human resources head. There, he created many management innovations that became standard, accepted practice. A second pioneer example, this time in the early–late 1960s, was George Raymond of the Raymond Corporation, a manufacturer of electric forklift trucks in Greene, New York. Here, too, it was the CEO who recognized the benefit of involvement in decision making to

product quality, productivity, and customer service. See *A President's Experience with Democratic Management in Interpersonal Behavior and Administration* (Turner & Lombard, Free Press, 1969).

Pioneers like Richard and Raymond turned to a small group of researchers for ideas. One group was National Training Laboratories (later, NTL Institute for the Applied Behavioral Sciences), which had started in 1946 and created the genesis of what we now call *team building*. Another source was researchers in a few universities. These included Ed Schein, Dick Beckhard, and Warren Bennis at MIT, Chris Argyris at Yale, Ken Benne and Mikki Ritvo at Boston University, and Dave McClelland at Harvard. From the activities of people like them, a management development industry developed by the early to mid-1960s, anchored by such training firms as the Managerial Grid and Kepner-Tregoe. By the late 1960s, these experiments had evolved to create the beginning of the consulting industry in organization development and leadership. One of the most important of the early consulting and research firms in this area was the Behavioral Science Center of Sterling Institute, which a few years after being founded became McBer & Company. Among the areas it pioneered were climate surveys, competency assessment, and onboarding (then called the *joining-up process*).

4. G. Litwin and R. Stringer, *Motivation and Organizational Climate* (Cambridge, MA: Harvard University Press, 1968).

5. J.C. Abegglen and G. Stalk, Jr., *Kaisha, the Japanese Corporation* (Basic Books, 1985).

6. Dick Beckhard was a professor at the Sloan School at MIT, and then an independent consultant. He was one of the handful of people who created what became known as *organization development*. Beckhard was a key member of NTL Institute, which was involved in the State Department training program in Africa.

7. Michael Watkins, *The First 90 Days: Critical Success Strategies for New Leaders at All Levels*, Harvard Business Press, 2003, p. 240.

8. Ibid., p. 260.

4 The Board's Role

I t is clear by now that we disagree that a senior-level transition can be handled as a routine event requiring no special management. Such a belief is a shortcoming that leads to the errors in thinking and execution that are described in the previous two chapters. When it happens with directors, it can be particularly problematic because of the key role they play in the transition. This chapter examines the role of the board further to see how both changed thinking and execution can lead to better outcomes.

To start, consider the handoff recently directed by the board of a large technology corporation, one that we believe will be problematic. The board had spent months on its succession duties. Directors had assessed many candidates and debated long and hard whom to choose. Yet they succumbed to the myth that their job was over when the preferred leader said, "Yes." They did this consciously because of their collective belief that the best way to help a new leader was to not interfere. "If he needs help, he'll come to us," was what one director said.

This board convinced itself that its direction was important up to the point that the search process was complete, but when the new leader accepted the offer, it would be inappropriate for directors to actively engage, that it would signal a lack of confidence. This assumption is commonly behind the belief of some boards that as soon as they hire the right candidate they should get out of the way and let the new leader and those in the company sort things out.

There is, of course, a sound rationale for directors to back off. When a successor is hired and the incumbent is in place, the board is not equipped to dictate the specifics of how the relationship should take shape or attempt to overly control it. Directors are not a full-time presence, and they only see the players in action periodically, usually in prepared settings. If the two executives are going to work together for any length of time, they must be given some freedom to form a relationship themselves.

The same holds true when it comes to the new leader being hired directly into the CEO spot without her predecessor in place. While directors necessarily will have been more hands-on in the hiring process than if a sitting CEO were in place, once the new leader is aboard they should be sure to keep some distance to allow her to get her bearings on her own.

The question is, how much distance should the board keep, and what are the consequences of not getting it right? One lesson from the tale of Alan and Wayne is that when the board backs off too much, the result could be a disaster for all involved. Too much distance can block the board's view of the all-important relationship between incumbent and successor, or the chance to pick up signs of operational problems that management is either unaware of or hiding. But that same distance could have the disadvantage of keeping directors from stepping in to recommend corrective actions before early-stage problems turn into more serious or chronic ones.

Backing off too much and too soon can also set a troublesome expectation for relationships. If the message is that the new leader has to be on his own in a sink-or-swim way, the corollary could be interpreted by the new leader that the board would consider it a sign of weakness if he showed any doubt or asked for help. In terms of the incumbent's role in the handoff, the same applies if he worries that the board will view him negatively if he does not take care of everything on his own.

In the technology corporation, the new leader was named CEO-designate for a short transition period, after which the CEO would leave the company. When asked why such an overlap was put in place, one director answered that it was to give the new leader the chance to take advantage of the CEO's experience and knowledge of the marketplace and of the company while he was still there, and even after the CEO left, the board hoped the new leader would call on him for advice.

When the CEO was asked if he intended to coach his successor, he replied, "I don't do coaching," adding that it would be a mistake for him to stay for even a brief period because it would be "confusing to have two of us at the top, and, anyway, [the new leader] is perfectly capable. That's why he was hired. He doesn't need me."

It was apparent that the CEO wanted to leave as soon as possible and had no intention to help, even if asked. It was probably a good thing for the new leader that the CEO leave as soon as possible since such an attitude is not likely one to produce useful counsel. But it revealed miscommunication, or worse, a disagreement, between the board and CEO, one that could come back to haunt the new leader. If the board expected the new leader to have the benefit of his predecessor's attention and advice, it would back off too much with a false sense of confidence; but if the new leader did not take advantage of it and something went wrong, the board could blame the new leader for the learning failure.

The board must avoid such miscommunication and, more important, find the right balance between being too involved and backing off too much. Many boards consist of current or ex-CEOs who believe that the best way to be helpful to a new leader is to not interfere. This view, combined with the historical dynamics of the relationship the board had with the previous CEO, seems to inhibit board members from getting too involved personally with helping or coaching a new leader beyond what is specifically asked.

Departing CEOs often operate under the same assumption, believing that a new CEO has the same requirements and abilities as a fully performing CEO at the end of his tenure. In deciding to keep a respectful distance, board members typically underestimate how much useful knowledge they have accrued about the company, markets, leadership challenges, and strategic opportunities, and how valuable their insights, experience, judgment, and opinions can be to a new leader in the organization. Their perspective, while unique, is often quite objective and their own personal leadership experience is often quite valuable.

If directors find the right range of involvement, they can learn a great deal. In the case of the technology corporation, as the board was selecting a new leader, it compiled a detailed analysis of the characteristics needed in the next CEO. As they went through it, several directors noticed that the current CEO would not be a good match for the profile they believed was needed. In other words, if the incumbent were a candidate, he would not get an offer.

There can be different reactions to such a realization. One might be that it's only to be expected since the company and market context have changed and the incumbent was obviously a match for what was needed when his tenure began. Another reaction might be that he may not have as much to offer his successor as it first seemed and it would be best if the new leader gets help with the transition in some other way.

Whatever answer the board decides is the correct one, there are two tasks it must take into account. The first is to pay attention to the knowledge that comes from putting in effort to think through the best path. The second is to turn that knowledge into learning that can increase the chances of the transition's success. In this case, by thinking the CEO would help his successor without being specific about what such help would look like and whether he was willing and able to provide it, the board came up short on this task. It had the right impulse, to get the new leader some help, but stopped short of a complete job. It failed to find the right balance.

Mistakes like this—which luck and special circumstances only sometimes prevent—can be avoided when directors work to ensure they are fully accountable for the transition's success, and when they go far enough to overcome thinking and execution errors. They can do this under two conditions. The first is that when they hold to the standard of extracting the right knowledge from their effort, they are not satisfied until they convert it to learning that will most help the transition. The second is that the other three players in the transition struggle in the same way and play complementary roles in making the transition a success. The first standard is squarely in the board's control and there is no excuse for not meeting it. The second is not fully in its control, but because of its powerful influence in the company, the board can and should stress to the other players that they expect them to do their part.

The first three chapters delved into the complexity of transitions, common thinking errors, and common errors in execution. This chapter begins a discussion of the specific role each player on the transition team should play in a successful transition process. We start in this chapter with the board, investigating instances where boards have managed transitions effectively and, as in the technology corporation, where they can take a more successful and systematic approach to ensuring the transition succeeds.

Directors as Major Players

Boards that take an active role and find the right level of involvement in managing transitions get the best results. This does not mean they meddle or intrude in what should be management's job, but that they find the right balance of backing off and assertively taking initiative in doing what only a board has the authority and purview to undertake.

They hold onto the reins when the transition requires their oversight. They monitor and guide it as only governing overseers can. They do what they have to do to get themselves or other players to get their roles right, from suggesting, on one end of the scale, to forcing, on the other. Most important, they work hard at finding the right formula to fulfill their mission of being accountable for the transition.

Consider three transitions that were unsuccessful because boards failed to find the right balance and remain accountable. After one, the board chairman blamed the executive search consultants and the CHRO who ran the search. The chairman, unhappy that the recently hired CEO did not live up to expectations, refused to accept any accountability. In another case, the chairwoman of a board complained that the transition had failed because the departing CEO never really wanted to pass the mantle to the person the board decided should succeed him. She complained that even though he said he would, he "didn't really mean it." As chairwoman, she had abdicated her responsibility in ensuring the incumbent leader exited in the right way. The lead director in the third case maintained that the person hired simply oversold her abilities and could not deliver what she said she could before being hired.

While the complaints in each case may contain some truth, the root cause of each failure was the board's poor job in accepting its accountability. The first board chose the search firm and oversaw its work. In the second case, the chair never talked explicitly with the departing CEO to agree on what was expected of him, but only sent an email that said the board expected him to do what would be necessary for a smooth handoff. In the third example, every director interviewed the person hired at least once but failed to delve into feedback from reference checks that should have raised questions about past performance problems.

Pointing fingers and assigning blame are not examples of stepping up to the plate and being accountable for results. Sometimes, ready excuses are simply a sign of ignorance about the transitions and the special role boards should play.

To raise the board's game in this respect, directors need to become students of transitions. They must involve themselves enough in studying the nature of transitions to understand what is required for a successful one as well as the common causes of failure. Such studying should be done in a way that ensures they grasp what will work best in their company's culture and its particular strategy and capacity to improve how it operates. While part of that learning should be about transitions, part should also be to gain a healthy level of familiarity with the processes and systems that form the company's central nervous system and with the employees who are most central to its effectiveness.

How directors can best come to know the organization is not always easy to determine. Presentations at board meetings or reviewing board materials are not enough. Directors can become more intimately knowledgeable by talking with managers and seeing them in action as well as by taking an interest in initiatives where their experience can be useful. As they find the right balance, directors must go about their learning with care since any sense that they are intruding on management's responsibilities can sour relations and make it more difficult to find out what is going on. They must balance the need to be sensitive to the CEO's expectations but also be willing to influence and shape those expectations for the good of the company.

Some companies make it easier for such familiarity to take place. In the case of a large reinsurance corporation, the CEO/chairman instituted a requirement that between board meetings each director would provide insight to the company's managers in the area of his specialty. For example, one director had founded and run an industry-leading information technology corporation; his task was to get to know the company's IT group and become a teacher and mentor. Another had been a senior executive at Lloyd's of London and had held high positions in the property and casualty insurance industry; he spent time with the strategy unit and the risk management department. A third was experienced in converting strategies to plans for operations and culture improvement; he counseled the head of strategy, head of operations, and CHRO. Each director joined the board knowing this requirement and willingly found the time to fulfill it. Part of the annual board self-assessment was feedback from the managers who had received the help each director had provided.

There were two benefits from this system. One was the improvements in the company stemming from the advice received by the company's managers. As one manager put it, "The chance we have to learn from these directors is very special. Most of us would never have the chance to even meet these guys, never mind have them roll up their sleeves and help us on a regular basis." The other benefit was the knowledge the directors gained about the company. When a strategic or policy issue came up at a board meeting, they knew firsthand how it would affect the way the company operated or whether the managers had the capacity to take advantage of it. This latter benefit was especially useful during the leader transition as the COO took over from the chairman/CEO.

Of course, this also meant that the directors knew more about the company than many chairpersons/CEOs want them to know. It took a mature and secure leader to create such a program, recognizing that the benefits outweighed the concerns.

Telstra, the largest telecommunications company in Australia, is a good example of a company where the board has worked hard to achieve the right level of involvement. Due to a remarkable partnership between the external chairman, Catherine Livingstone, and the CEO, David Thodey, the board appropriately inserts itself in strategic and business reviews, holds informal discussions with management, debates large resource commitments, and, most importantly, is fully able to assess internal managers when succession planning is undertaken because of their knowledge of the organization. In their most recent appointment of a new CEO, their ongoing relationship with the whole organization facilitated a clear choice and a smooth succession process.

When it comes to a leadership handoff, more involvement does not mean that the board does the bulk of the work on specific aspects of the transition. It does not, for example, manage the announcement of the new leader's appointment or take responsibility for the onboarding step in the process. But it can fulfill its accountability by working with the CEO to think through the type of person best for the future conditions the company will face. It can also schedule regular meetings to review progress, seek out the CHRO for her perspective, and ask for the plans by which the senior managers will be involved and the organization will be prepared for the handoff. Taking this level of initiative gives the board the chance to ask questions, pose optional ways to answer them, judge what has been left out, and weigh in with firm opinions.

This type of involvement is required of the board in other important issues it oversees, such as acquisitions. There, too, it has overall accountability but the CEO is responsible for finalizing terms, planning and executing the integration, and so forth. Why, then, would a board not be as active and attentive on a leadership transition, which has at least as significant an impact on the organization?

If a board's work on a transition results in a person as the new leader who is a mismatch with the culture and whom influential managers will not follow, the board should be called to account. If the right successor is found but the incumbent CEO decides he does not want to relinquish power, and in the process triggers a transition failure, the board should be called to account. On the other hand, if the transition goes smoothly and the new leader exceeds expectations, the board should accept accountability and welcome congratulations on fulfilling its duties.

From the data on the high amount of failure in transitions at the top, however, the evidence is that many boards are not on track to earn congratulations. There is a clear need to do better. Convincing evidence comes from incoming CEOs who have reported that they are not getting the support they need or getting it for as long as they need it. In a study of 23 major CEO transitions, 57 percent of CEOs promoted from inside and 83 percent from outside said they believe their boards were "less involved" than they should have been.[1] In other words, a lot of new leaders are left to navigate transitions on their own, with the board remiss in its duties. To be sure, many new leaders struggle their way to success and come out just fine, but the question is, how much potential value is lost in the meantime? And, of course, as we explained in the Introduction, a large percentage of senior-level transitions fail with high costs for the company and the individuals involved.

Putting off actively addressing the transition is another common board failing. Perhaps it is because directors lack experience with CEO transitions and knowledge of the available pathways to success. Or perhaps, as was the case of Alan in the previous chapter, directors put it off because the handoff will be contentious and it is easier to avoid it. Sometimes it is because they fall into the trap described in Chapter 2 and adhere to the myth that "our job is done when the one we want says yes." Whatever the reasons, and there are understandable ones, putting off confronting an important problem, one that will have to be dealt with at some point, is rarely a winning strategy.

The role of the board has two parts (see Figure 4.1): first, to accept overall accountability for the transition, based on being active and informed, and on becoming students of transitions so that they understand what makes a transition succeed or fail, and the necessary roles of the various major players, including their own; and second, to find the right level of involvement, in particular when to be involved and when to back off, and knowing the organization well enough

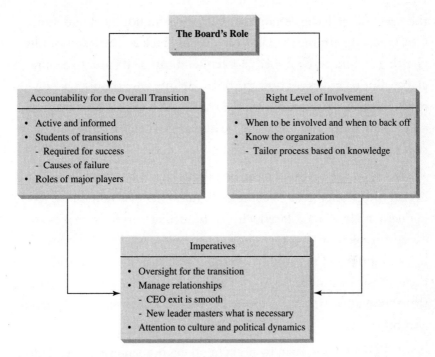

Figure 4.1 The Board's Transition Role

to be able to participate with the CEO in tailoring a process that is best for their company. To fulfill this role, the board must focus on three imperatives: to provide oversight for the transition; to manage relationships with the incumbent and the new leader so that the incumbent's exit is smooth and the new leader masters what is needed to meet the company's challenges; and to pay particular attention to the culture and its political dynamics.

Oversight for the Transition

Although the CEO should remain the central figure in managing the details of the handoff to a new leader, this can raise the temptation for the CEO to assume too much control, which can strain the incumbent's relationship with the board and hinder the one with the new leader. To be certain that balance is found, the board and CEO must determine the tasks each should tackle. The responsibility charting technique described in Chapter 3 can be helpful to ensure clarity. But regardless of how the board defines who should take on key tasks, it is most important that the board think about the transition and its role in the right way and be prepared when the time comes to step up and recognize its accountability.

In some cases, although the board intends to be accountable for overall direction, it fails to completely fulfill that accountability. This happens when a board faced with an immediate problem makes an expedient decision that turns out not to be the wisest one because it was unprepared to fulfill its oversight responsibilities. Consider the example of a midsized, multinational financial services company thrust into a transition unexpectedly when the chairman/CEO had to abruptly resign.

The CEO was known by peers in other companies for having done a good job of managing his board. A longtime director clarified how he did so:

> He controlled the board, he didn't manage it. He pretty much determined the things we'd take on and what our involvement would be with management. And any contact with even the most senior people had to go through him … and I found out after he left that each time there was any contact with a board member, [the executive] was grilled by [the CEO] … He wanted to know everything that was said. So, for us, when you say he was known as doing a good job of managing the board, it means he held us on a short leash.

Not surprisingly, the CEO had exhibited the same sort of need for control in managing the business. Information was held tightly and even upper-level managers could make few decisions without the CEO's involvement or approval. As a result, he created a culture with two defining features. First, he was the center of decision making where the de facto structure looked like a wheel with him at the hub. Second, information flow was vertical between him and the departments, which caused collaboration problems between units and communication across the organization to be difficult.

The net effects of this management style were threefold. Decision making took longer than it should have; when teamwork was required, the organization did not perform well; and the executives who came up through the organization tended to be narrow in scope rather than broad-based general managers.

Because he controlled board agendas with his chairman's hat on, the CEO had a similar effect on the working of the board. Items brought up in board meetings were presented only after they had been analyzed to the point that one or two options had been identified. Discussion of underlying issues was not encouraged. Directors came to expect when a suggestion was made that the immediate response would be, "We thought about that, it's factored in, let's vote." This history of CEO dominance and board acquiescence became an immediate handicap when directors faced a succession emergency.

The board met immediately after the CEO informed it of his decision to resign. It struggled through a long and difficult meeting but failed to agree on a path forward that satisfied every director. At the next meeting, directors were able to agree on three points: First, it was vital they name a permanent replacement as soon as possible. The longer the company went leaderless, the more likely that problems that were not visible to them would fester—and the more likely the board would be held responsible. Second, the next CEO should come from within the company, someone who understood the way information had been handled and knew the people and culture. Third, they would never again accept a leader who was both a chairperson and CEO. The new job would be CEO only and the chairperson would be one of the directors.

Four weeks after the CEO's resignation, the CFO was named to replace him. She had been at the company for most of her career and ran the finance, IT, and risk management functions. She understood how the organization worked as well as anyone. She also took over at a time when the industry had started to grow again. There was a burst of innovation as new products were developed to meet needs of both existing and emerging markets.

These advantages, however, made for a complicated competitive picture. With the emergence of new business opportunities came the emergence of new, entrepreneurial competitors offering creative niche products and services. At the same time, large well-financed corporations from other parts of the industry advanced into the market, offering traditional products that were directly competitive at discounted prices. The result was the company had to fight on two fronts. On one side, it faced a guerrilla war with small, nimble adversaries where innovation was needed to win. On the other, it faced a pitched battle with big competitors—well-equipped with large sales forces—offering lower prices and accepting lower margins.

Six months later, the company had not taken advantage of market-place opportunities while competitors on both fronts made inroads. Profit continued to grow modestly and revenues stayed flat as the new CEO managed expenses rather than growing the top line. The same level of performance continued over the next quarter, at which time the board talked about the lack of growth in executive session. The chairman then asked the CEO for her plans to solve the problem.

At the next meeting, the CEO and several of her senior managers presented their growth plans. After the meeting, several board members agreed that the plans basically added up to more of what the company had been doing. As one put it, "There was nothing new that was going to get us to the next level. Not enough punch … nothing hard hitting." They agreed to keep close tabs on the situation.

The mediocre performance continued over the next three months. After another meeting with the CEO, the chairman called an executive session. Over the next hour, the directors shared their thoughts and speculated on what was missing from their company. Toward the end of the meeting, one of the directors raised a question that was on the minds of most of them: do we have the wrong CEO? The question haunted the chairman over the next few weeks. The board soon decided that the CEO was indeed not the right one and arranged for an early retirement package. Two months later, a little more than a year after she had been named CEO, she departed. Her replacement came from outside.

It could be argued that this failed transition was just a matter of taking a calculated risk on an internal candidate during a time when the board had few options as it faced an unexpected departure from a powerful leader. To avoid a crisis, it had given an opportunity to someone who could keep the ship from sinking because of her knowledge and credibility inside, even though she had never run a business. As luck would have it, the marketplace became complicated, it proved too much for a first-time CEO, and the board made a change within a year.

A more accurate assessment of what happened is that the reason this transition failed is that the board rushed its decision to name a replacement for the former CEO. It became nervous because it was focused only on the current problem rather than taking the opportunity to pause and think through what was needed for the organization in the future. Part of the problem was that it knew so little about the details of the business, and when faced with its most important decision, chose the path that was most convenient. What other choices did it have?

An alternative it could have considered was a variation of the path it took—to promote the CFO, but with a change in how she and the board proceeded down that path. The CFO was not a total mismatch for the top job. In fact, while she was CEO, the directors were pleased and somewhat surprised to find she had broader and deeper capabilities than they had thought. They knew her to be accomplished in the finance and risk management areas, but during her first months they recognized that she was strategic, very bright, hardworking, open and transparent, and a good manager of her people. She was respected and listened to inside the company and she was not afraid to make tough decisions.

But she lacked two components that the company needed. She didn't have a good enough feel for the marketplace, especially its newer, emerging parts that were changing the most and held the most promise. Because she had worked in this company for so long, she also did not have a clear mental picture of the kind of people she should have under her versus the ones that she had been working beside for so long.

To help her make up for these shortcomings, the board could have invested in her and found ways to close both gaps. Directors could have constructed a program for her to better understand the changes brewing in the marketplace and also to grasp the talent needed to grow, perhaps including a new CHRO who could better find the right new people and train existing ones.

Another alternative would have been to install an interim CEO (either the CFO or one of the directors) while the board launched a careful search for a new leader. This would have been a more promising path because it would have provided the chance for a more careful strategic, forward-looking view. The board needed to become clearer about the strategic objectives that were best for the organization to pursue and also about what was necessary for the strategy that would achieve them. The current strategy had become muddled because it had been too dependent on one person who could no longer keep up with the size of the organization and complexity of the market, but who would not allow his people to be involved enough to help.

The board needed to set the tone for a new direction, and once it did, to hire the right person who had the experience to build on it by charting the right path, working with the board to make it specific, and then leading the organization forward. That would have taken time and effort on the board's part, which it was not willing to consider.

The core problem, of course, was one that should have been faced when the former CEO resigned. Had the directors taken the time then to think through the strategic and cultural issues facing the company, they would have been better prepared to make the wisest decision about its leadership. But they did not find the right point on the scale of board involvement. One of the biggest gaps was the lack of a grasp of the talent in the company. This board had not involved itself in this area until it faced major problems and then realized there was insufficient talent in the company to solve them. But even then, directors weren't entirely sure just how to proceed.

An example of the depth required to get it right comes from Walmart. Every year, the board asks an outside firm to provide a 10-year outlook on global trends. Among the questions it answers are what factors will affect the business model in the future, and what leadership characteristics will be most effective in a changing world. Then the board, guided by CHRO Susan Chambers, uses that trend outlook to update the CEO job description. One of the features that gives this process particular richness at Walmart is that the board has invested time and effort in getting to know two groups of top executives: the "next-generation CEOs" and the "next-generation executive committee members."

The board interacts with these leaders in several ways throughout the year. Directors attend presentations by them to their people as well as customers. Board members each become one-on-one "board buddies" to some of these executives. A psychologist interviews each executive, prepares an assessment, and shares it with the executive and with the board. This gives the directors deep knowledge of the critical talent pool. Because Walmart usually promotes from the inside, it means that directors have a good idea of what is available in the future CEO pool and of the personality, strengths, and weaknesses of the person who is finally named to the top spot.

Intensive involvement with the CEO continues after he is promoted. At his 90-day mark after being named CEO, Doug McMillon met with an external consultant to create his first scorecard based on a 360-degree assessment that came from interviews with a half dozen directors (including the chair, vice chair, and three committee chairs) and all direct reports.

In the most recent one, McMillon received good marks but the report also pointed out ways to improve. It was reviewed privately with McMillon for 30 minutes, after which the chairman joined for another 30 minutes. McMillon and the psychologist then shared the results with the compensation committee and, in summary, with the full board. Susan Chambers believes this level of depth and transparency not only educates the board but also accelerates the complete and successful transition of a new CEO.

Directing the transition comes down to finding that right balance between backing off too much and being too involved. Necessary to locate that point on the scale is the board working consistently at thinking about its role in the transition and being prepared so that, at the most crucial time, the board is ready to make the wisest judgments.

Managing Relationships

The board's next imperative to a successful transition is to manage the relationships between, first, the board and the incumbent CEO, and second, between the board and the new leader. The right type of relationship with the incumbent is a partnership, not a remote transaction-based connection. From the board's point of view, it should be one where "managing the board" means the CEO provides what the board needs to do its job in a constructive way, not withholding information it needs and keeping it at arm's length. From the CEO's point of view, it should be a relationship where he feels confident that the board supports him, is honest about its concerns, and has the same belief as he does in the mission and strategy of the company. These elements form a foundation that should have been built long before the transition.

The relationship between the board and the new leader is, of course, one that must be shaped as the new leader hopes for a chance to show what she can do for the company. She should expect a relationship based on feedback that is fair, timely, and accurate and on input and advice where directors think it would be helpful. Because relationships begin with first impressions, both parties should see the interview part of the search as the first step in a relationship, in addition to seeing it as a chance to market one's capabilities or to sell the benefits of joining the company.

The board should consider the establishment and nurturing of relationships with both incumbent and new leader as a primary responsibility. That conviction should be backed up in concrete ways: The board's annual objectives should include enhancing the relationship with the CEO and forming one with the new leader; there should be a formal plan for each; there should be scheduled as well as as-needed reviews of those plans throughout the year; and it should be a topic that is included in the board's annual self-assessment.

As far as we know, there has been no research showing a specific link between the nature of the board's relationship with the CEO and transition success. By this we mean research that proves, for example, that when the relationship between directors and CEO is a partnership versus a mistrustful one, the chances for a successful handoff increase by X percent. Hopefully, this book will encourage such research. In the meantime, conclusions in this regard are based on our own experience as directors and advisors as well as the experiences of the directors and executives we have counseled and with whom we have talked. We have neither heard anyone say nor seen a board–CEO relationship in action that suggests that a contentious, negative relationship between a board and CEO will lead to a successful leadership handoff or have a positive effect on the company. When we have asked whether a partnership based on mutual trust and open communication is likely to lead to transition success, the answer has always been, "Of course."

But true partnerships are not common between boards and CEOs. One reason is how much the governance landscape and expectations of the board's role have changed, something that has had a profound effect on a board's role in CEO transitions. Most boardroom relationships used to be dominated by the CEO, who handpicked directors and where directors agreed to join because of friendship with the CEO. Boards were much more likely to agree to whatever the CEO wanted, including whom he wanted to be the next CEO. That began to change in the mid-1990s with the growth of institutional investors. In 1980, total assets held by institutional investors was about $2.7 trillion, of which pension funds held about $870 billion. By 2005, total assets held by institutional investors had grown to over $24 trillion with pension funds holding about $10 trillion.[2] The effect of this change in ownership stakes was a much stronger voice from investors in who gets hired and how long they stay.

In addition to changing ownership patterns, there was increased media exposure of ethical lapses and poor performance by executives, along with threats of litigation. The scandals from 2000 to 2002 at Enron, WorldCom, and others thrust the boards of these companies into the public spotlight as they failed to detect smoke-and-mirrors strategy, false accounting, and criminal activity. In response, new federal regulations in Sarbanes-Oxley legislation and new rules from the New York Stock Exchange and others called for boards to increase scrutiny of management. Later in the decade, the credit crisis of 2008 brought more unflattering publicity about boards, this time in financial services companies that failed to closely enough monitor or even understand exotic new products or ensure adequate risk management. In both periods, directors were criticized for failing in two important responsibilities: operational oversight and governance practices.

Of course, these boards failed at a third responsibility, one more basic. They failed in their duty to oversee the talent process in the company, including leadership succession, when they hired CEOs and approved the hiring or promotion of other officers. That failure in turn set the tone for each company's organization culture, affecting everything from how open and transparent it was to the types of people placed in key posts and the decisions they made

One outcome has been a change in who becomes a director in a public company. There is much more emphasis on independent directors who will be more available, and perhaps sympathetic to, investors or other stakeholders. Companies listed on the major exchanges are required to have a majority of independent directors, and key committees such as compensation and nominating/governance must be entirely composed of independent directors. The upshot is that, to avoid the accusation of too much influence or cronyism, CEOs are also more cautious in influencing board decisions.

All of these changes have affected the relationship between boards and CEOs. Whereas the nature of a partnership in the past was often based on relationships outside the boardroom, it now must be shaped in different ways with directors who may not be known personally by the CEO and may have different backgrounds and interests. The potential for a true partnership may also be affected by the formal roles on the board that some directors have taken on due to governance changes. There are now nonexecutive chairs who have replaced executive chairs and are responsible for board meetings and executive sessions. There are also powerful lead directors in most companies with executive chairs. They must be independent and take on many of the tasks of the nonexecutive chair.

While new regulations and the changing role of directors have both affected the relationship between the board and CEO in ways that do not make it easier for a partnership to form, partnerships are possible nonetheless.

We have described the dynamics of one incumbent–board relationship in the case of Alan and Wayne. The political intrigue that led to Wayne's departure was Alan's doing, but it could not have happened without a complicit board. Alan divided the board and isolated John, the lead director, patiently and over many months, eventually creating a coalition of those few always loyal to him but also of several directors who had been neutral. This was done through a number of one-on-one conversations and informal meetings of small groups of directors. The whole board never met formally on this topic until its final decision to ask Wayne to leave. Apart from potential governance violations of such actions, it suggests a relationship between Alan and directors that was not open but depended on secrecy and clandestine meetings.

Contrast that with the example of Dave and Jim in Chapter 1. On most issues, Dave revealed his preferences and emotions openly and there was usually little question about what he was thinking, which in turn enabled the directors to better understand the concerns that would affect his behavior and not worry that there was a hidden motive or secret agenda. Also, directors did not hesitate to raise questions or give him advice. Because of their personalities, conversations could become heated, but the relationship could handle even the most intense ones. The picture is one of a CEO and board that communicated often, dealt with problems instead of avoiding them, and openly confronted emotional issues.

What caused things to work with Dave and not with Alan? It is a combination of mutual respect versus distrust, continuous rather than sporadic conversation where all parties have a chance to be involved, and dialog during those conversations that is open enough that not only are positions clear but so, too, are the emotions and motives that lie under them. These conditions occur only when both the CEO and the board put in the effort necessary to shape a collaborative relationship. This happens when the board, as the accountable player, sets the tone for the relationship.

Sometimes that is more difficult than it sounds, especially in the face of the financial ups and downs that all businesses experience. Certainly when they get to the point of serious cost cutting and sale of assets, pressure builds that can rupture relationships. In our experience, though, with the right leadership it is just as likely to pull people together as they confront a common threat. More pernicious is what happens to relationships after success. Because sustaining success is more difficult than becoming successful, the pressures that it brings can effect even the most durable relationships. Often starting with lack of communication between key players, problems can escalate rapidly but quietly if they are ignored because the business is going well. An example is provided by a large, successful pharmaceutical company that is currently just starting the transition process.

Peter, the CEO, was hired several years ago and, on his watch, the company has thrived. He skillfully brought to market high-growth products that he inherited, and also has improved the new product development process so that the company's pipeline has become the envy of competitors. Peter is trusted by analysts and investors, admired throughout the industry, and has earned the loyalty of managers. It is the best of times for the company and prospects are bright. It was then not welcome news when Peter told the non-executive chairman that he was considering retiring. He is 64 years old and even though the company has no mandatory retirement rule, he decided he will leave "within a couple of years." He explained that he is enjoying himself and will not leave until the new strategy, which he has committed to recommend to the board, is in place. But he added that "once the new strategy is set [next year], it will be time to decide who the next CEO will be. The company needs someone who can put in five or six years to get it done. I'll be over 70 by then."

The board is made up of scientists, engineers, and investors, several of whom have been directors for over 10 years. It is strong in the science and technology the company depends on and includes sophisticated financial investors. But, no director is a sitting CEO of a large public company. In addition, no one on the board has any direct experience in a CEO handoff at a company the size of this one.

At the suggestion of the CEO, the CHRO met with each director to discuss CEO succession, the results of which he fed back at a board meeting. Included in his presentation was an item that had come up in most of the interviews, even though the CHRO had not asked about it: a sometimes tense relationship between the board and the company's management.

The directors had noted that at the last few meetings tension appeared when management made formal presentations on topics where there is no obvious answer, and at the last meeting, it escalated into a heated argument. So, at a time when more discussion was needed, conflict curtailed it. As the CHRO recounted his feedback to the board, "When I mentioned it [as part of the review] there was silence. Eyes down. That kind of reaction. Then, [the chairman] said, 'Sounds like that's something for us to pick up on later. Anything else in your report?' And the meeting just moved on. It was quite awkward. But, it just reinforced that there is something to this and it is important to get to the bottom of it."

The CHRO talked to the director he knows best—the chair of the compensation committee. The director said that the CHRO had identified something very important that has started to affect the relationship, but that the board had never discussed it. He went on to say, "Some of this can be explained by how complex and very expensive these issues are. [Because of how fast we've grown] we haven't dealt with them before, and we feel a lot of pressure to get them right. But, I think there's something else behind this. You guys [in management] don't understand that this happens because of how you bring things to us. You tell us what you want or what you've decided [is best] instead of asking what we think. Some [of the directors] feel like they're getting a sales pitch instead of getting into a serious discussion that they can influence. That approach causes them to get their backs up. They get competitive and decide they have to take on management, sort of show you guys who's boss."

This communication problem is sure to get worse if nothing is done to reverse it. The board and the CEO have just begun to confront it, starting discussions to agree on the nature of the problem and what has caused it. Four root causes are emerging: rules of engagement; teamwork; experience/skill base of the board; and empathy.

- **Rules of engagement** are necessary in any professional relation-ship. They provide guidelines for the sort of behavior necessary for an outcome beneficial for both parties. When they are thought through together, the relationship is smoother and more positive. In this company, guidelines exist for behavior that is legal, ethical, and conforms to accepted best practices; but, not for relationships between the board and management that will ensure the right level of communication and coordination. One result of this oversight is teamwork problems.

- This board has not invested in becoming a well-functioning team or ensuring **teamwork** with management. There are essentially three benefits that come from team building: agreement on how those involved will work together, defining the barriers to doing so, and practicing the skills of communication and collaboration. This board has done nothing to accrue these building blocks, which are necessary to the success of any organization.

- The third root cause is lack of balance in the ***experience and skills of directors***. The membership of the board does not include people with two needed attributes: experience overseeing a company the size and complexity of this one and a deep appreciation of the challenges faced by Peter, the CEO. That means that contributing to this communication problem is that on the board there is no sitting CEO of a company of comparable size who can interpret for the other directors or counsel Peter.

- Lack of ***empathy*** is apparent in the way that the CEO has approached the board on issues where its agreement and approval are needed. Paradoxically, Peter has an interpersonal style that is quite empathetic, something noted by all with whom he interacts, including directors, at least one-on-one. But, when presentations are made to the board, he has not consistently consulted them beforehand or ensured that they believe their concerns and expectations are understood.

At this point, it is not certain whether this issue will be resolved. But, that it surfaced (thanks to the head of HR) and that the board is talking about it are the necessary first steps. What is certain is that without progress on rules of engagement and teamwork, this problem will not be solved. If progress is made on those two fronts, the way to make certain that it continues and the relationship strengthens is to ensure the full complement of abilities is represented on the board and to use team building to increase mutual understanding of what each party expects.

Importantly, because the board has skipped some of the basic steps needed for a smooth, collaborative relationship with their CEO and top management, there is an urgency to make such progress. If Peter stays to his current plan, it will be only a matter of months before the board and he will be forced to agree on who will be his successor and how power will be transferred. If the relationship cannot take the tension that comes with disagreement on strategic and operational issues, it could crumble when it comes to a decision about power.

If the board wants respect, involvement, and open dialog in its relationship with the CEO, it is up to the directors to establish the rules of engagement. This is true whether the board is chaired by a director or a CEO who is also chairman, in which case the lead director must take on a pivotal role.

The second important relationship for the board is with the new leader. Most important for a winning one are clarity on how performance will be judged and consistent expectations of each other.

Judging Performance

The simple view says that judging performance isn't that complicated. Objectives are set at the start of the fiscal year, steps are taken to ensure understanding, a system is put in place to measure progress, a midcourse check gives the chance for both parties to discuss where things stand and what's needed in the time remaining, and at the end of the year, judgments are based on achievement of the objectives.

While it is true that the mechanics of performance review are rational and useful, in the case of a new leader rising to the top it is more important for the board to view the chief executive's performance through a prism rather than through a microscope. A prism view will reveal not only achievement of quantitative targets but also progress on qualitative objectives having to do with how the new leader adds value in such areas as navigating the culture in his early days, turning the power structure to his advantage, challenging managers with new ways to think about growth or innovation, and shaping positive relationships so that the whole organization prospers. The board must find a certain balance between judging qualitative versus quantitative success.

A place for the board to start is understanding what the new leader goes through when first reporting to a board that will judge his performance. It can be quite an adjustment for even the most accomplished executive to be evaluated by a group rather than a single boss. Most people who rise to the top have had their reviews each year by a boss who determined adequacy of performance based on a company-wide system of standards, metrics, and measurements known to all.

But once the new leader arrives at the designated successor spot and is a step away from being CEO, all that changes. He is now evaluated both by a sitting CEO whom he was chosen to replace and by a board to whom he does not yet officially report made up of people he does not know. And if he ascends to the top spot rapidly, the first real performance review will be by the board. One brand-new CEO preparing for her first review likened it to being on trial: "Having a jury of people you can't influence decide your fate in a room where you can't go."

In any new relationship, each party seeks clarity about how the other views important issues. That understanding is partly responsible for the relationship going to its next stages. In the case of a board and new leader, objectives and how achievement will be judged are at the top of the list of pivotal issues. The objectives must be realistic to accomplish and stated in terms that are specific and measurable, with care taken to quantify signs of progress. Special attention must be given to objectives having to do with the organization's culture. Improving teamwork or ensuring a common vision are examples of cultural objectives that are difficult, sometimes impossible, to measure precisely by people who are remote from the organization. But because such tasks are important responsibilities for any manager at the top, if not made clear, they can be sources of tension at performance review time.

In the case of a designated successor reporting to the CEO, another question that should be clarified is how the board will participate in judging the new leader's performance. Will it be a sounding board to the CEO who will be the final judge, or will directors work closely together, aiming for influence? Will a director be present during performance-review feedback? If directors are more active participants, how will they gather information during the year? Will there be chances for the new leader to meet with directors without the CEO?

The board has a vital responsibility to assess the CEO's performance. In our experience, most fail at fulfilling that duty. They neither give useful, direct feedback, nor do they approach the task in a comprehensive way. We believe the ideal method begins with a detailed assessment of specific, quantitative objectives that are set as part of the annual operating plan, but the assessments should not end there. In addition, the board and CEO should agree to a set of qualitative objectives that lay out how the CEO should go about achieving the quantitative targets, including how she manages relationships, ensures loyalty, handles the political structure, and, in general, strengthens the culture. To measure such qualitative targets, the board should commission a 360-degree assessment where each director is interviewed by an objective, outside advisor and asked to characterize the CEO's behavior as he achieved the quantitative goals (this should complement the same type of interviews of the CEO's direct reports). Included should be areas such as how the CEO interacted with the board, how forthcoming he was, the degree to which he was open to criticism, and whether he told the board bad news as well as good news. These individual reviews should be combined in a report presented to the chairman, lead director, and/or executive committee. It should then be presented to the full board. Then, it should be reviewed in depth with the CEO. A copy of the review should be placed in the records of the board to establish its formal oversight responsibility.

While it is vital to clarify the format and details of the formal appraisal by the board, it is just as important that the board and CEO understand that it should be only one part of the board's feedback rather than being the only method to give feedback to the CEO; it should be the culmination of regular conversations and contact throughout the year. In a healthy relationship on the way to a partnership, there should be few surprises in the first formal performance review. If there are concerns about style, for example, they should be revealed as they are encountered through frank discussion rather than being bundled and reviewed all at once in a formal review. Indeed, one of the most important rules of feedback is to make it continuous, getting concerns and feelings out on the table as soon as possible after the event that brought them about.[3]

Expectations

The part that clarifying expectations plays in the new leader–board relationship is to ensure that the standards of the relationship and the ways that each party will contribute to it are as clear as possible. As simple as it sounds, a discussion about such expectations will be most helpful if the parties have a structure to support it, especially when a new leader is going through a transition for the first time. One way to structure the conversation is for the nonexecutive chair or lead director to ask the new leader to prepare her thoughts on three questions: (1) What information do you need from the board as a whole to be able to do the best job you can do, and in particular, what do you need from me (as the lead director or nonexecutive chair)? (2) What behavior on our/my part would best enable us to work together in a trusting relationship at board meetings, in between, and in one-on-one conversations? (3) From your experience so far, if there were one thing that could change in the way the board operates today, one thing that would have the most impact on making our relationship all it must be, what would it be?

As the new leader is preparing responses to these questions, the board as a group should discuss the same questions as they apply to the CEO (information, behavior, the one most impactful action on her part). Then the board and CEO should meet to go through their thoughts. Complete notes should be taken and used to continue conversations until each is clear about what the other expects. At the appropriate time, a summary should be prepared that lists the expectations for the relationship.

Beverly Behan is a former general counsel who is now an advisor to boards of directors. She wrote a book called *Great Companies Deserve Great Boards*, which is full of useful, practical steps boards should take, including the task of setting expectations with the CEO.[4] She describes how her board clients have clarified expectations of their CEOs, including one that listed these expectations:

- Be entirely open and honest in running the company and in dealing with the board. If there is bad news ... share it, don't try to hide it.

- Keep the board informed ... it should never be the last to know or see an item in the newspaper before hearing about it from management.

- Use the board as a thought partner and sounding board ... draw on directors' experience ... don't bring everything to the board fully baked.

- Give the board exposure to high-potential executives and facilitate board discussions on succession and talent.

- Create a corporate culture that is positive and energizing for employees ... take the same approach in your dealings with the board.

Managing relationships is tricky under the best of circumstances. Emotions, triggered by different objectives, motives, and needs, affect the behavior of both parties in ways that have profound impact on their ability to work together. When the context in which the relationship exists changes (as it does in fundamental ways in a transition of leaders), it becomes even trickier. Lack of clarity on how performance will be judged or on mutual expectations will complicate the task. Constant attention must be paid to the relationship by both parties, but the board is ultimately accountable.

Cultural and Political Attention

The third imperative for the board in a top-level transition has to do with the directors managing the cultural landscape. Because the company culture in general and the power structure in particular are most associated with failure, and since it is the directors as much as the new leader who will live with the consequences of their choice, paying attention to this area will pay healthy dividends.

There are seven ways the board can address this imperative.

- *Understand the nature of the culture.* Particularly important is how the organization communicates (and whether employees believe information they receive is accurate and useful); involves others (employees in decisions affecting them or where they have valuable input); cooperates (through a genuine willingness to help one another in ways that benefit the business); and manages power and influence (whether these always-present dynamics are employed for the good of the company rather than in a zero-sum, win-lose way). The board should have a sense of this through continuous exposure, questioning, and dialog well before a leadership transition.

- *Use cultural knowledge to determine the profile for the new leader.* If a search firm is used, it will generally prepare the profile under the guidance of the CHRO. Once it is drafted, the board should approve it and ensure that it describes the sort of person who fits with and can manage the particular culture of the company.

- *Choose the right recruiter*. It should be one who not only has experience with the unique conditions and needs facing new leaders but also understands the importance of the culture to a successful transition. One way to ensure this understanding is through reference checks; another is through discussions on the recruiter's beliefs regarding what is most important for effective leadership in general and for new leaders in particular.

- *Interview wisely*. When the search gets to the point of candidate interviews, stress questions on the culture and political structure. Ways to test cultural capacity include probing prior experience, philosophy of leading, and reactions to the board's description of the sort of cultural factors that the successful candidate will face.

- *Predict strengths and shortcomings*. These steps should enable the board to lay out for the final candidates strengths and shortcomings when it comes to the culture. One board used a simple chart prepared by the CHRO to summarize "cultural challenges" on one axis and the names of the final three candidates on the other. From interviews and reference checks, the board and CEO agreed on a high, medium, or low rating for each person for each challenge. They then listed the questions to probe for more clarification in a next and final round of interviews. At this point, a decision should be made on the need for a formal assessment of the final candidates' styles and personalities.

- *Review the plan to take hold*. Once a decision is made on whom an offer should be extended to and as negotiations are taking place, the board should review a taking-hold plan for the new leader, a topic we discuss further in Chapter 6. Prepared by the CEO, the taking-hold plan should cover three time periods: between an acceptance of the offer and Day 1 on the job, the onboarding plan for the first 90 days, and, finally, the period following onboarding where the leader moves as quickly as possible toward securing the loyalty of the organization. While the execution of the plan is up to the CEO, the board's oversight should ensure clarity on how progress will be measured, on the role of the CEO and CHRO, and also on plans to prepare for the new leader's entry.

• *Prepare the organization.* The CEO should review with the board a plan to prepare the organization for the new leader's arrival. This should include informing senior managers and the organization as a whole of the accepted offer and also ways for senior managers to prepare for their first meetings with the new leader. Chapter 7 lays out how one organization did so.

Summary

As much at the beginning as at the end of the transition, the job of the board is to find the right balance between involving itself in the transition and backing away to allow the new and veteran leaders to iron things out on their own. Directors face the same conundrum as overseers of any high-level event: They need to be good at both stepping in and stepping out of the day-to-day process.

This means they need to first become earnest students of transitions and make their judgments and expectations known. But they need to take their seats on the sidelines when all players are on task and engaged. In general, the board will find its right place by focusing on the three issues we've highlighted in this chapter: providing overall direction for the transition;

assuring they establish partnership-like relationships with the CEO and the new leader and will be ready to manage them; and troubleshooting problems as well as anticipating and where possible avoiding them, taking into account especially the culture and political structure of the company.

The board does not want to come up short on this task, as the board did in our opening example, when one director said, "If he needs help, he'll come to us." At times, indeed, the board needs to keep hands off. But at other times, when the success of the transition is at stake, it needs to be hands on. Directors need to be ready to say, "If he needs help, we'll go to him," supported by the access and, most important, the relationships that allow the board a clear view of situations where help is required. That is what board accountability is all about: knowing what's going on and finding the right balance of involvement so that when it is most needed, directors are welcomed by the CEO and new leader as they step in to do their part.

Notes

1. RHR International Executive Research, "Chief Executive Transitions: Keys to an Effective Transfer of Leadership at the Top," RHR International, 2012, accessed January 13, 2015, http://www.rhrinternational.com/100127/pdf/rs/ChiefExecTransitions-Research-2012.pdf

2. The Conference Board, The 2009 Institutional Investment Report, Trends in Asset Allocation and Portfolio Consumption, by Matteo Tonello and Stephan Rabimov (The Conference Board, 2009), p. 6

3. One of us became familiar with rules of feedback through workshops in the 1960s at NTL Institute. As far as we know, these rules were first defined by NTL for use in training programs in conflict resolution, organization

development, and interpersonal skills. Feedback as it relates to interpersonal behavior refers to verbal reactions to the behavior of another person that describes the emotions, whether positive or negative, that that behavior caused. It should be: given about behavior over which the other person has control; descriptive so that the behavior in question is clear; specific regarding the effect of that behavior on the person giving feedback; checked to ensure the person receiving the feedback understands it; and, given to the person as close as possible to the time when the behavior occurred.

4. Beverly Behan, *Great Companies Deserve Great Boards: A CEO's Guide to the Boardroom*, Macmillon, 2011.

5 The CEO's Role

The incumbent CEO's primary role in the handoff has two parts: The first is as transition director, which includes tasks that are necessary in any transition. Second, the CEO has the responsibility to ensure his successor assimilates effectively into the organization and ultimately moves up to the top spot. This second part of his responsibility must be tailored to each unique situation and is one that each leader approaches differently.

An example of how one CEO handled this dual role comes from a large international company that recently appointed a new CEO. After 10 years as chief executive and chairman, the CEO (whom we'll call Robert) passed the role to his successor, Greg, one of his direct reports who headed up the largest unit in this multinational conglomerate. Unlike some departing CEOs, Robert was able to create a feeling among his executive team that each member had a responsibility to help in the transition.

In most companies, "senior management team" is a misnomer. Too often, the people on it do not think like teammates, have not been trained in teamwork, and don't act in a collaborative, we're-all-in-this-together way. As a result, they fall short when they encounter a situation where teamwork is necessary, like a transition. When a CEO transition occurs, they mostly ask only, "What's in this for me?" and spend much less time asking, "How am I going to help make this a success?"

The what's-in-it-for-me reaction may be natural in many corporate cultures. But Robert, who remained chairman for a year after giving up the CEO title, encouraged everyone to support Greg. Robert stressed that a smooth transition was important for the enterprise and important to him. The message was simple: "Do your part to help Greg."

For the CEO, directing the handoff, staying in place, and helping his successor move up can be awkward, and it was for Robert and Greg. In board meetings, staff meetings, and employee meetings during the transition period, many people continued to look to Robert as the definitive decision maker. Greg, of course, was also at times in an awkward position since eyes also turned to him, wondering if he had a different opinion. And yet, Robert knew this was the appropriate role for him to play as the outgoing CEO.

For a decade, Robert was the corporate leader with full authority, and did a good job wielding it for the company. Even though he was used to that role as the executive of last resort, he now believed he had to discipline himself to lead in a different way.

Formulating a task list and role assignments for himself and others, Robert put together a profile of the key success factors of the CEO role as he had practiced it to review with Greg. One was his network of people and relationships critical to the CEO job. Another was the set of most important elements regarding the company's regulatory pressures, markets, competitors, products, talent, finances, and so on—along with how he used his knowledge in these areas to make policy decisions. A third was his thoughts on self-management—how he spent time, dealt with conflicting requests, managed the administrative system that supported him, kept his energy up, and balanced stress. A fourth area was how he utilized or shored up the strengths and shortcomings of his direct reports and viewed each given the challenges facing the company, including inevitable tensions or problems as their units overlapped. Fifth, he summarized his thinking about the directors, the governance pressure points, and the inside workings of the corporate board.

Then, Robert ran a series of one-on-one discussions on this accumulated experience and knowledge with Greg, including his opinions on how they would apply to the future. The two spent hours alone discussing these and other issues. They met in the office, for dinners, and travelled together to meet customers, government regulators, and alliance partners in the company's network.

Robert undertook the transition in an opposite way from that taken by the technology corporation's CEO described in the last chapter. Robert could have made a clean break from the company and told the board, "If he needs me, he'll call." During the year this transition spanned, Robert continued as chairman and CEO, then only chairman; but throughout, and with the board's agreement, he was the hands-on director of the transition. This included such steps as setting expectations, establishing roles of the various players, ensuring communication was accurate and timely, reviewing progress, and making sure an effective transition was on the agenda of all senior leaders as well as the board.

Robert took on another role to help in Greg's ascent: a "counselor," more a coach than the boss. That choice was critical to the success of this handoff for a few reasons. One was because of Robert's belief that it was vital to the handoff's success that he visibly step back frequently while still in office to allow Greg to be in the spotlight. He knew he was the one to be responsible for directing the transition, but he also realized that his successor had to tackle difficult tasks on his own with Robert on the sidelines but available.

Second, Robert believed he had a duty to offer his opinions and what he had learned as CEO, while also allowing Greg to figure out his own way of doing things. This transition was not easy for either, but both had the personality in interpersonal skills to deal with it. Robert was able to give feedback to Greg regarding parts of his approach and style that could reduce his effectiveness as CEO and lay out clearly what he needed to prove to the board. Also, he was open about the mistakes he made in his decade as CEO.

The third reason this approach succeeded was Greg's ability to be the client as Robert acted as the counselor. As with any helper–client relationship, the person who receives help must be a willing and skilled advice taker translating what is offered in a way that works for him; deciding what to accept and what to reject, all the while preserving the overall relationship with a mentor. Greg as a new CEO passed that very challenging test.

These are three success factors without which the model of CEO-as-counselor will not be as successful as it was at this multinational. But regardless of the way the departing CEO shapes his role, he must see as his last big objective before leaving to ensure his successor has all the help needed.

When a CEO immerses himself in the details of his successor's transition, he deepens his commitment to making the new leader's tenure a success. This is true whether the board names the successor directly to the CEO post or if she starts on the senior team and earns the top job over a year or two. Intensive involvement in the transition provides the opportunity for the CEO and the new leader to more quickly forge a relationship. That is important because, as we have seen, a close working relationship between the CEO and the number two is a hallmark of successful handoffs. The CEO's influence also helps ensure the support of senior managers who will be peers of or report to the new leader. This influence is even more powerful if, as was the case with Robert, senior managers respect the CEO.

By taking on the job of transition director, CEOs must ensure that their primary responsibility of being the company's executive of last resort is not compromised while they are CEO. As the transition progresses, they must adeptly perform both roles in the early stages, and as they relinquish portions of their formal authority, gradually get to the point of only being the transition director. Robert believed that could best be done by staying on at the company as chairman to continue to manage the necessary balancing acts of the transition and to advise Greg. This is the same decision made by two out of every five CEOs, according to a 2012 study.[1] CEOs in those companies stayed for an average of eight months after the point where their successors officially took the CEO title.

As we've pointed out, the specifics of each transition vary, affected by the company's financial pressures, culture, and the personalities involved. Robert took all this into account. He had the skills and help to successfully navigate through his transition's challenges in a way that was best for his company and for him; and Greg had the patience and advice-taking skills to make the most of the help available to him. Other equally capable CEOs will succeed at this transition challenge using a different approach that suits their circumstances. But regardless of how they do it, they will recognize this responsibility is the CEO's alone; it can be delegated to no one else.

Essentially, the CEO's role comes down to three imperatives that must be handled, albeit in different ways, for a successful transition: controlling steps and pace; ensuring the other players do what they must; and practicing self-management and self-awareness to manage his or her own exit.

Controlling the Steps and Pace

As the director of the transition and to ensure the transition stays in control, it falls to the CEO to lay out the steps of the handoff and control the pace of their implementation. Anyone who has reached the top job knows how to control steps and pace of a complex process, and that the strategy for doing so must be tailored to the unique conditions she faces. In the case of a planned leadership transition, an added wrinkle

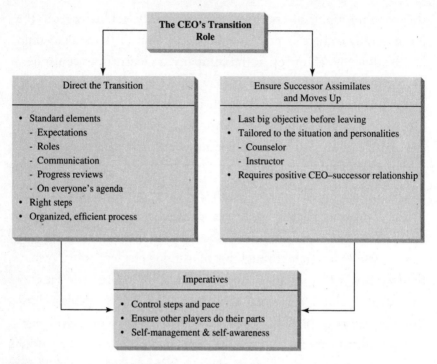

Figure 5.1   The CEO's Transition Role

is that one certain outcome of the transition for the CEO is that she will leave her job, and everyone involved knows it. It is for this reason that the way the CEO handles this management task will set a tone for the entire transition, and in particular for how it is perceived (and perhaps accepted) by influential managers. Given the ways that this process should be controlled by the CEO, particularly important is the role she chooses for herself as the transition begins. Just as important is the way she coordinates the steps of the transition with the steps of the search for a new leader.

Role

Often, the first decision of the CEO as transition director is the position the new leader will occupy. In a planned transition, the person who eventually accepts an offer enters the organization in a position reporting to the CEO, one that may exist on the organization chart or may be created for the transition. The position should meet several purposes.

For the company, it should be an important job with substantive responsibilities and with objectives closely tied to strategic and operational success. For the new leader, it should be the chance to prove his abilities and provide the platform for rising to the CEO spot. For the board, it should offer a proving ground for the new leader, a chance under controlled conditions for the new leader to perform while the CEO is still in place to verify that he has what it takes. For the CEO, it should show that the new leader is indeed ready to step up and also identify the areas that must be filled or shored up for the new person to be a great CEO.

If the position meets these needs, the CEO's thoughts then turn to what a smooth transition should look like, thoughts that fall into three categories of images that form in the mind of the CEO. One is the type of person best for the company given the future strategy. What are her capabilities? What knowledge must she bring? What functional or technical skills must she have? How should she behave, that is, what interpersonal, influence, and decision-making styles should she have? What should be her core beliefs and values, the basic attitudes that underlie her behavior? In shaping this image, it is vital to determine the match with what the company will need in its next era rather than what has been needed in the past.

A second image category is how the CEO will interact with his new subordinate who will replace him. On what issues will they collaborate? Which decisions will she pass by the CEO before she makes them, which without his involvement, and which will he expect to be informed of afterward? On what issues will they meet apart from the senior team, and how frequently? Will he want the board and the senior managers to view them as partners? How will the CEO want that partnership described? Or will he want to convey that a true partnership is a step to be achieved, that while the new leader is the putative successor, there are still things she must prove to win the partner label?

In the third category of thoughts, the CEO will begin to consider what the handoff should look like. What phases should it go through? Which of his current responsibilities should he retain and which should the new leader take on? Should it be gradual as he offers a few of his duties at a time, or should he wait to see how the new leader handles her initial tasks and then promote her? What role should the board play in general? What should be avoided as the board becomes involved? Which directors can be most helpful? Of the CEO's direct reports, who can take on tasks that will most help the handoff be a success? What contribution must be made by the senior team as a whole? What will the CEO see and hear that will tell him that the organization is ready for the handoff?

Clarity of the transition's image can help define the two parts of the CEO's role. The first part is transition director, where the CEO is responsible for setting the objectives and ensuring the right steps are carried out to achieve them. The outcome of this part should be an organized, efficient transition process, and, as pointed out above, is one only the CEO should play in a planned transition. If this part is constant, the second part of the CEO's role meets a different purpose: the most useful assimilation of the new leader. There is no universal definition for this second part; what is best is a function of the situation and the personality and abilities of the CEO.

For Robert, this second part was counselor. But when the CEO does not play this role, he must ensure that someone does. The new leader should have someone to turn to who provides coaching and advice. That could be an outsider, or as we saw with Wes in the case of Dave and Jim in Chapter 1, it could be the CHRO. We will explore this further in Chapter 6.

CEOs who do not have the personality or skills to do what is required of a counselor find other ways to meet the needs of the transition. Some become "instructors." For this role, the CEO makes sure information that the new leader must have is gathered, screened, and presented in a way to best prepare the new leader to take hold, and in particular, to achieve early successes.

One CEO who chose this route tapped a manager in the human resources department who ran the company's learning and people development department (L&PD) and had been a curricula developer for an international education company and the editor of a business journal. When the search process began, he asked her and her boss, the CHRO, to prepare a learning plan for whoever was to be the new CEO. As the search progressed and interviews were scheduled, the CEO asked four people—his CFO, head of strategy and business development, chief engineer, and CHRO—to work with the L&PD manager to develop a program (or as he referred to it, a course) to cover important issues in their respective disciplines.

Two weeks before her official start, she met with the executive in each area on consecutive days. Each senior manager taught his or her course with the new leader being the student. Each course was preceded by the L&PD manager meeting with the new leader to review the content of the course, and in general, for the new leader to prepare. On the fourth and final day, while the material was still fresh, she and the CEO met from late afternoon through dinner to discuss reactions and questions.

As the new leader put it later,

> "I'd never heard of something like that before, but it turned out to be enormously useful. It wasn't the content ... I could have read that. But it was that it was just [the senior manager] and me talking one-on-one for hours about the content and getting into some depth. Maybe we'd have done that once I started, but probably not ... and certainly not with the preparation each of them put in."

She went on to distinguish these courses from a general orientation. "It did a couple of things. Each of those people and I connected in a way that would have taken a lot longer otherwise. I've been through onboarding kinds of things before, and of course, they're on the surface because the information is standard and there isn't the one-on-one, give-and-take with the department head. It also made it clear where the [opportunities] were for me … where I could tackle something right away." In fact, in her case, there was one problematic process that she learned about during these sessions that frustrated all of the senior managers. She made it a priority to fix once she joined, giving her a significant early success and winning fans throughout the organization.

There isn't a single way for the CEO to handle the assimilation of the new leader. Robert became the counselor/coach to his successor because it came naturally to him and because it was what he believed was most useful for Greg. This CEO did the same thing, but in a way that was more natural for him.

The Search and the Transition

As the CEO finds the right formula for his role, his thoughts should turn to the next issue involved with controlling steps and pace: the best juxtaposition and overlap between the steps of the search and those of the transition (as shown in Figure 5.2). For a time, the two processes go on in parallel, with the transition beginning well before the search ends. Starting the transition too late puts CEOs, their organizations, and the new leader at a distinct disadvantage.

There are two broad phases to the search (preparation and agreement) that are also shared by the transition. There are two additional phases (onboarding and taking hold) as the transition continues. The preparation phase on the search side begins with the decision

Phases	Search	Transition
Preparation	Decision to hire.	Draft broad outline of transition plan.
	Draft of requirements and expectations.	
	Decision on how the search should be conducted (search firm or not).	Identification of strategic and operational hindering factors and facilitating factors to transition success.
	Finalize specifications.	Match candidate profile with strategy, culture, and factors affecting successful handoff.
	Determine roles in the search (board, CEO, CHRO).	Draft of roles in transition: board, CEO, CHRO, senior managers.
		Plan to prepare organization.
	Locate candidates. Do initial vetting. Revise specifications if necessary.	Identify derivative defections, which should be avoided or managed.
Agreement	Decide who interviews. Decision on use of psychological/style assessment.	Draft sequence of process over expected length of transition. Also draft onboarding plan (first 90 days).
	Formulate offer.	Finalize onboarding plan.
	Present offer. Negotiate terms.	
	Agreement, "yes."	Finalize steps between "yes" and Day 1.
Onboarding		Implement first 30-day plan. Check in/adjust as necessary
		Next 60-day plan implemented.
Taking Hold		Continue transition plan over the next 12–18 months, from building credibility to earning loyal followers.

Figure 5.2   Transition Phases

to hire a successor and to draft requirements and expectations. As those steps are being taken, a broad outline of the transition should be drafted.

The next step on the search side is to decide whether a search firm should be used. Sometimes, a formal search is not necessary as candidates are identified through contacts of directors, the CEO, or others. A particular person may also have been already identified as the target as was the case with Jack in Chapter 2. As this step is taking place, it is time on the transition side to assess strategic and operational factors in place that are likely to facilitate or hinder the success of whoever is hired, with particular emphasis on the political structure.

The final specifications and profile of the successful candidate are next on the search side while the transition should proceed by matching that candidate profile with the company's culture to identify the organizational and political factors that will affect the success of whoever wins the job, particularly the influential managers with the most to gain or lose with the arrival of the new leader.

Next on the search side, the roles in the search should be determined, especially for the board, CEO, and CHRO. In parallel, roles should be drafted for the major players once the transition starts (the board, CEO, CHRO, and senior managers). Also, it should be determined how to best prepare the organization for the arrival and early days of the new leader.

The final step in the preparation phase of the search is the location of and initial vetting of candidates (revising the specifications and profile if necessary). When that step is complete, it is time on the transition side to identify the people in the organization who may leave because the new leader is hired (that is, the derivative defections).

The agreement phase begins in the search stream of activities with decisions of who in the company will interview candidates and in what sequence. Also, it is by this point that a decision should be made of whether an assessment will be done of the final candidates, resulting in a psychological and leadership style profile and an estimate of the personal characteristics that could hinder the new leader successfully taking hold. While that step is being taken, on the transition side a second draft of the overall transition plan should be prepared, and also a draft of its initial phase once the new leader is aboard in the form of an onboarding plan spanning the first 90 days.

Once the offer is made to the candidate, and terms are negotiated, the 90-day onboarding plan can be finalized. When the offer is accepted and it's clear who the new leader will be, the steps on the transition side that should take place between "yes" and Day 1 should be finalized.

The transition process continues by carrying out the onboarding plan for the first 90 days (with a check-in after the first month). At the end of the onboarding period, the overall taking-hold plan for the remainder of the transition should be reviewed and updated as needed.

In addition to the role the CEO chooses and the coordination of the search and transition processes, the selection he makes of the mechanisms by which he handles both contributes to the tone set during these early days of the handoff and the pace of the overall process. By "mechanisms," we mean the vehicles by which information about the transition will be shared, where decisions will be made, how senior managers will be involved, and so on.

Mechanisms answer a variety of questions. Will information be shared in the CEO's senior team meeting? Will the CEO inform his people about progress individually on a need-to-know basis? Who is part of drafting requirements and expectations for the new leader? Who is responsible for finalizing roles? Will the board be involved through one of its existing standing committees or will the CEO ask one or two directors to be most involved? An example of one approach is described in Chapter 1, where Dave utilized Wes as a mechanism to run interference with the board rather than dealing directly with directors on a couple of important issues. The choices made are a function of the CEO's style and the situation, but the CEO should be aware that whichever mechanisms he chooses will signal to all involved the CEO's objectives and opinions about the transition.

The image of how the transition should proceed should have begun to form in the CEO's mind when considering the position the new leader will occupy once she is aboard. If that image is of a smooth, collaborative handoff, the mechanisms should enable the major players to meet often and encourage collaboration, involvement, and communication. If it is one where the CEO is in tight control and prefers to have contact between him and the new leader without others involved, the mechanism should be one-on-one meetings limited to contact between the two of them. Whatever image the CEO forms, it should be shared as needed with the CHRO and relevant directors.

Ensuring Other Players Do What They Must

As the director of the transition, the CEO has the responsibility to make sure that other major players do their part—and as the CEO he has the power. The question is how best to exercise that power. As with any part of the transition, the answer depends on the situation and the personality and style of the leader. There are, though, a few principles on which to base a plan.

The first principle is that the major players must believe it is important to the CEO. The CEO must say it is important, and even more vital, he must prove it by the effort he spends on the transition. The example of the CEO arranging for four days of courses for the new COO is an example. Just before the new COO's first day in the company, she reflected on what the experience said to her about her new boss,

> "It told me a lot about [the CEO]. He had gone over every course. Most people wouldn't have put the effort into this. I'm sure the guys I reported to in other companies never even looked at the onboarding stuff. But the thinking and time that went into this told me that he cared a lot about me starting in the right way..., and it said that when he asked me for something, I'd better approach it [carefully and do a complete job], because like any good instructor, that's what he expects."

The CEO must also use the bully pulpit of his office to talk about the benefits to the company of a smooth entry for the new leader. If he has described his mental image of how the company would look and feel when it is operating at its best, he should now make the link clearly between that optimal organizational state, a successful transition, and the major players doing their parts. It is best to do so with a steady drumbeat of information about the handoff in normal forums that happen in the organization as a matter of course. Having an item on the senior team agenda, including the topic in a business update, or merely remembering to bring it up in a one-on-one conversation will cause the director or senior manager to keep it in mind and reinforce that it is on the CEO's agenda.

In addition, the CEO must be personally persuasive, as Robert was at the large multinational company described previous. Robert's interpersonal skills helped as he listened carefully to the questions and reactions of his senior managers and directors each time the topic of the handoff or of who was to be his successor came up. If he sensed that there were doubts or worries that lay behind questions, he quickly surfaced them. By doing so, he could understand the true position of someone important to the handoff and also have the chance to address concerns directly. The net effect of these discussions with each direct report and the directors was that everyone knew that he was squarely behind this handoff of power to Greg.

The second principle is that the CEO must link support for the handoff to the company's reward system. Just as with any other important part of a senior manager's job, doing one's part in the transition should be reflected in the end-of-year salary and bonus calculation. That should also be something the board does with the CEO's compensation. If the board holds itself and the CEO accountable, the CEO should do the same with the people who report to him and on whom he depends to play important roles in the transition.

In one case, an executive vice president of operations opposed going outside to hire the head of a new, centralized information technology department. Instead, he favored the promotion of a person who reported to him and ran IT for Operations. The EVP was one of the most senior people in the company and someone whose opinion carried a great deal of weight. The CEO, however, had a different opinion, which set up an opportunity for the CEO to make an unmistakably strong point about the importance of supporting the transition.

The EVP lobbied aggressively for his candidate, but the CEO told him that the decision had been made that the new IT person would be an outsider. The EVP persisted, having judged that if he gained support, the CEO would change his mind. It came to be so well known that the EVP did not support the decision that the CEO instructed the head of Human Resources to tell the EVP that the CEO expected "everyone to be behind the plan."

The search progressed and final candidates came for interviews. The CEO learned from the CHRO that the EVP had made comments to the candidates that implied that he believed it was not necessary to go outside the company to fill this job. The candidate the CEO preferred was hired and set to begin at the start of the fiscal year.

At the same time, the CEO made recommendations to the board's Compensation Committee regarding salary and bonus adjustments. When the discussion came to the EVP and after the CHRO had reviewed the results of the formula that factored in achievements of quantitative goals, the CEO recommended a much lower bonus figure. He explained his decision by referring to the EVP's behavior, using terms like "obstinate" and "approaching insubordination." He said he wanted to a send a message that "gets his attention, and everyone else's" so that when the new person began there would be nothing but help and support, especially since Operations had to contribute quite a bit to the new unit and was one of its primary clients.

When the CEO informed the EVP about his decision, the conversation was at times heated, but the CEO got his message across. The EVP was fully supportive of the new IT head from that point on, as were each of the other senior managers.

The third principle is to involve and educate. When it comes to the organization under him, it is not news to any good manager that if he expects people to be supportive of changes he wants to implement, they should be involved in determining how those changes will be made and feel prepared to execute their parts. It is also true that the more involved they are, the more they will be willing to convince others whom they influence to be supportive as well.

An example comes from a company run by its founder, an iron-fisted patriarch. He had hired most of the current senior managers at the start of their careers, and they had worked nowhere else. He had devoted most of his time to the company for the 30 years he ran it, and had kept the organization structure flat, with only a few layers between him and the lowest level. There wasn't much that went on that he wasn't aware of or did not control. He had concluded that none of his children or their cousins was capable of taking over the business. As he got older, he began to think about how succession should be handled. Then, he was diagnosed with cancer. He decided to sell the company to a private equity firm.

One of the board members took over as CEO. Because he was in his early 60s, the new CEO made one of his objectives to revamp the senior manager group and hire a set of executives from which he could select a successor within a couple of years who could then run the business to the point that it went public. He arranged for early retirements of managers he judged could not do what he expected and hired five executives who could. He believed two of them could be successors.

In his first 12 months, he had created a new strategy, brought in operations consultants to recommend and install new processes and systems, and established a new organization structure as well as a new management ethic. He had a senior team of nine people, four of whom had been in their jobs before the sale. The CEO told these four that he would not recommend any of them as his successor, but stressed that he believed each was important to the future of the company and that he wanted each to stay and work for whoever would be the next CEO.

He then set out to convince the board to give them special financial rewards and the chance for a onetime bonus when the company completed an IPO, all as part of a revamped long-term incentive plan he was introducing. The board agreed. He then told the managers about the financial awards and said, "I told you that I want you to stay and that you are important to making this company all it can be. I went to bat for you, and the sign that the board agrees are these awards. Now, I need something from you."

He went on to say that he wasn't sure whom he would recommend to replace him, but he wanted the senior managers to throw their support behind his successor. Over the next six months, he talked to this quartet of company veterans regularly, asking about the reactions in the organization to the changes that were being implemented, and as much as anything else, educating them about the details of a transition (something none of them had experienced) and how important it was that they get the organization to support it. When he settled on who should succeed him, they were the first ones whom he told after getting the board's approval. He asked them to put together a communications plan to introduce the choice.

The handoff in this company was smooth and positive. The CEO returned to his seat on the board and as he helped steer the company toward its IPO 30 months later, stayed in close touch with the person who replaced him, and occasionally, with the four managers. One reason this is a success story was the careful decision making and maturity of the CEO. He made the right calls on talent, and perhaps most of all, was honest and forthright in how he dealt with and communicated with the senior managers who played a major role in the handoff by preparing the organization. As much as anything else, success came from how well this leader involved those who ended up reporting to his successor.

Lack of educating senior managers about the steps and dynamics of a transition and lack of informing them about what is at stake for the company, and in particular, what is required of them, will construct barriers to progress that will be as formidable as they are unnecessary. We will explore the role of the senior managers in Chapter 7.

Self-Management and Self-Awareness

The third imperative of the CEO in a transition is also a key success factor for the first two: the CEO must manage his own emotions and sharpen his awareness of his impact on other players as the handoff proceeds. To the degree that the CEO can do a good job of both will determine how well he relinquishes authority and helps the new leader as she takes hold of that authority.

The CEO's success at self-management and self-awareness does not mean that the transition will necessarily be a success, or even that it will be a positive one. In the example of Alan and Wayne in Chapter 3, Alan managed himself carefully with a good deal of discipline and once he recognized he wanted to remain as CEO was fully aware of his emotions and the impact of his behavior.

But, just as the CEO's self-management and awareness can contribute to a transition's failure, it can play a significant part in success. They are particularly important to the departing CEO because the emotions that come with giving up a role at the top can have a big impact on behavior.

While it is difficult to move to the top spot, it can be just as hard to leave it. For a new hire, the emotions of starting involve confronting the uncertainty of a visible, powerful role in an unfamiliar culture working for a new boss (or a group of directors). For the departing CEO, the emotions of leaving involve confronting questions of accomplishment (Did I do all I should have?), of what is left behind (Is it in better shape than when I took over?), and of what's next (What's my next challenge?).

The chance of finding satisfactory answers to these questions diminishes as the leader gets closer to the actual handoff and it becomes more apparent to him just how limited is his control over organizational accomplishments and personal legacy. It is at that point that he may become more frustrated, especially if he is used to controlling events rather than facing limits. While some CEOs navigate this juncture in a positive way, and others in a way that cause difficulties for successors, every long-serving CEO experiences strong emotions when departing a place he has run. Many are used to commanding the attention of those around them, controlling an agenda of problems thrust before them, and being in the position to marshal the resources needed to make the difference they wish to the company's situation. But as the transition moves forward, the new leader begins to take hold with more confidence, and the attention of the directors as well as subordinates turns to her.

Even for the departing CEO who has fulfilled his responsibilities to encourage this shift, the realization can be jarring that he no longer can effect changes he wants to see implemented. Some departing CEOs, in the midst of feeling eclipsed by the new leader, nonetheless try to make a final, momentous addition to their legacy. The rationale is often, "I have the information and know the capacity of my organization, I can get this done now." But often the unspoken thought is, "This is my last shot to put that final piece in the puzzle."

In one case, the CEO of a transportation company accelerated pursuit of an acquisition target once he and the board had agreed on a planned transition. The strategic effect would be an impressive increase in the size of the company and more dominance in its traditional market as well as significant share of a new one. The transition was to unfold over 23 months and by the time the successor started, there were 15 to go. By that time, the CEO had gotten the acquisition to the point that it was official and negotiations had begun.

The CEO told the new leader that discussions were entering a critical stage and introducing a new face might affect progress, " ... and, anyway, as I concentrate on this, you should concentrate on getting to know the organization."

The deal took place and the handoff happened on schedule. Left unsaid by the CEO was that one of his objectives was to garner the credit for landing this impressive catch. As it turned out, however, the estimates of economies of scale proved unrealistic, as were revenue objectives in the face of an economic downturn. The new leader, now CEO, had to devote an unexpectedly large amount of time to the new division as he unwound and sold off a portion of it. As he put it,

> "If I'd been more involved, it could have made a difference. We could have still done the deal, but the terms could have changed, and I would have been more prepared. The big difference would have been that I'd pay attention to things that [the former CEO] didn't because I would have known that I'd have to live with the consequences."

As we have suggested, the reasons that transitions fail are complicated and overlapping, usually involving cultural and political elements that exist in the organization the new leader joins. But when a careful autopsy is done, there is often another reason that lies even deeper in the root of the problematic handoff—the inability of the CEO and the successor to form a positive relationship. When that appears, going one layer deeper reveals certain emotions of the departing CEO that block her from a collaborative bond or from helping her chosen successor overcome more obvious barriers. Those emotions are not usually obvious to people other than the CEO, and sometimes their destructive potential is not even recognized by her. But they are powerful. In the transition situations where they are at play in the mind of the CEO, it is essential that the CEO, the board, and perhaps the CHRO recognize them and understand their source.

A book called *The Hero's Farewell* is a thorough treatment of the personal, emotional issues that surround the CEO's departure.[2] In it, Jeffrey Sonnenfeld explores the self-image of leaders who are exiting the organizations they have led for some time. He points out that many develop the self-concept of the hero because of their accomplishments. Their personal identities are so intertwined with the leadership roles they occupy that it is difficult for them to leave.

To make departure easier, Sonnenfeld suggests the need to come to terms with two barriers to leaving. The first is "heroic stature," the special place the leader believes he occupies apart from and above others. Taken to an extreme, it hinders the retired leader from reintegrating into a normal role as one of the many rather than the chosen one who is admired and listened to. The second barrier that must be overcome is "heroic mission," or the belief that the leader embarked on an epic quest that he is uniquely qualified to achieve. It will be more difficult to exit for someone who holds such beliefs, especially if all that she wanted to do was not accomplished. Of course, that is a hurdle that just about every CEO will face because very few believe they have achieved all they set out to do.

How can such barriers be overcome if these beliefs are so strong and so intimately intertwined with one's sense of self? The glib answer is gradually and carefully. In a planned transition, the leader has the benefit of time to prepare for his exit. He must use it in two ways. First, he must recognize that leaving will cause strong emotions. Whether they are positive feelings of pride and satisfaction of a job well done or negative ones of regret, anxiety, or anger, he must understand them, recognize their signs, and respect the influence they can have over his behavior in his final months.

The second way the CEO should take advantage of the time afforded by a planned handoff is to think carefully about his next phase after leaving the CEO position. The question to answer is: how can I best utilize my energy, experience, and skills to do something that will be satisfying and that will make a contribution? It is not necessary (and is often unwise) to try to be too specific before leaving. Only a direction is needed until he has more time to think through a destination, but it should be a direction that is intriguing enough that he wants to devote time to explore it.

A consequence of the CEO recognizing emotions and considering questions of accomplishment, what's left behind, and what's next is recognition of the issue of legacy. *Legacy* is a freighted word for many leaders facing their final months on the job, especially for ones who have been viewed by employees as dealing with being the top leader with some humility and who have not sought personal credit for what has been accomplished on their watch. These CEOs have carefully avoided signs that they were thinking of themselves as important decisions were made, and wish to avoid any hint of that as they plan their departures. But however much they avoid the word, everyone who has devoted his full time and energy to leading an organization for any length of time thinks quite a bit about what he will leave behind and how he will be remembered.

There are two broad categories in which thoughts of legacy fall: rational and emotional. The rational thoughts often come down to satisfaction with strategy, financial health of the business, people, and culture. The leader will feel good about the rational part of his legacy if the company has achieved its mission and grown profitably, if a group of people are left behind who can competently sustain success, and if the organizational culture is a healthy one.

The key on the emotional side is whether the CEO is leaving with the sense of fulfillment that comes from recognition of her efforts, a certain affirmation, and admiration she believes she has earned, especially if she is the type of CEO who has worked tirelessly for the company and accepted the tradeoffs that come with the role.

CEOs who are diligent and dedicated trade off personal time for the 24-hour-a-day attention they devote to their duties. They also accept the solitary nature of leadership. The axiom that it is lonely at the top is true. Anyone who has spent time as CEO learns quickly that only people who have been in the top spot fully grasp what it is really like. For one thing, good leaders more than anyone else associate themselves with the organization they run. Because their decisions affect everyone in the company, their work provides a sense of purpose that is not as strong with those not in the top job.

Many leaders respond by maintaining a certain distance; something others notice. It is common that when promoted to CEO, former peers and bosses experience the new leader as remote and less attentive to the relationship. Part of the reason could be due to increased time demands, but it is also often because the longer the CEO stays in charge, the less she and old acquaintances have in common. Even those leaders who work hard at maintaining longstanding friendships learn to compartmentalize to keep them going. All of this adds up to a certain isolation.

In spite of that isolation of leadership, the CEO who is preparing to depart after a long time at the helm looks for a certain recognition of the time and effort he has devoted. Whether it comes, of course, is a function of what has happened well before the time of the transition.

The evidence of legacy in the rational category comes from carefully putting in place certain foundation building blocks in the years prior to departing such as the right acquisition, cost reduction efforts at the right times, and the right decisions about whom to hire and let go. Similarly, the emotional part of legacy requires building blocks put in place over time, and as carefully and deliberately. Admiration and loyalty come from the connection that is made with employees as they and the CEO grapple with tough challenges, from the feelings that result from events when the boss helped people succeed at difficult tasks they thought they couldn't do, from listening and helping to sort out problems, from wise and caring advice and counsel, and from making the right call when no best answer was clear.

It is for these rational and emotional reasons that the leader looking toward her exit must pay attention to the task of self-management,
including becoming more aware of the impact of leaving. Ancient
Greek legend holds that at the entrance to the Temple of Apollo on
Mount Parnassus those who sought the advice of the Oracle of Delphi
first saw engraved near the entrance, "Know Thyself." Just as it was
true for those seeking wisdom then, so it is today for departing CEOs.

Summary

Although the CEO remains foremost the transition
director—controlling the steps and pace, ensuring others
do their parts, managing his or her own departure—the role
of "director" should not imply that success comes just from
being behind the scenes. Success also depends on the intensity
of the CEO's involvement. He must be active and visible in his
direction. The more he becomes involved in the details of his
successor's transition, the more he deepens his commitment to
making the new leader's tenure a success.

An engaged CEO also provides the entrée for more quickly
forging a relationship with the new leader. That is important
because, as we have seen, a close working relationship between
the CEO and the number two ranks among the foremost hallmarks of successful handoffs.

The CEO's hands-on involvement also helps ensure the
support of senior managers who will be peers of or report to
the new leader. Witness the involvement of the CEO engaged
in the four courses for the new leader he hired, the influence of

(continued)

(continued)

Dave in Chapter 1, and Roberts's behavior at the multinational over a year of transition described at the beginning of this chapter. Dedication by the departing CEO translates into a greater chance of dedication by the board, CHRO, and senior managers—the entire transition team—to the new leader's success.

Notes

1. RHR International Executive Research, "Chief Executive Transitions: Keys to an Effective Transfer of Leadership at the Top," RHR International, 2012, accessed January 13, 2015, http://www.rhrinternational.com/100127/pdf/rs /ChiefExecTransitions-Research-2012.pdf.

2. Jeffrey A. Sonnenfeld, *The Hero's Farewell: What Happens When CEOs Retire*, Oxford University Press, 1988, p. 114.

6 The CHRO's Role

Bruce Broussard was hired by Humana in December 2011 from McKesson as the new president and designated successor to CEO Mike McCallister, who had run the large health insurance company for 12 years and who had announced his intention to retire. Under McCallister's leadership, Humana had become one of the largest and most respected companies in the industry. In fulfillment of the company's succession plan, Broussard became CEO in January 2013 and McCallister retired from that position, although he continued to serve as the company's chairman of the board. By then, Broussard had had time to develop a point of view on the company's strengths and shortcomings, including its people and culture.

Shortly after the passage of the Affordable Care Act (ACA) in March 2010, McCallister had overseen a complete strategic review. The most far-reaching ACA provisions were not scheduled to go into effect until 2014, but in anticipation of them, McCallister and the board asked Broussard to judge what changes were necessary for Humana to implement its new strategy and continue its preeminent role in the industry, changes that he would be responsible for when he became CEO.

By the time Broussard was promoted, he had outlined a strategy to broaden the company's offerings to better take advantage of the new healthcare environment. He also recognized that, for that strategy to succeed, changes were necessary to the company's top management and its culture.

Under McCallister, the corporate decision-making style had been careful and systematic, and the information and measurement systems (the essence of that type of business) had been tightly controlled. The model had worked well for some time. McCallister was focused externally as a voice of the industry on national healthcare policy, the company's strategist, and the overall conductor at the board level; the company's financial health was managed by the CFO; while operations and systems that propelled the day-to-day workings of the company were overseen by the COO.

The calculus adopted by Broussard and the board was that because the external environment was changing so much due to the ACA, so too must Humana's management capabilities and structure and how the company operated. This meant shifting to a flatter structure, which, in turn, required a more team-based style. It also meant hiring five new executives for a new ten-person management team, including ones from very different industries in important new positions (chief consumer officer, chief medical officer, chief innovation officer, chief strategy officer, and chief financial officer).

This presented CHRO Tim Huval with the sort of challenge that heads of human resources departments long for, but few have the chance to tackle. The HR team was charged with coordinating the hiring of essentially half the senior management team in a relatively short amount of time, and to ensure these new executives took hold in such a way that they directed core parts of a new strategy under a new first-time CEO who was also relatively new to the company. If the quality of people determines the success of the company, Huval had one of the most pivotal roles in Broussard's plan to remake Humana's role in healthcare delivery in the United States.

Broussard sought people who fit Humana's traditions and overall company values, but also who could help him meet the needs of this new, emerging era. Each candidate was matched to five operating values: cultivate uniqueness, pioneer simplicity, inspire health, rethink routine, and thrive together. In addition, the candidates were assessed against important attributes such as humility, acting as a team player, and being a thought leader. During interviews of candidates for the new positions, Broussard laid out expectations for translating these operational and personal imperatives into how Humana had to operate day-to-day in the post-ACA marketplace.

Once these new managers started on the job, the team worked closely with each to be sure his or her actions in the company were consistent with the new strategy and operating values. There were detailed, customized onboarding plans for all new executives. Huval regularly asked how their onboarding was going, their impressions or ideas about the organization, and where they noticed what might be improved. They discussed mission, culture, behavior, company history, mindsets, and people. And he offered feedback when one of them moved too fast without collaborating (violating the "thrive together" principle) or suggested a solution that was too complicated (not the way to "pioneer simplicity"). He and Broussard also stressed a central tenet of how the senior teams should work with the phrase, "egos fail fast," meaning that taking credit or forcing one's own views on others would not be tolerated.

Because Huval started the same day Broussard was named CEO, and since Broussard had hired Huval while he was still the designated successor, he was in a good position to describe the new CEO's style and preferences. One example is that Huval could help new managers understand Broussard's method of clarifying his thinking on complicated decisions—to hear himself talk about pros and cons, occasionally testing various ways to approach a problem in multiple conversations with different people.

Huval devoted his effort to the sorts of areas a CHRO should in top-level transitions: Understand and interpret the strategy and translate it in ways necessary to shape a new culture. Find ways to ensure behavior is consistent with core operating principles. Integrate new people into the management structure. Become an advocate and resource for senior leaders responsible for moving strategy and policies to actionable tasks. Provide senior leaders with a way to interpret the political landscape and shape it to be consistent with the desired culture. Serve as a sounding board and senior advisor for new executives, for the CEO, and for the top team. And act as the CEO's primary executive officer in implementing the steps in the succession and transition processes.

So far, each of the new executives has stayed the course, the four who stayed to work for Broussard are adapting and contributing, and the new structure is working. Huval has been an important part of the management team, in addition to being the CHRO. He contributes as much to the operations of the business as he does to talent matters. Even though the task he faces is anything but easy or straightforward, it is one of the most important to ensure a top-level transition is successful.

Many heads of human resources departments have neither the experience nor the ability to handle the delicate coordination challenges required in a planned transition. They have not earned enough stature in the eyes of their CEOs or directors to have a seat at the table on complex issues like who will be the next CEO and how she will win the loyalty needed to lead. This is the reason that a 2013 study by the Moore School of Business at the University of South Carolina found that "many CHROs don't participate in CEO succession at all."[1]

The opportunity in front of CHROs today is unique. As pointed out in Chapter 3, the areas of organization culture and relationships, traditionally considered "soft" and less important, are now recognized universally in well-run companies as essential ingredients for financial success. The political structure that has always been recognized was rarely acknowledged. As the softer issues come out of the shadows, CEOs, and increasingly directors, are demanding that people-related issues be factored into hiring decisions and performance reviews, and that the development of the culture be a bigger factor in strategic and financial decisions; and in the best companies, they are.

To take advantage of this opportunity, CHROs must be able to not only clearly define the strategic and financial case for the importance of culture but also to be specific on how to change the current one in practical, measurable ways. They must be as adept at making hard-nosed decisions on costs and operations as they are at compensation and hiring. If the CHRO cannot pass these tests, he will not gain the credibility needed from the CEO and board to be considered the right person to play the central orchestrating role in the transition at the top.

While the board is accountable for the transition and the CEO responsible for directing it, the CHRO's part is to ensure each step operates as it should and that they all fit together appropriately into a general system. While the CEO carries the primary authority for the results of the search and transition processes laid out in Figure 6.1, the CHRO should be responsible for the efficacy of each step and for the efficient, effective execution of them all. In the terms of the Responsibility Charting model explained in Chapter 3, the CEO has the authority for doing what is necessary to achieve the right results (the A) while the CHRO has the responsibility for implementation of the process that will lead to those right results (the R).

In this sense, the CHRO fulfills the same role for the CEO during the transition that a chief of staff fills for a general in the military or a cabinet secretary in government. It is he who ensures the right preparation for key decisions, that necessary information is clear and provided on time, that the CEO always feels prepared, that the critical path is laid out with clear milestones, that progress is tracked, and that whatever blocks can hinder success are either dealt with before reaching the CEO or are flagged with optional ways to deal with them.

The CHRO position is the right place to expect efficiency and effectiveness of all tasks because how well the search and transition

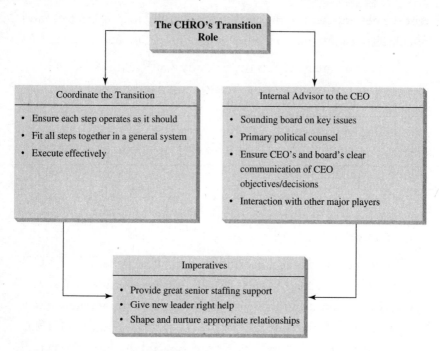

Figure 6.1   The CHRO's Transition Role

processes go has a profound impact on the areas that the human resources department is intended to handle: the organization's culture, the credibility of the company's leaders, and motivating employees to all move in the same direction.

Also, the CHRO should be the primary internal advisor to the CEO on the transition. This includes being a sounding board on the most important issues, providing counsel on the impact of the transition on the company's culture, in particular it's political structure, and being the person who handles communication with the other major players and within the company in general.

One example of a CHRO who has been effective at guiding a transition at the top is Peter Fasolo at Johnson & Johnson (J&J). Fasolo has been CHRO since 2011, playing a central role in the sourcing, selection, and transitions of executives in the company, and in particular, in the transition from former chairman and CEO Bill Weldon to the current one, Alex Gorsky. His effectiveness has been a function of his abilities as a human resources executive as well as his success in four other areas: shaping solid working relationships with members of the J&J board; being a sounding board to Weldon as he made the decision to promote Gorsky and then advise Gorsky as he took over; a thinking partner to Gorsky as CEO and then chairman; and then as a trusted colleague as well as advisor to his peers on the executive committee.

Performing well in each area requires a certain balance that few CHROs master. On one hand, he must be viewed as a key, equal member of the executive team who understands the business as well as the line executives do, and demonstrates the ability to make the tough strategic as well as operational decisions required for the company's financial success. In addition, he must have the interpersonal, political, and influence skills necessary to be trusted and listened to by his peers even though they realize that he is part of assessing and planning their career next steps with the CEO and the board as part of the talent planning process.

CHROs will master this balance by skillfully coordinating the transitions' various parts as they provide sound advice. Performing that role requires that they master three imperatives: (1) providing great senior staffing support, (2) giving the new leader the right help from the point that she says "yes" to the point that she has earned the loyalty of key managers, and (3) formulating ways for the right relationships to form that are necessary for the transition's success.

Great Senior Staffing Support

The first imperative of the CHRO during a transition is to provide to the other major players the structure, information, analysis, and options necessary for each one to contribute in the best way to the transition. When the board must be informed of progress, it should be the CHRO who prepares the materials for the CEO to fill in directors. When it is time to prepare the senior managers for the new leader's start, the CHRO should think it through and make sure it happens in the best way. When the search is launched with the decision to hire a likely successor, the CHRO should find the right recruiting firm and be its main contact. When the organization as a whole should be informed and the time is right to take steps to prepare it for the changes about to happen, the CHRO should do what's necessary to bring this about. And when the right person is hired, it should be the CHRO who not only manages her entry but also continues to counsel her through the transition to the point that she has earned the loyalty of employees and the handoff is complete.

Because of the central role the CHRO position should occupy in a top-level handoff, the CHRO is in the middle in more ways than one. Certainly, information should flow through his office and it should be the center of communication about various aspects of the transition. In addition, since the CHRO is in the middle between the board and the CEO and between the new leader and the CEO, the two relationships that must be positive ones for the good of the handoff as well as for the company, his performance has a major impact on overall success.

As the overall coordinator of the transition, the CHRO has the responsibility to keep the board informed. And as he is in contact with the directors most involved in the search and then the transition, he will have the opportunity to hear their expectations and also concerns. If some of those concerns have to do with the CEO's behavior or anything else about which the CEO will want to know, the CHRO faces the decision of what to do with the information. Similarly, once the new leader is aboard, the CHRO should be the person who talks with her and the CEO about their relationship. To do that well, he should have the abilities to improve collaboration and, on a regular basis, to give feedback to both parties as they shape their relationship.

An outcome of great staffing support is the effective management of the executive search firm retained by the company to secure candidates. An example is provided by the CHRO of Best Buy, Shari Ballard, who has managed multiple senior-level appointments as part of CEO Hubert Joly's transformation efforts. She points out that when CHROs engage an executive recruiter, they must ensure that the search firm understands completely, as she put it, "who you are as a company," and then manage the recruiter tightly to be sure those candidates who are presented are truly enthusiastic about the company's mission and the nature of its business. In addition, it is equally important that the recruiter grasp the culture that the transformation is designed to create, that is, grasp the CEO's image of the optimal way the company should operate, including the types of people who will thrive in that environment.

One of the most important parts of this imperative is to ensure the CEO is kept informed about progress in the transition, and in particular, about the issues to which he must attend and the problems (both actual and potential) he must address. While specific topics will vary in each situation, the way the CHRO prepares for this task is all-important. It requires a deep understanding of a few topics. The first has to do with what motivates the CEO.

Because transitions at the top involve the CEO, the person who will be CEO, and the board, perhaps the most important item on the "things to understand" list is the topic of power—more specifically, the reality and experience of the CEO who has it and what affects his use of it.

As suggested in the last chapter, the role of the CEO can easily lead to a sense of isolation, one that can be especially acute when it comes time to pass the reins to a successor. Because the attention of most people will be on the ascension of the new leader rather than the departure of the old one, the CHRO has a unique opportunity to help. Doing so requires an understanding of the pressures felt by the CEO, what he focuses his attention on, and how he judges his success. Carefully reading signs in each area reveals that the person who is in the top spot worries about and approaches things in a way that is somewhat different from the way others do.

David McClelland is known for his research on why some individuals and groups tend to achieve extraordinary results while others who are just as capable do not.[2] He posited that there are three basic social needs or drives that people have in varying degrees: achievement, affiliation, and power. People who score high in achievement are driven by a need to win, to compete, and to do things that are unique. High affiliators, on the other hand, may accomplish a lot but it is because they are driven not by a need to win but by a more powerful need to be accepted by others. Those who are high in a need for power are driven by a strong impulse to control others to do what they want them to do. When people encounter the same situation, they will judge what is important and how to best react based on their dominant drives. It is not surprising that people who are in charge and thrive in that role often tend to be high in power and as high or moderately high in achievement, and somewhat lower in affiliation.

This is relevant in two ways for the CHRO who wants to be the primary internal advisor to the CEO. First, it opens up a window to what motivates the boss in a way that can explain his behavior and how he decides what actions to take. Second, it can be useful as he is preparing to leave, especially if he is departing with some difficulty. If his "motive profile" is typical of the people at the top, not being able to influence or achieve what he wishes will be particularly frustrating.

The second topic the CHRO must understand is the readiness and capacity of the organization to change. Some new leaders inherit CHROs who have worked for some time in the company the new leader has entered. The combination of knowledge of what drives the CEO and familiarity with the company's people, culture, and processes provide obvious advantages. When the CHRO has been in place long enough to be that familiar, it is easier to tap into the power system for support and to counsel the new leader on the most important but subtle keys to early wins. Also, by then a relationship would have been established with the CEO, which will make it easier for the CHRO to facilitate a positive relationship.

Often, the new leader who wants to institute changes that are significant enough to affect the culture imports a head of human resources with experience and abilities more geared to the image the new leader has of what he wants to create and to the changes that are needed. In these cases, the new CHRO must come up to speed quickly to understand not only his new boss but also the new organization's capacity to change and barriers to progress, including his own team.

Tim Huval worked at Humana for more than a year and a half before completing the searches that brought the five new executives to Broussard's new top staff. That was long enough to get a working knowledge of Humana's traditions and values, to get to know at least the upper-level managers, and importantly, to locate the veterans on whom Huval could rely for balanced viewpoints and in whom he could confide. The credibility of the CEO as well as the transition's success depend on the new CHRO's ability to quickly become familiar with the company and to rely on the right advice.

In addition to understanding what drives the type of person who thrives as a CEO and the organization's readiness and capacity, the CHRO should understand thoroughly the nature of transitions at the highest level. Until the late 1990s, little research focused exclusively on CEO transitions; much good work had been done on "manager transitions" (vice president, general manager, etc.), but as far as we know, not on ones at the most senior level. As we have suggested, the dynamics of each are so different that experience at midlevel management transitions will not be transferrable easily to ones at the CEO level. The CHRO must become a student of CEO transitions just as other major players should, but in his case there is also the need to be the in-house expert on the top-level handoff's implementation and the impact it will likely have on key people as well as on the culture.

The place to begin the quest to master the implementation of transitions is with a set of propositions and related prescriptions for the CHRO.

- The various information that is necessary for the major players and for the new leader must be gathered systematically, described at the right level of specificity, and prioritized. It must be packaged with the needs of the major players in mind and geared to the particular situation of the company and the people involved.

  While some of this work can be delegated, the CHRO must attend to this task directly. He is the one who talks most frequently to the CEO on the topic of the transition and to the relevant directors. And it is he who should have the strategic view and cultural per-spective necessary to provide the right flavor to the information provided about the transition.

- The appropriate amount of time must be devoted to coordinating the transition. At certain junctures, the CHRO will have to spend full time on some transition steps. Also, because parts of this task are unpredictable, the CHRO must maintain a degree of flexibility to ensure she is able to respond quickly.

  When the decision is made to hire a successor, the CHRO should take a hard look at the structure and talent in the human resources department. The wise CHRO will use that opportunity to adjust the structure and to upgrade so that he has the time to concentrate on the transition.

- The CHRO must always remember that he works for the CEO, but because he is in many ways the person in the middle, he must operate in such a way that the board trusts him and can talk to him in confidence without sacrificing the trust of the CEO.

Usually the best way to handle this need for balance is directly and transparently. At the start of the transition, the CHRO and CEO should discuss ground rules, including what information might not be sharable. The CEO must be sensitive to the CHRO's position in the middle between two powerful forces, each wanting control.

- The number-one job is the success of the new leader. The number-two job is the smooth exit of the CEO. They are in that order of importance. While the CHRO has an important responsibility to the CEO, an even more important one is to the company overall. The new leader's failure will be expensive in financial terms but even more expensive in the long run in cultural and leadership credibility terms.

  Prioritization is a key theme that runs through the various tasks for which the CHRO is responsible. His ability to do this with the needs of the organization in mind will be an important ingredient for the transition's success, and ultimately will be of the most benefit for the CEO as well.

- Senior managers depend on the CHRO to look out for their interests and needs. Because he is one, the CHRO is more attuned than the CEO to the reality of the pressures and requirements faced by the senior managers.

  It will fall to the CHRO to remind the CEO and board to not forget about the senior managers when deciding who will be their next boss and when they should be informed. It will also be his job to follow up from the CEO's message to remind his peers that they must keep the needs of the whole business in mind as they decide whether and how to support the objectives of the transition.

- Part of the CHRO's mastering of the implementation of the transition process should be a clear grasp of best practices, including knowing which apply to his organization. A related benefit will be the help that such a grasp will provide to the CEO as he formulates an image of the best possible top-level handoff.

The CHRO should read all he can find about top-level handoffs, judging what is worthwhile and relevant. Also, he should seek out those from other companies to ask about their experience, and through these contacts to find sources for the CEO and directors to do the same.

Help for the New Leader

The second imperative for the CHRO during a transition is to ensure the new leader receives the help she needs to have the best chance to succeed. This should fall to the CHRO because, as the search process manager, he will likely be the first to meet the person who eventually wins the job, or at least the first to get to know her. In that role, he will also be the person to guide her through interviews and, once hired, through assimilation into the company. Such exposure gives the CHRO the opportunity to size up the new leader more closely than anyone else. If style and personality fit with the culture appear to be clear and potential problems, they can be identified early to both the CEO and the new leader.

In order to effectively carry out this imperative, the CHRO must have a full understanding of what the new leader must do in order to have the best chance for a successful transition.

What the New Leader Must Do

There are three broad areas that any new leader must master when entering a high-level position: learning, visioning, and coalition building.[3]

Learning Any executive in a new job faces strategic and operational situations not encountered before. For a leader hired from the outside, the situation is made complicated by systems that contain essential information but are unfamiliar and processes that are familiar but operate differently from what she is used to. When the systems and processes are added to a unique culture and political structure, what was just complicated becomes complex and even treacherous, especially when she faces the need to shape relationships with the CEO whom she was hired to eventually replace but who may not be ready to leave. Also adding to the complexity are peers whose support she needs who may not be in favor of her success, and a board to whom she'll eventually report that the CEO may still control. One result is stress that comes from trying to act in a way that shows she belongs in the top job, to meet the expectations of self and others, and to achieve impressive results quickly.

One effect of all this is to block efficient learning. Many blocks to learning are self-imposed. Some new leaders misinterpret the advice to gain early wins when they believe they must take action on their own to achieve them and go for one that will be dramatic and visible. If they haven't learned enough, it can be like sailing in a dense fog at too high a speed: The risk of making the wrong move is high, with the possibility of turning a hoped-for early win into a damaging early mistake. The subtlety of early wins is such that it is often more fruitful to attempt small achievements or ones that enlist others. In such cases, the "win" comes not from being the person who has the answer or the solution to the problem but the one who points out an opportunity that is only apparent to someone who is new and looks at the situation with fresh eyes. Early successes often come not from solitary, heroic acts as the new leader rushes toward a solution but by galvanizing people in the company to action and allowing them to take credit for a success.

Another self-imposed block to learning is waiting too long to start. When the time between accepting an offer and Day 1 is wasted, the new leader begins unprepared. It is common to attend to family relocation or adjustment and take time off before starting a new job. One new leader remarked, "I knew this job was going to be a meat grinder, so I wanted to be rested and with my batteries charged before I started." As much as that seems a good idea at the time, it often turns out to be a bad one. Being rested but unprepared is not a formula for success.

The weeks before starting should be the time to shift the learning process into high gear. Strategic, operational, and financial information will be available after accepting an offer that should be studied carefully and, as a result, hypotheses should become clear that the new leader is ready to test on Day 1. Also, it is a time to talk with the CHRO and CEO about the culture, with the CEO about expectations, and with managers who will be peers or subordinates.

The reflection offered by this new leader demonstrates the danger of not taking advantage of this precious time. "In terms of my family, it was a win, but in terms of starting my new job, it was a disaster. I had to work twice as hard to get up to speed once I started." To maximize learning, it is generally best to take time off after the onboarding step, usually 90 days after Day 1. By this time, the leader should have done what is necessary to enter the company successfully, and is ready at that point to take some time off. As we point out later in this chapter, taking time away from the office after the first 90 days to reflect on what has happened is an ideal way to learn from that important initial period.

Visioning   Visioning is the mental process the leader goes through to clarify an image of an optimal future state of the organization when it has achieved its mission and carried out its strategy. It should be descriptive to the point of being vivid and attractive enough to motivate the leader, and eventually his followers, to do what must be done to make it happen.

Importantly, to best ensure this mental process has the most positive impact, it is vital to understand what a vision is not as much as what it is. It is not a statement of the company's mission or broad objectives. Rather, it is an image of the organization that has achieved those objectives and realized that mission. To be effective, it must answer the question: Given what this place has to do (its mission and priorities) and how it expects to achieve it (its strategy), what will we look like and how will people act when it has succeeded? It should be clear enough that the leader can describe what she will *see*, *hear*, and *feel* when the organization is operating in this optimal, best way. For the new leader, a vision of her being in the organization begins during interviews. As she learns more and it becomes clearer, it is a primary way she decides whether to accept the offer. Visioning is the mental process behind the comment, "It just felt right," or "It just seemed I'd fit well here."

As the new leader settles in and more adequately grasps the nature of the challenges and the capacity of the organization to meet them, a new image should form. Drawn from her past experiences, from those of others she talks with, and from what she has learned about her new organization, she should be able to form an image of what she most wants to see, hear, and feel when she has succeeded the CEO.

As in the case of learning, blocks to shaping such an image can come from within. Some people do not easily envision an optimal state because they find it difficult to see anything other than what is in front of them. Others are reticent to share what they are thinking and keep their thoughts private because they are not sure whom to trust, with the effect being that the vision is narrow and undeveloped. Still others try to be too specific or continually refine the image to achieve perfection, only to end up never being satisfied.

Other blocks to a leader's vision come from the culture, especially the political structure. As one new leader colorfully put it, "If I'm up to my neck in water that's filled with sharks, I may want to be on the distant shore, but I can't really spend much time thinking about what it will be like if I ever get there."

Of course, for the leader with a change agenda, the next step after clarifying his own vision of an optimal state is to expand it to a shared vision. When a vision is commonly held and shared by a critical mass of employees, it "pulls" people toward a desirable future state, it aligns behavior as they move in that direction, and it helps lessen anxiety about what the future will bring. It is unlikely this is something that the leader will be able to accomplish during her transition period, but it is there that the foundation for a shared, common vision should be laid. As the vision starts to be a common one, the political support from coalitions supporting the leader becomes all the more important.

Coalition Building   Effective learning in the early days of the new leader's tenure, along with a clear, attractive vision, provides the foundation for the transition's success. Without coalitions that support the changes needed, however, even the best learning and visioning will not be enough for success. Coalitions mean a critical mass of loyal followers who will support the new leader in good times and bad. The support of the board and the CEO is not enough on its own. The new leader must have behind and around him a coalition of people who are committed to and share his vision of what the organization should become. They also should have enough influence to draw in others the leader will not have the time or pulling power to attract.

This is where coalition building comes in. Unlike learning and visioning, which are largely private activities, coalition building is a public and political task. It requires a firm grasp of the company's political structure, which includes who is most influential, why they have the power they have, and who benefits or is threatened by the success of what the new leader wants to put in place. This firm grasp must begin as soon as the new leader starts in his new job by learning about the culture and about what influential people want and what they wish to avoid.

A major part of coalition building involves the hard work of building "winning coalitions," or cohorts that have the ability to take action and also the staying power to survive inevitable opposition.[4] Coalition building also involves the equally hard work of preventing "blocking coalitions," which are the groups made up of those who want to see the status quo survive or want the organization to proceed in a different direction.

The difference between winning and blocking coalitions sometimes stems from external realities the new leader can do little about changing. One example is a poisonous inherited culture that has been in place for a long time, or a threatened CEO who is forced into the transition and resists. In other cases, the difference between winning and blocking is a function of style and personality and comes down to the new leader's behavior and the way he tackles problems or deals with people.

Whether it is external realities or internal lapses, they should be identified early and steps should be taken that will result in strengthening winning coalitions and minimizing the power of blocking ones. This is a task for which the new leader will have neither all the knowledge required nor enough political capital in his early days. Just as is the case with learning and visioning, the CHRO should be able to help.

If the CHRO has a good idea of the power structure, he will be able to shed light on the objectives of the most influential people. Doing so will give the new leader a better chance of forming winning coalitions and lessening the resistance of blocking ones. And as the new leader approaches the point at which new programs and systems are designed and plans to attract new talent are laid out, the new leader should rely on the CHRO to anticipate roadblocks and sources of resistance to change.

The management of organizational change has been a topic that has been well researched and widely explored for decades, from many different angles. But when such change coincides with a transition to a new leader, success essentially depends on capturing the commitment of people with influence so that they support changes the new leader is advocating and so that they contribute essential detail that the new leader has not yet mastered. Capturing commitment, in turn, depends on how accurately and wisely the new leader reads the culture, in particular its power structure, an area in which the CHRO should be thoroughly familiar. As such, it is she who should be the primary coalition building advisor to the new leader.

Learning, visioning, and coalition building are the enabling technologies for new leaders to navigate successfully through the dangerous waters of the transition. Simply put, if the new leader does not do well in each area, he, and therefore the transition, will most likely fail. The CHRO should play an important and helpful part as the new leader masters each one. A key success factor is the ability to form the right relationships.

Methods and Mechanisms for Relationships

The third imperative necessary for the CHRO in a top-level transition is to ensure the methods and mechanisms are in place for the relationships required for the transition to be a success. Constructive relationships are the most important facilitating factor for a successful transition. Even with a style or temperament tailor made for the strategy and culture of the company, and even with experience or skills that fit well with the changes necessary, the new leader will not succeed without positive relationships. It is only from them that comes the support needed for the new leader, support that comes in different forms.

The board must support by making sure that expectations of the transition by the CEO and the new leader are clear and realistic. Included are timing of when the new leader is likely to replace the CEO, the circumstances by which the CEO will leave, and the metrics and measuring methods used to judge the new leader's readiness to be CEO.

The CEO must support by directing the overall transition process (as well as the search). In doing so, he must ensure the new leader has all the information necessary to understand what she is committing to and what it will take to succeed. Support from the CEO is necessary to help the new leader to prepare to enter and assume responsibility, and to get up to speed as quickly as possible so that she can show her leadership capabilities.

Support from the senior managers includes doing what it takes for an informed organization that is prepared to contribute and to handle the pressures that come during times of change. Perhaps most of all, support from the senior managers will be apparent as they show a willingness to give the handoff a chance to succeed by, for example, being willing to adjust operating plans, processes, and systems they are invested in to accommodate changes the transition brings about.

The CHRO also has a responsibility to display support. Her support touches everyone directly through management of the steps of the transition process, as well as the search, and ensuring the appropriate coordination within and between them. By being the senior staff aid to the CEO for the transition, and helping the relevant directors with their transition duties, the CHRO also ensures the board's accountability is fulfilled. In addition, the CHRO must support the new leader through several phases as she takes hold: before she says "yes"; between "yes" and Day 1 on the job; through the onboarding program of the first 90 days; and during the all-important months that follow as the new leader secures the loyalty that is given by followers to the effective leader.

Role	Primary Relationships	Secondary Relationships
Board	CEO	CHRO
CEO	Board, New Leader, CHRO	Senior Managers
New Leader	CEO, CHRO, Senior Managers	Board
Senior Managers	CEO, New Leader	CHRO
CHRO	CEO, New Leader	Board, Senior Managers

Figure 6.2   Roles and Relationships

These forms of support, all necessary for a transition that is a success, come from the nature and quality of relationships between the various major players. Figure 6.2 offers a simple way to consider these various connections, denoting primary and secondary relationships. By secondary, we do not mean unimportant. Each of these relationships is vital. But the primary relationships are the ones that the most time should be devoted to because, if they go well, the secondary ones will also have a better chance of going well.

For the board, the primary relationship must be with the CEO. The CHRO has an important role to play in sharpening and getting the most from that primary relationship. For the CEO, the primary relationships are with the board, the new leader, and the CHRO. The CEO's direction to the senior managers has important consequences that will be easier to achieve if the three primary relationships go well. For the new leader, the primary relationships are with the CEO, CHRO, and the senior managers. The new leader's relationship with the board is more remote as it goes through the CEO. The CHRO will help if she has developed the right relationship with the CEO who controls access to the board, and if she has made the most of these opportunities with directors. The senior managers' primary relationships are with the CEO and the new leader. The CHRO here plays a supporting role. For the CHRO, the primary relationships are with the CEO and the new leader, with relationships with the board and senior manager being secondary.

The necessary support for the transition that comes from constructive relationships must be facilitated by the CHRO. The methods and mechanisms that she uses and the skill with which they are implemented will go a long way toward determining how these relationships take shape. Two methods can be particularly useful to meet the transition challenge. The first is to constantly stay in close connection with the major players as well as with the people who control constituencies in the organization. The second is to listen, listen again, and listen some more—but do so in a way to have the best chance to shape a winning relationship.

Connecting

As an example of connecting, one CHRO rearranged his schedule once the incoming new leader accepted the board's offer. He allocated one evening a week for dinners to be devoted to the incumbent CEO or one or more of the senior managers. Next, he suggested more time for one-on-one meetings he had with the CEO every other week. These hour-long meetings had been devoted to the human resources department's objectives and various top-team topics. But with the transition to a new leader moving into a more active phase, he recommended they set aside 90 minutes and include a regular update on the transition.

He also contacted the new leader the day after he accepted the offer. The CHRO explained that while they had spent time together through the interview phase, it would help ensure a smooth entry if they met soon on two topics: plans for onboarding and the company's culture, in particular its political structure. The CHRO traveled to the city where the new leader was living and spent two days reviewing both topics. In addition to the information shared, both remarked later that the time spent together had been useful. To the new leader, it clarified and enabled him to plan more effectively. "Once I'd accepted, all my thoughts were on how to leave [the company where he was CFO]. I wanted to do it in the right way. But when we met, it refocused my attention on what was ahead. There was a lot I didn't know and the onboarding plan he went over was a good start."

The CHRO had a similar impression of the importance of the meetings:

> Talking to him on his turf was important and I wanted it to be informal and away from our offices. It gave me a chance to see a part of him that [hadn't been as apparent] when he went through interviews. He was anxious about talking to his boss about leaving. I went through a couple of times when the same thing happened to us and just reacted to his ideas about an approach and what he would say. I didn't know we'd talk about that, but he really appreciated it ... It was a good ice breaker and I think he got a sense of how I would be of help to him.

Following their meeting, the CHRO took the initiative to stay in touch with the new leader, including sending a summary of the onboarding plan they had discussed. It enabled the new leader to tailor it so that it would include information that he believed was most important.

> The start [of the onboarding plan] had some stuff that I could wait for until I started. But as we talked more that weekend, it occurred to me that I didn't really know anything about how innovation had been handled and how they'd measure it and whether it was clear that when it had happened it paid off financially. Given [the strategy], that ended up being something I spent a lot of time on once I started. Maybe I would have done the same things if this hadn't come up, or maybe not. But I was more prepared to ask the right questions.

In this case, the CHRO took the initiative to manage the transition in the period before the new leader joined. He was disciplined and systematic about it, and he allocated enough time to be in constant contact.

Listening

The second method that will best leverage the contribution of the CHRO is the master skill for relationship building—listening. Even though it usually makes the difference in relationships, it is an ability that is rarely taught anymore. Positive relationships do not form between people who do not listen to each other carefully and sensitively. Relationships suffer because of it.

One way to listen is *passively*, that is by saying nothing. It could mean lack of attention or disinterest, things that the person talking picks up through nonverbal cues such as lack of eye contact. But if the listener is paying attention, passive listening can be a way of communicating acceptance. Therapists use this method with patients as they maintain silence. Saying nothing can communicate an understanding and enhance the chance for a relationship to form.

But passive listening has two drawbacks: its effectiveness is limited because the person talking needs to hear the listener say something to verify he has been understood. Moreover, the person talking tends to not learn very much. Some people clarify their thoughts by hearing themselves talk about something. The problem is that they don't gain new ideas or different perspectives.

There are two other ways to listen. For each, the key is what the listener says, and at least as important, how he says it. One of those other options is to *listen aggressively*. There are various ways the listener can respond in this way. She can be prescriptive ("Well, obviously, in that situation, what you should do is … "), or be moralizing ("You shouldn't do that; you should always do what you'd want someone to do with you."), or lecture and logically analyze ("There are three things you just said that give you the answer you're looking for, or let's look at the logic of this situation."). Or she can be reassuring ("You'll figure this out, and you'll feel better about it in the morning."). Or perhaps she will try to identify with the person who is talking ("That happened to me once.").

There is nothing necessarily wrong with the listener choosing these responses as long as they are offered sincerely. But they all have the drawback that they can be conversation-stoppers. They can inadvertently cause the other person to feel guilty or inadequate or defensive. A third way to listen, though, is: *listening actively*.[5] The person who listens actively responds in such a way that the one talking is encouraged to talk more, and as that happens, there is an interaction that enables him to see the situation he is concerned with in a different way, to gain more clarity. That new level of clarity often comes because the listener has accurately interpreted what the other person means, that is, what lies at a deeper level than what was said, something that frequently the person talking is not even aware of.

When people get at that underlying meaning, the chances increase of a positive result to the relationship. The listener has a better grasp of the issues faced by the person talking. Because of the skill of the person listening, the person talking has a clearer idea of what the underlying issues are that have been bothering him and both have participated actively.

As an example of active listening, a new leader we will call Ruth was hired into a troubled retail services company that had been battered by investigations of its purchasing and pricing practices. The CEO had survived but several senior managers had left. State and federal authorities had pressured the board to reorganize the company. One result was that Ruth was hired as COO. At the time, Ruth faced a host of challenges: new customers stayed away, employees feared the company would go out of business, morale hit new lows, finding new talent became increasingly difficult, and pending fines froze money that had been budgeted for expansion and bonuses. One of the executives let go was the head of HR, who was replaced by a new CHRO we will call Steve.

Ruth had been an assistant federal prosecutor, had worked for the U.S. Securities and Exchange Commission, and had been a general counsel. She was tough and smart with a legal, regulatory, and business background. Steve had preceded Ruth in the company by six months, enough time to have gotten a good sense of the CEO and of whom to trust among the managers. Also, because of the situation, Steve had unusually frequent contact with the board. He became one of Ruth's allies and confidants quickly.

Six months after joining, Ruth asked Steve to come to her office. When he walked in, she was sitting behind her desk, hands gripping the arms of her chair, face red with anger. "Close the door," she ordered. "I need to vent."

For the next half hour, Ruth described the "week from hell I'm having": unreasonable demands from regulators; a large customer defecting to a competitor even though the CEO had "promised me to my face that he wouldn't"; word from auditors about a mistake they had made that she would have to disclose to regulators and the board; a report due the week before for the board from the CFO that wasn't done.

Ruth was convinced two district managers were still doing some of the things that had gotten the company in trouble, but she couldn't prove it. She was also sad about having to order another layoff. On top of it all, she had had a disagreement that morning with her husband that she was still upset about. "And it's only Wednesday!"

Steve let her talk, thinking that she had much to get off her mind. He said very little for 30 minutes but acknowledged what she had said by nodding his head, keeping eye contact, and taking notes, not about the steps that had to be taken to resolve the problems Ruth faced, but about the emotions that seemed to lie under what Ruth was saying.

When he thought she was ready to listen, he said, "Each one of these things is huge. It probably feels like you're facing a tsunami."

"Yes, it does," said Ruth, "and I'm standing on the beach in front of my house with nothing to protect it."

Steve: You feel sort of overwhelmed.

Ruth: Yes, and there are still guys here who caused this getting paychecks.

Steve: You'd really like to nail them.

Ruth: I sure would. It's not fair that people who didn't do this are losing their jobs while those clowns are still here.

Steve: You're angry at [the district managers] because they're still here.

Ruth: I'm way past angry, especially about the guys who are at the bottom of all of this.

Steve: You're not angry at all of them, just a few.

Ruth: Yeah, some of them didn't know what was going on and others are just lemmings that followed. But throughout this, there was a place where the buck stopped.

Steve: You mean Russ [the CEO].

Ruth: He's a snake. I've gotten to the point that I don't believe anything he says. But he's convinced the board and [the regulators] that he didn't know anything about this and that he's a big part of the solution.

Steve: You're stuck with him but don't trust him.

Ruth: Yeah. You know what he did this morning? We were on a call with the regulators and they gave us some good feedback about progress—that was a first—and he went on for 10 minutes how it was his idea and how tough it was to put in place. He lied about all of it. He had nothing to do with it. And those idiots believed him.

Steve: You got angry at him for taking credit but also at [the regulators] for not asking about what really happened.

Ruth: It's just not right. I'm working 20 hours a day here, my
        husband's mad at me for never being home. I haven't talked
        one-on-one with my daughter in weeks. I'm not sleeping
        well. And this snake Russ is getting pats on the back from
        the Feds.

Steve: You aren't getting the credit you deserve with all you've done
        since you've been here. But you're the one doing the dirty
        work and the heavy lifting.

The rest of the conversation revealed Ruth's fear that while the company's situation would continue to improve and its credibility slowly won back, Russ would stay on as CEO and she would neither replace him nor get the credit she deserved.

In this interchange, Steve avoided prescriptions, moralizing, lecturing, identifying, and being reassuring—the five blocks to communication mentioned earlier. Instead, he was more helpful by listening in a way that got to what was really at the root of Ruth's concerns and how she felt about it. That kept the responsibility for finding the solution in her hands but enabled her to talk through her anger to the point that it was clear to both of them what the core issue was. Listening actively requires responding, as Steve did, in a way that avoids being judgmental but shows empathy for what the leader is experiencing. It also takes a strong desire to help the other person resolve what is bothering her. Doing it well requires time and patience because of the emotions involved.

The psychotherapist Carl Rodgers pointed out that the main barrier to communication is evaluating and judging what another person says before understanding it. And that understanding is blocked when emotions run high.[6] There are several mechanisms that the CHRO can use to improve communication.

- *Leadership and executive development programs.* These programs
  must be specially designed for the issues faced by the company

where the transition is taking place and tailored for the culture and individuals involved. They fall into two categories, each with its own purpose: education and training.

Education programs increase understanding of core concepts involved in the transition, provide a sense of involvement, and are forums for two-way information sharing for the CEO. As an example, one corporation conducted a two-day program for the top 50 managers. It covered the nature of transitions at the top, case examples of successful and failed handoffs, the financial and cultural impact in this company of a failed transition, and expectations of the major payers. *Training programs* designed for specific team-oriented purposes are particularly useful for natural workgroups (a boss and direct reports) or an ad-hoc team brought together to address a specific challenge. In both cases, they should either anticipate and avoid the interpersonal and political factors that block collaboration and communication, or in cases where these blocks exist, minimize their impact on the group's ability to function effectively. For a transition, these sessions are necessary if teamwork problems are blocking the preparation for or execution of the transition. Rather than going over concepts and information to increase knowledge, these programs deal with the behavior of the individuals in the group and the relationships between them as they impact the common goal of a transition. Often required is to identify in advance the usually unspoken issues that block teamwork and to design ways to bring them to the surface and resolve them.

- *Whitepapers.* These are papers written especially for a particular element of the transition. Their purpose is to thoughtfully delve into the details of a particular element and to leave a paper (or electronic) trail of the transition's evolution. In one company, five whitepapers were either written by or commissioned by the CHRO. Their titles were: "On the Nature of Transitions," "The Role of the CEO," "Tips for Benchmarking as We Visit Other

Companies," "Why New Leaders Hired from Outside Fail," and "What We Learned from the Transition." An example of the use of a whitepaper is that Steve wrote a seven-page whitepaper for Ruth on what he had heard during their discussion and the questions and issues it raised that she had to address.

- *Journals*. Research in 2006 revealed that learning takes place when we reflect on what we have done rather than as we are doing it.[7] The senior scientist who conducted the research said, " ... while there is certainly some record [in the brain] that's occurring [while acting], the actual learning—what was important, what should I keep and throw away—[happens] after the fact during periods of quiet, wakeful introspection." Keeping a journal during a transition is a mechanism to force reflection and ensure there is learning from what has just happened.

  One CHRO began her own journal after the board meeting where it was decided to begin the steps of a planned transition. She convinced the person who became the new leader to do the same after he accepted the company's offer. Once he joined as COO, they sometimes compared entries of the same event as a way to get another perspective.

- *Responsibility charting*. As described in Chapter 3, these charts are a mechanism to ensure roles and expectations are negotiated and clearly understood. If done well, the resulting RASI chart is useful as a record of the agreement reached regarding who will do what. But even more helpful is the benefit the charts bring to relationship building. Thinking through one's position on responsibilities, authority, support, and information forces a mental image of the optimal handoff. Following that with hearing the opinions of others, and then participating in the give-and-take of deciding final roles, offers a chance to enhance relationships.

  The competent CHRO should have no trouble tailoring and employing these mechanisms. When they are inserted into the transition process and wrapped in the core methods of connecting and listening, the CHRO should be better able to maximize her impact on the transition.

- *Digital media.* The rapid advance of blogs and other means of electronic information sharing has meant that much communication now occurs in ways other than face-to-face, on paper, or in training classrooms. In many companies, podcasts, blogs, Facebook posts, or some combination are the common means through which senior leaders communicate to employees events such as transitions. Digital media has also affected the way that learning is handled. At American Express, for example, Chief Learning Officer David Clark has revamped the company's learning model and protocols through innovative employment of electronic media. CHRO Dennis Berger at CDW has guided the company down a similar road. Both provide examples of innovative ways to make use of the latest technology to make communication and information sharing more effective as well as reach a changing workforce.

Summary

This chapter describes the role the CHRO should have in planned transitions. (See Figure 6.2.) It comes down to two parts. The first is to ensure each facet of the transition operates as it should and that all the individual facets fit together into a coherent process that is both tailored to the organization and key players and is practical enough to be implemented effectively. The second part of the CHRO's role is to be the internal transition advisor to the CEO and to the new leader; and also, as needed, to the board and senior managers. In order to fulfill this role, the CHRO must have the skills and temperament of an excellent chief of staff, must win the confidence of the new leader to help for the entire length of the transition (from the moment she accepts the board's offer to the point where she wins loyal followership), and must ensure the relationships between the major players and with the new leader are solid and effective.

After looking at one company's effective transition where the CHRO played a pivotal part, we identified a half dozen propositions for HR heads to master their transition responsibilities; and for each one, a prescriptive action necessary for successful implementation. Also in this chapter, we suggested that, to be of most help to the incoming leader, the CHRO must have a complete understanding of the tasks and challenges facing the new leader. Finally, we highlighted the central task of facilitating relationships by suggesting that strategically solidifying connections between the major players and with the new leader combined with careful, skillful listening (the master ability for relationship building) will produce the best results.

The techniques, models, and suggestions in this chapter point to a central belief about transitions: essential facilitating factors are the right relationships, the most supportive culture, and a power and influence structure geared for the new leader's success. They are "people issues" which have important effects on every part of the transition. They are also the purview of the human resources function and should be areas of particular expertise of the person who runs it. While there are technical or functional contributions the CHRO must make to the transition that are important to the final result, such as executive compensation and recruiting, we have not dwelled on them in

(continued)

(continued)

this chapter. They should be basic and core skills of any CHRO. However, these other areas of relationships, culture, politics, and power are more important for transition success at the most senior level. But, they are not areas of high-level competence of all CHROs.

Sometimes, that lack of competence is because the CHROs do not have the requisite background and experience. Sometimes it is because they have not put in the effort to master these complex people issues at the most senior level in the organization. However, often it is also because CEOs do not expect their heads of human resources to contribute in these ways and fail to demand that they become expert in these areas.

The message is simple: people issues are essential to the success of transitions at the top and the human resources head should be the major player with the knowledge and expertise to enable the other players to deal with them in the best ways. If they are not providing such help, either they are the wrong people to be in the CHRO position or the CEO does not have expectations that are sufficiently high. If either is true, the transition from one CEO to a successor will be in jeopardy.

Notes

1. Patrick M. Wright, "The Critical Role of CHROs in CEO Succession," University of South Carolina, 2013, p. 2.

2. Dave McClelland ran the Social Relations Department at Harvard in the 1960s and 1970s. He identified three basic social motives, or underlying needs seeking to be filled to varying degrees: achievement, affiliation, and power, research very influential in the organization and leadership areas. Beyond his research, his teaching and mentoring influenced a number of individuals who

had great impact on the management development, culture, and leadership areas that ranged across generations. Included were academics and practitioners such as Timothy Leary, George Litwin, Dave Kolb, Dave Berlew, Irv Rubin, Rick Boyatzis, and Daniel Goleman, and also, one of us (Dan). McClelland was also the founder of McBer & Co. (the first two letters of which represent his name). For a description of his motivation theory, see *Human Motivation* (Cambridge University Press, 1987), and, with David Winter, *Motivating Economic Achievement* (New York: Free Press, 1969).

3. D. Ciampa and M. Watkins, *Right from the Start: Taking Charge in a New Leadership Role*, Harvard Business School Press, 1999, p. 35.

4. David A. Lax and J. Sebenius, *Think Coalitionally: Party Arithmetic, Process Opportunism, and Strategic Sequencing*, in Negotiation Analysis, ed. H. Peyton Young (University of Michigan Press, 1991), 153.

5. Dr. Thomas Gordon, *Parent Effectiveness Training*, Three Rivers Press, 1970, p. 49.

6. Carl R. Rogers, F. J. Roethlisberger, "Barriers and Gateways to Communication," Harvard Business Review, November 1991, accessed November 19, 2014, accessed January 13, 2015, https://hbr.org/1991/11/barriers-and-gateways-to-communication/ar/1

7. C. Goldberg, "Is 'instant replay' a learning tool?" *Boston Globe*, February 20, 2006, accessed November 15, 2014, http://www.boston.com/news/science/articles/2006/02/20/is_instant_replay_a_learning_tool/

7 The Senior Manager's Role

T he most memorable of lessons about successful transitions often come from companies least prepared for a new leader. That was true of a major retail chain known for its growth. The company was started by an ambitious founder who had devoted 30 years of his life to make it one of the largest retail chains in its category. As committed to the business as to his family, he was either in his office or walking through stores (his own or competitors') seven days a week. His hard work paid off as his company earned a reputation as a constant innovator, one benchmarked and emulated by other companies.

As the fortunes of the company grew, however, the founder's health took a downward turn. The first stroke was a minor one, but it got him thinking about succession. He considered carefully the sons, one daughter, and a son-in-law who worked in the business. None of them was capable of taking over. As he recuperated, his thoughts returned to the business, including issues such as same-store sales and financing for the new distribution center. Then the second stroke came. At that point, he decided to sell the business so that he could be sure his family was financially secure regardless of what happened to him.

Two private equity firms bought the company and formed a board that included several retired retail veterans. One of the board members, who we will call Mitch, agreed to take over as interim CEO while a search was conducted to find a permanent leader. Mitch joined the board during the fall of the same year he retired as chairman/CEO of a large, profitable retail company. It had been his second stint as the head of a retail corporation, and he knew he enjoyed that life but didn't know how much until he retired. Perhaps it was the pace of retail and closeness to customers. Or just that he had been in it for most of his life, starting at 15 as a stock boy.

Even though Mitch had decided his days as a CEO were behind him and was enjoying retirement, he accepted the challenge to take over the company that had made essentially no preparation for a new CEO. He made it clear, however, that he would lead the company only until a permanent CEO could be found, at which point he would return to being only a director.

Four problems became apparent in the first weeks of his new role. One was the lack of an adequate management information system that tied together the various departments. This poor interconnection made it hard for even high-level managers to implement changes. Mitch also learned that the founder/owner had tightly controlled both information and decision making. Empowerment was an unknown concept. The scope and pace of the business, however, demanded sharing accurate, timely information so that decisions could be made rapidly.

The second issue that Mitch noticed was the capability of the senior people who became his direct reports, ones he would have hired in either of the companies he had run. Their competence made it all the more striking that they had not been allowed to make local decisions.

The third noticeable problem was that the term "senior team" was misleading because the group he inherited had never operated as a team. It did not meet regularly, and when it had met, it was not to collaborate to run the business but to be given instructions by the founder, who made the decisions and instructed each executive what he wanted them to do.

The fourth problem that became clear to Mitch was that the group of executives reporting to him did not understand the changes that would come from being owned by a private equity firm. Financial metrics and the measurement of success would change. Depending on short-term results, oversight and monitoring would increase, probably by financial analysts of the private equity firm who had no industry experience. Plans to take the company public would bring systems, programs, and pressures that the managers had never experienced. Although Mitch would not be the one to take the company public—an event that was a few years into the future when a new CEO would take over—he would have to prepare senior managers.

Within a few months, Mitch had begun to transform the way the company operated. Weekly senior team meetings were punctuated by first-ever training programs in teamwork. A new information system was approved by the board. New written performance expectations and objectives were formulated for the senior managers, emphasizing their interdependence and responsibility to make the decisions in their areas they believed best for the business. Decisions once made at headquarters were more often pushed down to store managers.

As all this was going on, the search for a permanent CEO moved forward. Mitch shared with his direct reports some of the specifics of the search's progress. As he got to know each executive well, he recognized the entire team's anxiety, which came out clearly at a weekly staff meeting that Mitch extended to better understand their concerns, mainly the many changes thrust upon them.

As capable as they were, these executives had been controlled by a paternalistic owner. Some had never worked for anyone else. In a short period, they'd seen his health deteriorate, the company sold, a new group of owners take over, Mitch move into the CEO position, significant changes that expanded their responsibilities, and now a new CEO would soon arrive. They were worried how they'd come across to the new boss—whether they'd be able to live up to his standards and how to prepare. Mitch knew that the organization had to be prepared for the transition, and these managers had to do the transition work.

Mitch also knew that, before the senior managers could play an appropriate role in a transition, something had to happen to get them ready so that they could get the organization ready.

Whether it is a situation like this retail company where the senior people become direct reports to the new leader, or one where the new leader enters as a peer to the senior managers, the group of unit, business, and function heads we refer to as senior managers must be both ready for and supportive of the handoff. It is they who should prepare the organization for the new leader's entry and for being ready to adapt to a new style as well as to new strategic priorities. This task falls to them because of the influence they have over rank-and-file employees who will be asked to implement changes and because their knowledge of the details of the business will make those changes more practical and easier to take effect. Taking on this role has the advantage of bringing them into the transition process, offering the chance for them to be invested in its success.

Being a senior manager on the top team is often the most complex position in the organization. It carries more responsibility than any other position except the CEO but often with uneven policy/direction-setting involvement. Depending on the style of the CEO and culture of the company, senior managers may or may not be included in deliberations that result in the company's strategy and policies. They must nonetheless communicate the strategy and policies vertically so that their staffs execute effectively. They must also ensure alignment horizontally so that the company's departments and functions are in sync.

It is to this senior manager group that falls the task of adapting plans, systems, and processes when strategic and operational requirements change. As they are performing these forward-facing and managerial tasks, their attention must also be riveted on the short term, so that whatever is necessary to meet the next month's financial targets is accomplished.

Any senior manager faced with such needs prefers a set of rules of engagement and protocols that are as stable and predictable as possible. But, nothing creates more disruption than the entry of a new CEO with a change agenda. When that happens, ambiguity and uncertainty touch important strategic and operational requirements, which depend on certainty and consistency. Carefully crafted annual operating plans and tactics must change, ones that departments have been staffed and organized for and told to execute.

In addition, senior managers have personal concerns when CEOs change. "Will I measure up?" "Does the new leader already have someone in mind to import to replace me?" "Will our styles clash?" "Will everything I've been working on change?" "Will he think that my team is good enough? That I'm good enough?"

These concerns were top of mind among the managers who reported to Mitch as they waited for the arrival of their new boss, the third in nine months. One of them had been hired just several months earlier and wondered if his brief tenure and low institutional knowledge would be a minus. Another, whose whole career had been in the company, worried if that would be a mark against him. Another was planning to retire in a couple of years and had no answer to his wife's question of whether he would complete his career at the company. Still another had recently joined the company but hadn't moved her family.

Senior managers are expected to adapt to continuously changing conditions and disruptions beyond their control. But when these sorts of personal concerns increasingly take up "share of mind," even senior managers get distracted. When that takes place, mistakes happen, just at the point that these managers want to impress a new leader with their performance.

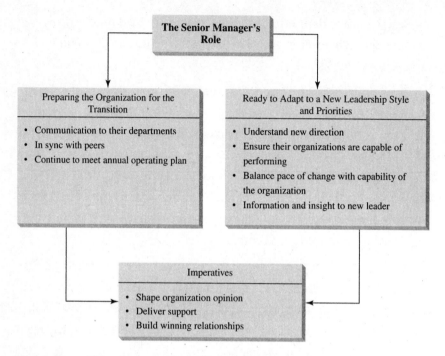

Figure 7.1   The Senior Managers' Transition Role

Facing these conditions, the role of senior managers is to prepare the organization for the transition and adapt to a new leadership style and priorities. Fulfilling this role well includes three imperatives: shaping organizational opinion, delivering support from the people who report to them, and building a wining relationship with the new leader. (See Figure 7.1.)

Shaping Organization Opinion

The first imperative for senior managers is to ensure that the various parts of the organization line up in support of the transition and its objectives. If there is no change in strategy that comes along with the leadership handoff, efforts should be devoted to supporting the handoff process. If, along with a handoff, there is also a strategic change in direction and the operational changes it brings, ensuring the right level of support requires more effort. In either case, it is necessary for the senior managers to understand as much as possible about the handoff and to effectively communicate both information and expectations.

The first step for the senior managers is to think through what the pending change means for the organization as a whole and the part they run in particular, its impact on what they have planned in the current fiscal year, and its implications for their career prospects. Sometimes to do that they have to assert themselves. An example comes from the experience of Janet, a trained biologist who, after earning a Ph.D. at Harvard and during postdoctoral work at a large Boston teaching hospital, took an unexpected career turn.

It all began when Janet began dating an executive at a small biotech company. As the relationship grew so did her interest in the business of drug development. Within a year, she took a job as a scientist at another company with a pipeline of three drugs in different stages of regulatory approval. The staff's dedication to getting a lifesaving drug approved and the resulting climate of colleagueship was a welcome contrast to the isolation and competition of academic research. Two years later, after the first drug was approved and a second in phase II trials, she grabbed the chance to move to the commercial group, which was just forming to market and sell the company's new product.

Janet enjoyed the commercial side of the business and was especially pleased that her scientific background gave her a high level of credibility with nonscientific colleagues and customers. She discovered she was good at negotiating the alliances the company needed to further its commercial activities, at formulating commercial strategy, and at managing people. These were all challenges she had had no experience with, but meeting them boosted her confidence that this was the right career for her. Moreover, as its drugs proved to be successful, the company grew, as did Janet. Within seven years, she had become an executive vice president and head of the commercial part of the company. Her salesforce, marketing team, and the medical/scientific affairs group she shared with R&D were staffed with people she had hired or known since she had joined.

The time came, however, that the CEO she worked for planned to retire. She respected her boss, who had overseen the company's growth from the informal organization he had taken over from the founding scientist to what it had become. He was 63 years old, in good health, and had a good working relationship with the board. It came, then, as a surprise when he told his top team that he had decided to leave. He said that he enjoyed his role and gained great satisfaction from the company's success, but that the business was at a strategic crossroads. It would be unlikely to continue to succeed without acquisitions to fill the drug development pipeline.

That reality led to his decision for two reasons. One was that he had promised his family that he would retire at 65; if he stayed to make this change, it would take three to five years to see it through. The second reason was that he believed someone with skills different from his should take the company into its next era. At the size the company had become, the acquisitions would have to be sizable ones to make an impact. And that was something that he had neither the experience nor the desire to manage. It was time for someone else to take over who had gone through what the company faced. He had talked this over with the board and a search was about to start.

Janet did not want to leave the company. She did not see herself being happy going to a startup, and she had little desire to leave to seek a CEO job. Her compensation was much more than she ever thought she would earn, and her long-term incentive plan and stock options meant she would be financially secure. She was very pleased with the capability of her commercial staff and loyal to them, as they were to her. The one fear she had was that the new CEO would be someone she did not want to work for. She believed that, especially if he or she came from one of the big pharmaceutical companies, the culture of her company would suffer.

Janet wanted to learn more about the specifications for the new leader. But the board controlled the search and said little publicly about it. At an open meeting of the company's scientific advisory board, which some members of the board of directors attended, Janet talked to the director she knew best who had been one of her professors in graduate school. She did not raise the question of the search directly, but she did talk about some of the strategic issues she was involved with that required strong CEO leadership, hoping the director would bring up the search on his own. He did not.

Next, she asked the CHRO about it. She knew he was involved with finding the search firm that was being used. He told her that the search partner had said she was pleased with the starting list of candidates, but beyond that even he had little information. Frustrated but now even more determined, at an executive team meeting, Janet raised the question, "Why don't we know more about this?" She went on to say that the senior team should be getting ready for this change. "If we're going to have a strategy shift and get more active with deals, what will we around this table have to do differently? And what kind of person will we get as the next CEO? A deal guy? Probably someone from big pharma. And we've all had people ask us about it. It's on their minds."

As the conversation continued, the CEO learned that word had spread throughout the company that he was going to step down. It had come up at the staff meetings of the senior managers and was a topic of conversation in the cafeteria and in car pools. Rumors began to spread. One executive said someone had asked him if the CEO had been fired. Another said that she had heard that a pharmaceutical giant was going to buy the company and install a new CEO. As they talked, all were surprised to hear how widespread the rumors were and agreed on the need to stop them.

The CEO explained that the board had been very clear to him that the search should remain as secret as possible, but at all costs the strategic options being looked at should remain confidential. The board believed that both were important to avoid the stock price being affected and competitors gaining an advantage. He added that it was not easy to get the chairman's agreement to let him tell the top team. But if rumors had gone this far, he knew they had to do something. He left it that he would talk to the chairman and get back to them.

The next day, he called the executive group to his conference room and said that the chairman had understood the CEO's concern and asked for a plan by the end of the week of how he intended to handle the situation. He asked each of his direct reports what he or she thought should be done. He then said,

> Before you start discussing this, I want to be clear about something. I will do nothing that could hurt this company, I love it too much for that and the work we do for patients is too important. But, I also have a responsibility to our shareholders, and as corporate officers, you do, too. We have to look at strategic options, and if there's a way that we can increase value, as long as it doesn't hurt our mission for patients, it is our duty to look at it. It is likely as we open that door that there will be a new strategic path that the company will take. Maybe new deals, maybe more than that. I don't know where this could lead. I have got to work with the board to open that door, but I'm not the right person to lead this company down whatever path lies on the other side of it. Our task here is not to try to convince me otherwise or to try to get the board to do something else. It is to figure out how to deal with the results of this situation that we are in right now. What we should be focused on is how to handle this so that it's best for morale and best for productivity, and whatever we do has to be consistent with our values and our operating principles.

With that framing of the task and the CEO's marching orders, Janet and her colleagues discussed options as the CEO listened. The next day, he took to the chairman the plan his senior managers had agreed on, which he had approved. It was based on a core operating principle of the company: to share information openly as much as possible, and when there was some that couldn't be shared, to say that. Because the anxiety about a change at the top was at the point of distracting people from their jobs, the CEO would address this at a town hall meeting that was scheduled for the following week. He would say that he had decided it was time to step down, that the early steps of a search had begun, and that he would keep them informed of progress as much as he could. But he would also stress that he could not tell them much as the search was going on, adding, "You have to trust me on this."

The chairman told him to add that this was the CEO's decision, not the board's, and that he was not being forced out, and that a date had not been set for the CEO's departure. Also, he instructed the CEO to say nothing about the strategic review.

Because the senior team had agreed to say nothing after their meeting, the CEO's announcement at the town hall meeting came as a surprise to the attendees. Because of the credibility of the CEO, however, after the town hall meeting, rumors stopped and anxiety subsided.

A few months later, a new leader joined, but as COO rather than CEO. Over the next eight months, he spent much of his effort on the strategic review and reshaped the company's strategy. During that time, the senior managers were fully involved. Under the COO's leadership, the senior manager group had divided into two task forces, each investigating a different, competing strategic option. Janet chaired one and the CFO chaired the other. Monthly meetings with the board enabled each option to be fully vetted. Ten months after the new leader started, the CEO retired.

The most apparent benefit to the company was a new strategy that eventually enabled it to add to its drug pipeline. As important were two other benefits that came from the way the top team handled this situation. One had to do with the transition. As was everyone's fear, the new leader had indeed spent his career up to that point in two large pharmaceutical corporations. As a result, he was viewed with suspicion by people in the company who believed passionately that the culture needed in biotech was incompatible with what they derisively referred to as "big pharma."

The original notion was to bring in a new leader as "president" who would become part of a temporary "office of the CEO" that would include the new leader and the CEO. Then, within six to eight weeks, the CEO would retire and the new leader would assume that title. When the chairman became aware of the depth of the concern among the senior managers and the senior scientists, he approached the CEO. Worried about a decline of productivity in moving new drug candidates forward, the chairman suggested that there would be much less risk if the CEO were to stay longer. "If [the senior managers] see you working with whoever we get, given your credibility with them, they'll calm the scientists and everything will go a lot smoother. The handoff will go better if it's more gradual. You've got to stay longer, but not so long that it will scare off whoever we want."

By that time, of course, the specifications for the search had been described to the candidate pool, which was in the process of being narrowed down. When it got to the point of identifying the person who was everyone's first choice, the chairman and the CEO talked with him about changing from a handoff over a month to one that would last nine months. They explained that the extra time would enable the new leader to concentrate on the strategy and not also on running the entire business right away. The new leader agreed after the company added to his contract a payment if he was not made CEO in 12 months. Also vital to his acceptance was a private dinner where the CEO emphasized that this extension did not mean that he was reluctant to give up the CEO title or was trying to find a way to stay longer in power. He emphasized that he was firmly committed to the new leader becoming CEO.

By flagging the problematic reaction that would likely greet the new leader, the senior managers played an indirect but important part in the board adjusting the terms to lengthen the overlap of the CEO and his successor. By pushing to be involved, they played an important, direct part in creating the new strategy. That enabled them not only to have a hand in shaping a plan that was practical and actionable, reflecting their knowledge of the organization, but also to get to know the COO as he managed the strategy process.

The senior managers' role enabled them to communicate the new strategy to their people with conviction that only comes from deep involvement. As important as anything else, since the company was just becoming familiar with the COO who had driven the strategy process, the endorsement of Janet and her peers was essential to the organization as a whole lining up behind him as well as the new strategy.

Delivering Support

The second imperative necessary for the senior managers to fulfill their role is a step beyond shaping organization opinion: to deliver the support of the people who report to and are loyal to them. To do so, they must accept that the change agenda and the new leader who is charged with its implementation are best for the organization and best for them. Frequently, while the board may cheer the announcement of the new leader and the CEO may be relieved that he is one step closer to his life's next phase, those who will be the new leader's peers or subordinates see the situation in another light.

As they prepare for the arrival of the new leader, the nature of the relationship that the senior managers anticipate is different from that of the other major players. Unlike the board, they must work for the new leader (either immediately or eventually). Unlike the CEO, they must shape a collaborative relationship that will last over time and will determine their career paths. And the CHRO (even though he may also report to the new leader) will have had the chance to get a read on and perhaps start a relationship with the new leader well before the senior managers have the chance to meet her. The difference compared to these others is that the senior managers have less control over the relationship, something that can determine fundamental reactions to the new leader's entry.

The board and CEO have obvious levers with which to shape the relationship and the CHRO has important information the new leader needs as well as the ability to help the new leader in ways that are crucial to her success. But other than performing their jobs, what the senior managers bring to the relationship may be less apparent to the new leader, to the other major players, or to the senior managers themselves.

In fact, there are two areas the senior managers occupy uniquely and that represent significant assets for the transition. One is that they know the details of what happens in and what is important to the organization as it does its day-to-day work. It is uniquely the senior managers who can fill in the gaps in knowledge about the short-term targets and who can explain the organization's capabilities, shortcomings, practices, and habits. The second asset over which they have control is the support of a critical mass of people in the organization for the new leader and for the changes that her arrival may bring. Both areas are important for the new leader, but the chance to use them will be wasted unless they are expected and valued by the new leader and each of the major players. Otherwise, resistance by the senior managers may replace help.

Resistance to the new leader by the senior managers is rarely overt but concealed in passive-aggressive behavior where there is agreement on the surface but resistance underneath. Causes lie in the emotional reactions of the senior managers. Because of the strength of negative emotions and because resistance is concealed, they pose significant blocks to a successful transition. Sometimes these negative emotions are the result of a senior manager hoping to have won the CEO job only to see it go to someone else. The disappointment, and the resistance that it can cause, can be avoided.

It is not unusual for the board and CEO to encourage senior managers from within the company to apply for the top job, even though they have made up their minds they want an outsider. Perhaps they want someone who has been or is a CEO, or they want an outsider because new skills are needed. Often, they are unable to envision an insider whose weaknesses they know well being able to step up to the top job. When they disingenuously open up competition to insiders it can backfire and demoralize the senior managers who compete. One director candidly put it this way:

> We all agreed that we should have someone who was a CEO somewhere else. But [a few directors] made the case that we should let [two inside senior managers], who were really good guys, very competent at what they did, put their hats into the ring. It seemed like a waste of time to me, but the general feeling was that they'd be demotivated if we didn't give them the chance.

This is an example of wrongheadedness on the part of these directors—as well as the CEO, who did not try to convince them otherwise. As the outside search was launched to find qualified candidates, the board continued to allow the senior managers to think they had a chance to be CEO. The director continued, "We had them go through it all—the assessment, interviews with the board, the whole thing. We didn't want them to think that they didn't have the same chance that an outsider did."

To add to this folly, these were the most talented of the senior manager group. It seems the board convinced itself that avoiding the possible disappointment of these managers at not being able to compete for the CEO post was preferable to the certain disappointment of not winning the job after putting in effort and raising expectations. They also ignored the impact of the negative reactions toward the outsider who did win the job by both these senior managers and those loyal to them. Within 18 months after the new leader took over, both senior managers had left the company.

Negative emotions can also come from senior managers viewing the transition as a threat to their influence in the organization. One executive vice president, whom we will call Tom, ran all of operations in a large family-owned corporation. He had everything under him except for finance and legal, having worked at the company his whole career, starting as an electrician's assistant. His ascent wasn't easy. He moved up the organizational chain of command as a sailboat struggles to make progress against the wind, tacking back and forth and eventually finding a way forward. He went from manufacturing services to maintenance to production to quality assurance to engineering to sales services to sales and then back to manufacturing as the plant's superintendent. Only then did he move up rapidly to control all of operations.

The family patriarch and longtime CEO had been one of his biggest supporters because, as he put it, "He's had just about every job in the damn place, and he could have gone somewhere else, but stayed with us." The CEO saw in Tom a rare combination of loyalty, hard work, tight control over what he was responsible for, and the ability to get everyone around him to follow his lead whether or not he was their supervisor. The CEO made him the only non-family member ever to become an executive vice president. The organization saw it merely as a way to recognize his contributions since he was already the most powerful manager in the company. To Tom, the executive vice president position was recognition that he was the best person to run the company.

When the family patriarch retired, his son left a large consulting firm and took over the business. Tom didn't expect much to change. The business was going well and his team was made up of veterans,

all handpicked, and firmly in control of their areas. Tom paid attention, though, when the son said he had been putting together a new
strategy to double the size of the company. When he said nothing
more over the next couple of months, Tom thought to himself that he
should either forget about it or be worried.

He started to worry when the CEO told Tom that he had asked the
longtime CFO to retire. He went on to say that he was trying to recruit
someone he had known at the consulting firm, who was presently CFO
at a multinational company in London. If he succeeded, she would
join as CFO and, because of her strategy skills and her knowledge of
the European market, she would start a strategic planning group and
a business development group to locate acquisition targets in Europe.
The CEO added, "But you don't have to worry, Tom. It won't affect
the United States much. What you have will stay on its own."

Tom found Sarah smart and quite capable financially. She was
also careful to respect Tom's position. Tom noticed that he was the
first person she called when she accepted the job and the first one
she introduced herself to when she first visited the company. Sarah
also did something that impressed Tom more than anything else: She
asked if she could work in the main plant for a week on the third shift
before she officially started as CFO. She said she wanted to be in a
department such as maintenance or inspection that would give her the
best understanding of the plant's capabilities and of what was necessary
to improve. Also, she did not want the supervisor to know she was
about to step into the CFO position so that she could get a sense of
what it was like to be an hourly worker there.

When Sarah decided to design a new financial planning and
control system, she came to Tom to talk about why it was needed. She
had taken the time to make up a sample report of the system she had
in mind compared to a current report for operations. She asked for
Tom's ideas to tailor it to his needs and managed the vendor so the new
system incorporated them all with no additional cost.

Sarah also kept Tom up to date on her thinking about revenue growth through acquisitions. She walked through the nature of the markets in Europe that the company could enter, the type of companies she believed should be targets, and the benefits and risks. She also explained how the deals might best be financed as well as the tax implications for the company.

Over the next 18 months, two acquisitions were completed, putting the company on a track so that, in five years, its revenue would grow substantially and its earnings would increase much faster than without the acquisitions. But unlike the first thoughts of the new CEO, they were not standalone units able to operate entirely independently of the core business under Tom. To make the investment work, parts of them had to be sold off, which meant the U.S. business would have to use its excess capacity to make up the difference. This meant Tom's ongoing support was necessary.

Organizationally, things changed, too. The CEO promoted Sarah to executive vice president as the two acquisitions reported to her. The CEO had expected Tom to resist or at least be unhappy that there was another executive with that title in the company, but he was pleased that, instead, Tom strongly endorsed the move.

Tom could have thrown up roadblocks to the strategy either directly or through his loyal organization, and he could have fought the promotion of someone else to become EVP with whom he would have to share influence. But he took the opposite route. By that time, the working relationship between the two executives was close and collaborative. They talked every day, and there was not a major decision that one made without informing the other. As important as anything else, Tom marshaled his forces to help ensure Sarah's growth strategy would succeed.

There were two reasons this situation worked out as it did. The first was that Tom cared more about what was best for the business than about remaining the manager with the most power, and he made sure

Sarah had the same priorities. He said he had two tests that he put Sarah through when they first met:

> The first was whether she was competent enough. Well, that didn't take long—she's the best [financial person] I've ever seen. My next test was whether she cared more about herself and getting more power [at my expense] or about what was right for the business. I found out that she's all about what's best for the company. She's backed off on some things because they weren't right for the business, but that didn't help her [politically]. If there's ever a [non-family member] who runs this place, I'll fight hard to make sure it's her.

The second reason this situation worked out is because of how Sarah handled herself, and in turn elicited Tom's reactions. She had entered the company because it posed a complex business problem that required an intricate strategy, the sort of situation that she found most interesting. Like any ambitious executive, she wanted to move up and be in a position where she controlled as many resources as possible. But she was motivated more by a need for achievement than by a need for power. Controlling resources meant having more at her disposal to accomplish bigger, tougher goals, not just having control for control's sake.

Satisfaction to Sarah meant tackling an intractable problem, especially one that others thought overwhelming. It meant not resting until it was solved. Just coming up with the solution without actually solving the problem would be more frustrating than satisfying. In this way, she recognized that she was unlike many of her business school classmates and consulting colleagues who were content with merely identifying the ideal solution whether or not it could be realistically implemented. Further, she realized that the satisfaction of achieving a tough goal required more than the right solution and resources. It required convincing the people who were in a position to implement necessary steps that the goal was important enough for them to dedicate themselves to achieving it. For that, she discovered that relationships were the key success factor.

Sarah had worked hard to understand what motivated people, studied the research on relationship building, and used her vacation time to attend training programs to be exposed to the skills of building trusting relationships. By the time she entered the company as CFO, she was good at it. She recognized Tom as someone whose support she needed to do what she wanted to do for the business and worked at forging a relationship. It helped that once she met Tom, she liked him. As she summarized, "He's straightforward. He knows how to play power politics. He's a street fighter and good at it. But deeper than that, he's a solid, trustworthy person. If you don't play games with him, but respect him and deal with him honestly, he'll do the same with you."

The examples in this section describe the impact of organizational, political, and personal dynamics on ensuring support of senior managers during times of change. While each of the people in these examples set out to do the right thing, the results varied. The case of the board that encouraged two high-performing managers to compete for the CEO job makes the point that not laying out clearly the rules of engagement or revealing positions already firm is a formula that guarantees resistance from senior managers. The case of Tom and Sarah, on the other hand, is one that underlines the central role played by relationships in whether a new leader receives support or faces resistance.

Building Winning Relationships

For senior managers to contribute what is necessary for a successful transition, they must be prepared to build solid working relationships with the new leader as well as with one another. Doing so is partly in their control and partly in the hands of the organization, particularly the CEO. In planned transitions, the sitting CEO will set the tone that will convey to senior managers the expectations for their involvement. If the actions of the board are complementary with the messages from the CEO, so that the senior managers know they're in agreement, the stage is set for the managers to contribute their part.

Of course, to shape relationships that will substantially increase the probability of a successful transition, more is needed than information and expectation-setting from the CEO or board. The right preparation of the senior managers is part of the puzzle. To explain, let's return to Mitch and the situation introduced at the start of this chapter. We left Mitch as he was making good progress in getting the business to run more effectively. He was realizing, however, that the senior managers needed help to prepare for their new boss.

The search had been going on for a few months when summer arrived, a time when recruiting activity tends to slow down. Mitch thought he had some time to figure out the best approach. However, it was at that point when the company found the right candidate, Marcus, the COO of a retail corporation that, although in a different market, had features similar to the company. Marcus was considered the designated successor, but his boss was not close to retirement age, and there was no indication that he would leave. When the recruiter contacted him, the chance to be CEO and the reputation of the company were immediate attractions. As he learned about the new owner's plans and timing to take the company public, his interest increased.

When the private equity firm partners who oversaw the company interviewed him, they called Mitch to say they believed they'd found the person they wanted. Mitch interviewed him and was impressed. But he cautioned that Marcus had never been a CEO and had not been in a business as complex as the one Mitch had temporarily taken over. There would be a necessary learning curve he would have to go through. They agreed that, if Marcus accepted an offer, Mitch would work with the new leader and provide any help needed to get him prepared. They also agreed that an independent assessment of Marcus's personality and leadership style would be done to suggest the hurdles that could hinder success. As it appeared that progress might be rapid toward an offer and negotiations, Mitch's thoughts turned to how to get the senior managers and the organization ready.

Mitch formulated a two-pronged plan. One was to put together an educational program for the new leader. It would include a detailed profile of the company, its strengths and weaknesses, and what Mitch had done to improve it. Mitch also outlined a plan to prepare the senior managers who reported to him.

Marcus accepted the offer and informed the CEO of his current company that he planned to leave. Until that meeting took place, it was unclear how hard his current CEO would try to convince him to stay, and therefore when, or whether, Marcus would become the next leader of the company. After a few days of negotiation, an agreement was reached. After having gotten through that step, Marcus was anxious to begin the next chapter of his career. That meant that Mitch had to put his preparation plans into high gear.

Three sets of notebooks were constructed. One was a comprehensive binder on the company's history, strategic plan, the last three annual budgets, 36-month financial performance, and market and competitive data. Also included were the strategic big bets that had been placed over the last several years for large capital projects. The second set of notebooks contained detailed information about each department, including staffing, objectives, operating goals, and recent initiatives as well as planned ones. The third notebook contained the assessment report that had been done and Mitch's notes on what he believed to be the big leadership and cultural issues facing the company.

Marcus and Mitch met for two days in the city where Marcus lived. Mitch had interviewed Marcus once when he had judged his experience and competence to run a large, growing company. Now he wanted to get to know him. Mitch said, "I wanted to see him on his turf because he'd be a bit more relaxed that way and it would give me a better measure of the man."

As Mitch settled into his seat for the flight to the meeting, he put together what he called his "make-sure list." There were three items: (1) that Marcus realizes the anxiety of the organization he's about to take over; (2) that Marcus is prepared to take the time to understand the culture, including the habits and practices unique to it; and (3) that Marcus listens to feedback from the assessment and takes it well.

One of Mitch's impressions from his interview with Marcus that had been reinforced in the assessment was a tendency to quickly size up a situation, determine what he believed was the best approach, expect others to have the same clarity, and drive relentlessly for execution. He told Mitch he had studied the formative era of the late 1970s to the early 1990s when American manufacturing remade itself by learning to operate in a way that avoided the tradeoffs traditionally accepted as necessary between cost, quality, and efficiency. A core accomplishment was learning to compete on the basis of time, that is, to use speed as a competitive weapon. He trained himself to make decisions quickly and to demand that others do the same.

Mitch admired that trait but went to his meeting prepared to prove that for a CEO an emphasis on speed only translates into financial results when the organization is able to perform at a faster speed. If followers don't understand or aren't prepared to move faster, the leader will fail.

To prepare for his discussion with Marcus, Mitch had also studied the history of that period in the evolution of U.S. companies. He learned that manufacturing companies that had thrived were ones where the senior-level managers had caught up with their leader's conviction about what was needed to compete in a new, global marketplace. Mitch was worried that a style that demanded action right away instead of pausing to learn about the organization would cause the senior managers to fall far behind Marcus's lead, and that would cause early problems for Marcus rather than result in early successes. Instead, Marcus had to understand the anxiety of the senior managers and ask questions and listen to them so he could learn, rather than arriving not knowing the company but coming across as though he had all the answers.

Mitch's time with Marcus on the first day of their meeting was devoted to information/discussion sessions from early morning through the afternoon. That was followed by a long dinner meeting that evening. The next day, they delved into detail on the people, culture, and state of mind of the senior managers, none of whom Marcus had met. That was followed by another long dinner discussion. The two days had been designed to enhance and quicken the relationship process. The two dinners centered on background, family, and leadership philosophy. The evenings were also the time to talk about the family that had owned the company and the environment in which longtime employees had spent their careers.

On the morning of the second day, Mitch fed back the results of Marcus's style/personality assessment. The majority of it was very positive, but Mitch knew that the few items that suggested areas where Marcus might run into problems were the areas they had to focus on. The two had gotten to know each other only a bit by then, and Mitch was concerned about Marcus becoming defensive about that part of the feedback. He was relieved that Marcus received it willingly and agreed that the conclusions of the assessor could indeed be derailers of Marcus's success as a CEO.

As Marcus drove Mitch to the airport, he asked for Mitch's help after he took over as CEO. Because Mitch had been a CEO previously, had run this company and knew it well, and had proved to be someone Marcus could talk to easily about topics he revealed to few people, he asked Mitch to be his advisor for the first six months. They discussed the sensitivity of Mitch being a board member and agreed how to handle it.

As Mitch flew back home, he was more optimistic than he had been a few days before about how Marcus would handle his entry. Now he had to turn to making sure the senior managers were prepared. Mitch had asked an advisor who had helped him prepare up to this point to meet with the senior managers, believing it would be helpful to them to talk about their concerns with an outsider. Mitch decided that there would be two full-day meetings, one week apart. The first day took place as Mitch and Marcus met.

The meetings had two objectives: Provide a forum in which the group could discuss concerns openly about a new boss entering soon, and suggest a framework by which they could prepare for Marcus's arrival. The first day began with a two-hour meeting of the whole group to discuss the nature of transitions at the top level and how they are different from any other handoff. The advisor then met with each senior manager through the afternoon. That was followed by a dinner of the whole group. At the end of Day 1, each senior manager agreed to prepare for the meeting the next week by thinking through three items: the questions he or she would most like answered about senior-level transitions; the questions that each wanted answered by Marcus; and to outline a presentation to Marcus to describe not only each manager's department but also the issues and concerns it faced.

A week later they met again, this time with Mitch. Mitch had briefed them on Marcus prior to the Mitch-Marcus two-day meeting, and he had involved them in the construction of the notebooks that he had reviewed with Marcus. This day was divided roughly into thirds. It began with Mitch reviewing the meeting he had with Marcus.

That fed into the questions senior managers had about Marcus and about relevant transition principles. During the afternoon, the senior managers went over their thoughts on how each would describe the unit he ran in the first presentation to Marcus. During the intervening week, the CHRO had met with each of his peers to help in the preparation. Mitch stayed for the whole day, and during the mock sessions in the afternoon, he role-played Marcus, giving the senior managers a sense of how Marcus might react and the questions he might ask.

When Marcus arrived, the onboarding program prepared by the CHRO called for a combination of senior team sessions and one-on-one meetings for the first two days. Marcus had asked Mitch to be present at all of them. Each senior manager went through a presentation of his department, how it operated, the major issues it faced, the plans to deal with them, and questions that had to be answered as well as how the senior manager intended to find those answers. At Mitch's suggestion, included in each were steps the department was taking or intended to take to improve problem identification and the speed of resolution. As his first week as CEO came to a close, Mitch had dinner with Marcus and asked him what had surprised him so far. Marcus said, "How prepared the people who report to me are. I'm very pleased about what I have to work with here."

The case of Mitch describes a transition that succeeded because a mature, competent CEO made the time and effort to prepare his senior managers. Mitch showed patience and empathy toward the senior managers and listened carefully to their concerns. He recognized that each was necessary to ensure these managers were prepared to be productive in the face of the inevitable disruptions of a transition plus the pressures of a new owner aiming at an IPO in the future. He also recognized that having a prepared new leader had to go hand-in-hand with a prepared organization.

Summary

By being prepared for the transition, senior managers are able to shape organization opinion to the benefit of the new leader. (See Figure 7.1.) The first step to being prepared is for the senior managers to understand as much as possible about the nature of top-level handoffs in general and about the one about to happen in their company in particular. Two related key points emerged from the case of Janet. One is the close link between senior manager involvement and the ability of the executives to influence the people who report to them. The other is that senior managers must sometimes assert themselves rather than passively waiting to be informed. They should not be bystanders in the transition. Nor should they sit back as judges who control a jury of direct reports. They should act as champions of a new era of management.

This may not always come easily. As senior managers become knowledgeable about the nature of transitions and the more immediate one in their organization that will produce a new leader, they must get to the point of accepting that the transition will be good for the organization and for them. That requires clarity on the senior managers' contributions to the success of the new leader, knowledge of the organization's capacity and problems that is not only clear to the senior manager but also communicated effectively to the new leader, and influence over a critical mass of employees to support the new leader's agenda.

(continued)

(continued)

Indeed, senior managers control the assets critical to a new leader. In a planned transition, they must be expected to help the new leader leverage the assets of knowledge and organizational support. They will not benefit the new leader if the senior managers do not deliver them … and they will only deliver them if they believe they have much to contribute, that their contributions are valued and wanted, and, in particular, that they have some control over shaping a positive relationship with the new leader.

Because emotions rule relationships, the CEO must act in advance to ensure positive, constructive emotions of the senior managers toward the new leader. The senior managers must meanwhile take a positive approach themselves. Working together, the CEO and senior managers—as in the cases of the senior managers reporting to Mitch and Janet and her peers—can defuse resistance and assure the new leader enjoys support needed in the first days on the job. In the example of Mitch, we saw the role education plays in preparing senior managers to contribute and to shape a relationship with the new leader. In parallel, the preparation Mitch afforded his successor helped on a few fronts—the senior managers were ready for their new boss, Marcus was much more prepared to take over than he would have otherwise been, and Mitch could return to his role as a director confident that he had done all he could to ensure the success of this handoff.

We looked at the case of Tom and Sarah to investigate this question of emotions as they impact the formation of relationships. Tom had many reasons to resist Sarah's arrival. But, instead, he showed the maturity to support a new leader and the ability to put what was best for the company ahead of the urge to act in a competitive way. Meanwhile, Sarah showed the maturity to elicit that support, as well as the competence and foresightedness to appeal to Tom's sense of fair play. The interaction of the two created a relationship that ensured strong backing for Sarah throughout the company.

We now see how all the parts fit together. The four players in a top-level transition—directors, CEO, CHRO, and senior managers—must each fill a distinct role in making the transition a success. Any one of them, ignoring or neglecting the roles defined in the previous four chapters, can trigger a cascade of unfortunate events that leads to a new leader's failure. When all players step forward with empathy and energy to make the new leader a success and when the new leader does his part, the company has a solid foundation to handle the complexity of a top-level transition.

8 Summary

In an ideal world, the organization in which a transition at the top is about to take place would have these features.

- The board would be knowledgeable about the company and its talent, aware of the challenges it faces, a partner of the CEO to meet those challenges, and dedicated to making the company great in every way as well as profitable in the near term. It would be wise in its counsel and know how much to be involved and when to back off. The CEO would know the board supports him as the transition proceeds and directors would grasp their unique role in the handoff. Some of the directors will have gone through their own CEO transitions as designated successors and as departing CEOs.

- The CEO would not only be a skilled executive but also a wise, mature leader. He would have earned the trust of the organization. He would be thoroughly grounded in effective CEO transitions, and have been himself a designated successor. He would have strong interpersonal skills and the ability to communicate in a way that both informs and inspires, and be personally secure with who he is and what he has accomplished. He would be attuned to the cultural and political forces of his organization and understand what motivates his people. He would be ready and able to help his successor and enjoy working on it with the board because their relationship would be based on not only respect but also trust.

- The CHRO would be strategic, practical, tough-minded, and thoroughly grounded in what's necessary for a business to survive and then grow. She would know how to create a culture of achievement that attracts and keeps the best talent, and be a wise advisor to the CEO as well as to her peers while also watching out for the needs of all employees. She would have the ability to make as well as to help others make tough decisions that face up to hard choices. She would be trusted by being seen as politically astute but not as a "political" person who is self-serving and not open. She would be widely respected as a skillful manager, be able to handle complex systems, and be an effective project manager who is able to coordinate all the moving parts of the transition.

- The group of senior managers would be knowledgeable about the complexities and dynamics of top-level handoffs and understand the perspective of the CEO while also having the appropriate degree of empathy for the new leader entering the organization. While ambitious themselves, they would welcome the chance to learn from and work with the right new leader. They would be able to adjust when needed to changing strategic conditions while maintaining predictable operating results. Most of all, they would be able to prepare their functions or departments for the transition in a way that ensures the CEO and new leader have unified support.

- The new leader would be poised to enter the organization ready to learn about his new company, knowing how to best envision the optimal organization as well as the optimal relationships with the company's major players. He would have already developed coalition-building abilities so that he can read the new power structure and manage it to his advantage. He will have also developed the skills of the great advice taker and be ready to learn from his new colleagues. He would understand with empathy the position of the CEO and have the interpersonal and influence skills to shape a relationship with him that meets both their needs. He would have been a director himself in a company that went through a CEO transition and so would have firsthand experience with the paradoxical responsibilities of a board. He would have realistic expectations because he grasps completely what the company should do for a successful transition and what he must do himself.

Of course, we do not live in an ideal world. Rather, we live in one that is imperfect and where, whenever a group of people come together to achieve a complex task, they will not align in just the right way because the abilities of each will not be ideal and their motivations and perhaps values will vary. Even if the board and CEO think through carefully and lay out in detail what should happen for the transition to go flawlessly, the pace of change, eccentricities, and quirks of the real world and, in particular, the emotions of the people involved will render these plans as less realistic in practice than they appear on paper. The most we can do is to work as diligently as possible to understand what is needed for success in any particular situation and, through well-considered, relevant principles, prepare to adapt to conditions that sometimes we can predict, but often we cannot.

Experienced leaders look to guidelines to help them deal effectively with the real-world conundrums they face. The principles and propositions contained in this book are offered in that spirit. Rather than prescriptions that will cure the illnesses affecting transitions, they are guidelines that the major players should take the time to understand and to tailor to their particular situations.

To make the best use of these guidelines, there are certain key success factors that should be kept in mind.

The first key success factor has to do with teamwork, people's ability to cooperate to achieve a common objective. Just as there are different types of transitions, there are also different kinds of teamwork. Depending on the contest a group is engaged in, one kind of teamwork works more effectively than others. It is sometimes best for each player on a team to concentrate only on the job assigned and where there is little need to actively coordinate. The collection of individual actions and performance is enough to produce the result the various players desire. To use a sports analogy, baseball requires this sort of teamwork.[1] Other times, teams must operate in a top-down way, with the leader devising the game plan and passing it to the various players, who are expected to follow orders and execute that which the game plan calls for as the leader ensures they do so in a disciplined way. Winning at football depends on this kind of teamwork. Either of these approaches can be successful, depending on the rules of the contest. But, neither is appropriate for a transition, which calls for a different type of teamwork.

In a transition, as we have seen, the major players on the company side of the equation and the new leader on the other side must understand their particular roles but also must coordinate and communicate continuously with trust and transparency. The CHRO must gather and coordinate information from their communication and have the skills of the chief of staff while also being close enough to the board, the CEO, and the senior managers to anticipate their needs. The board must walk the fine line of accountability while also being close enough to the CEO to read her mood as she prepares to pass the baton, and to coordinate its communication with her so that the new leader receives consistent messages from both. The CEO must not only master the ability to direct the whole process but also empathize with the new leader as he steps aboard, read the needs of the senior managers well to ensure they are ready to prepare the organization, and be able to make best use of the coordinating abilities of the CHRO. The senior managers must show flexibility as they face the inevitability of change while still being held to financial objectives previously set. And they should do what is necessary to prepare their departments as well as themselves for the handoff to a new leader.

Each player must be skilled at specific duties but, in particular, must operate together fluidly and in a way that allows all to adjust and change direction in unison to adapt to new conditions. This fluidity is essential and stems from trust in one another's competence as well as motives.

The type of teamwork that is required of the transition team is more like a basketball team or hockey squad where each player has a well-defined role and specialties but the game is won by all players being on the court or on the ice together, reacting as a unit to always-fluid conditions, moving from offense to defense as necessary and, importantly, as a unit. Teams that succeed at this game are made up of skilled individuals committed to winning but also to one another's success.

The second key success factor is to learn about transitions. Just as it is essential for leadership in any role today to learn continuously, to contribute to the success of transitions at the top requires that the major players become continuous students of transitions. There are five necessary tasks. The first task is to understand the general requirements of effective handoffs at the top, what makes them succeed, and why the ones that do not succeed fail. The second task for the major players is to avoid seeing general principles as universally applicable but instead must see them as needing to be tailored to their own unique circum- stances. They must figure out how to apply those insights in their particular organizations and to do so in a unified as well as timely way. The third task is to extend that analysis to understand how transitions at the top are unlike those at any other level. They impact each part of the organization in some way as they have an effect on strategy, operations, the political system, and the overall culture. The fourth task essential for learning about transitions is open conversation about the assumptions, goals, hopes, and fears of each player. The more there can be an honest dialogue, the greater the chance that the right learning will take place. The fifth task is to embark on a disciplined lessons-learned process after the transition. We have not encountered an organization that has not experienced at some point a failed handoff from one leader to another. What distinguishes high-performing companies from average ones is the willingness to objectively analyze what happened and why a transition worked out the way it did. An open, transparent conversation about who did what, why, and its effects will increase learning so the chances will greatly improve that the next one will be better.

We have said frequently in this book that the major players must become students of transitions. The same advice is offered to the new leader. The more the major players on the company side of the transition equation and the new leader on the other side know about handoffs at the top, the more helpful each will be in shaping a successful transition.

The mindset of a serious student comes through in curiosity, doggedness, and discipline. Each player must constantly ask questions and seek the right level of detail in answering them. Talking to executives in other companies is one way to do so. Hearing the experiences, mistakes, and lessons of those who have gone through senior-level transitions is invaluable as long as one listens carefully and actively. Reading whatever is available about transitions is another way to learn. This includes noticing articles in the popular press reporting on handoffs of CEOs in other companies. A third way is to keep a journal of thoughts and questions. After a few weeks of doing so, patterns begin to emerge and areas to delve into in more detail become more apparent. They provide the targets for further reading as well as for conversations with executives in other companies. Throughout this process, major players must keep an open mind, a mind available to learning other approaches and other perspectives.

A third key success factor is to recognize when the transition is at a critically important crossroads and as much as possible to be prepared to react in the best way. There are four important crossroads. One is the step in the transition process outlined in Figure 5.1 that calls for matching the profile of the most promising candidate with the company's strategy and culture as well as with the facilitating and hindering factors affecting a successful handoff. If the various components of this step are correct and if the CEO gets this step right, the best road to follow lies ahead.

Another crossroads is related to the final factor about learning. As the CEO learns about what is necessary for a successful transition, he should recognize the gap between the way his organization behaves versus how it should behave for the transition to go well. Perhaps it involves the type of teamwork or the political structure. Whichever it is, how the gap is closed is a test for the CEO as well as for his leadership group. The choices are to try to act in ways that are unfamiliar just for the life of the transition, use the transition as a vehicle to make permanent changes, or do nothing differently at the risk of the transition's success.

A third important crossroads is the point at which the board and CEO agree on when and how the CEO will leave. Handling this well enables the CEO to depart on the right note, the board to concentrate on the relationship with the new leader, and the new leader to focus on taking hold. Leaving this to chance heightens the risk of taking the wrong path. If the CEO feels cast aside or that her needs are not being taken into account, there will be unnecessary hard feelings that will distract from the transition. The board plays a key role here, and the CHRO should have the sort of relationship with the CEO that he can help. The new leader must also show empathy for what the CEO is going through. In the end, of course, as we pointed out in Chapter 5, the CEO must take the responsibility for his own emotional management.

The fourth crossroads that must be handled well is the period between the new leader saying "yes" and his first day in the company. As we have pointed out, that should be a time of preparation, not only of relaxation. New leaders as well as the company's major players make the mistake of assuming the job begins when new leaders show up on the first day. In fact, the moment that they said "yes" the next phase of their careers began. Also, during this pre–Day 1 phase, the CEO, CHRO, and relevant directors have important parts to play. This is the time when the relationship starts. All the players must be ready to make the most of it.

As we said in the preface, it's never smooth or easy to transfer power. We have tried in this book to provide a balanced, complete, and objective guide to effective management on the company side of the equation of a top-level transition. The propositions and conclusions are the way we see it. We welcome others to weigh in with their points of view. There are no definitive how-to manuals, no easy answers, and no single best approach. The more well-thought through perspectives that boards, CEOs, CHROs, and senior managers hear, the better.

Note

1. For a useful treatment of this analogy, see Game Plans by Robert Keidel by Dutton, 1985.

INDEX

A

Abegglen, Jim, 99
Accountability, acceptance, 12
Achievement, social need/drive, 188
Acquisitions
  completion, 232
  target, CEO acceleration, 172
Active listening, 203, 204, 207
Aetna, 30
  executive committee, 74
Affiliation, social need/drive, 188
Aggressive listening, 203–204
Agreement phase, 163–165
American Express, 30
  learning model/protocols, change, 210
  senior manager candidate, formal
      style/personality assessments,
      57–58
Annual operating plans, 96
Assumed knowledge, arrogance, 79
Attention (cultural/political), 148–150
Authority, challenges, 2

B

Ballard, Shari, 101
Beckhard, Dick, 106
Behan, Beverly, 147
Behavioral Science Center of Sterling
      Institute, 99
Behavior layer, understanding, 42
Behavior patterns, policy support, 41
Beliefs layer, understanding, 42
Berger, Dennis, 210
Best Buy, 30
  recruiters, 101

Biogen-Idec, 30
Boards
  accountability, 128
    fulfilling, 125
    management, 1
  accountability, acceptance, 12
  adjustments, 27–29
  agenda, control, 129
  blame, assignation, 122–123
  buddies, 133–134
  Chief Executive Officer (CEO)
    collaborative relationship, 142–143
    management, 128
    partnerships, 136
    relationship, 22–23, 135–138, 200
    struggle, 63
  complexity, increase, 29
  confidence, absence, 117–118
  decisions, 120–121
  direction, setting, 133
  director search, 28
  discussions
    facilitation, 147
    tension, 87
  distance, requirement, 118
  experience/skill base, 141
  failure, causes, 123
  feedback, 124
  formal appraisal, format/details
      (clarification), 145–146
  forward-looking view, 132–133
  handoff, example, 117–118
  involvement (Telstra), 124–125
  job completion, mistake, 28–29
  knowledgeability, 245

Boards (*Continued*)
  leader, relationship, 135
    formation, 12–13
  management, 135
  meeting
    blindsiding, 23
    outside counsel, presence, 63
    requirement, 123–124
  members
    CEO role, 169
    sensitivity, 239
  miscommunication, avoidance,
    119–120
  open dialog, 143
  plans, agreement, 130–131
  primary objective, preparation, 35–36
  relationships, 222
    strain, 64
  respect, 143
  responsibilities, 10
    failure, 137
    sharing, 64–65
  roles, 11–13, 65, 117
    fulfillment, 13
    parts, 126–127
  self-assessment, 124
  specifications, draft, 32
  succession plan, development, 5
  tension, relief, 87
  transition
    failure, 122
    role, flowchart, 127f
    work, 125
Boston Consulting Group, 99
Bower, Marvin, 103
Breakwaters, institution, 57
Broussard, Bruce, 179–181
  Huval hiring, 182
  style, 182
Businesses
  commercial side, enjoyment, 221–222
  financial ups/downs, 139
  growth, 66
  management, control (requirement),
    128–129
  reorientation, 112
  strategic crossroads, 222
  strategic/operational objectives,
    113–114
  takeover, 230–231
Business units
  combination, 37
  impact, 40

C
Candidates
  recruitment process, 51–53
  specifications/profile, 164
  style/personality, external assessment
    (company usage), 70–71
Career
  examination, 48
  example, 81
CDW, 30
  learning model/protocol, 210
Chairman, promotion, 86
Chairwoman, responsibility (abdication),
    122
Chambers, Susan, 133
Chief Executive Officer (CEO)
  acquisition target acceleration, 172
  adjustments, 8, 25–27
  agreement phase, 163–165
  assessment, 37–38
  assistance, provision, 61
  assumptions, 70
  behavior, 60
    characterization, 145
  board
    collaborative relationship, 142–143
    partnerships, 136
    relationship, 22–23, 135–138, 200
    struggle, 63
  CEO-as-counselor model, 156
  CEO-designate, naming, 119
  communicator, role, 31
  core beliefs/values, 159
  credibility, 189
  crossroads, 251
  day-to-day business, 40
  decisions, 225

departure, 3–4, 171
  assumptions, 120
  desire, 119
diligence/dedication, 175–176
direct reports, 33
disagreement, 69
discussions, tension, 87
effectiveness, 155–156
efforts/schedule, 26–27
emotions, management, 15
execution-related work, 29
executive skill, 245
expectations, clarification, 32
foresight, 56–57
frustration, 59
global public company exit, 3
growth plans, 130–131
handoffs, 160
  support, 167
hiring, 51, 139
imperatives, 14–15
interim CEO, installation, 132–133,
    215–216
interpreter, role, 31
involvement, 134
job
  responsibilities/objectives, 159
  search, 222–223
leadership, strength, 223
learning curve, 235–236
management style, net effects, 129
mastery, 248
meeting, 131
motivation, 189–190
next-generation CEOs, 133
objectives/directives, communication
    clarity, 16
overlap, lengthening, 227
pacing, 70
performance, 64
  board assessment, 145
  tailoring, 14
personal issues, 67
persuasion, ability, 167
planning, absence, 60
promotion, 86

resignation decision, 129–130, 133
responsibilities
  fulfillment, 172
  sharing, 64–65
retirement, 226
  date, agreement, 27
review, first draft, 110f
roles, 13–15, 65, 158–162
search, 162–166
  phases, 162–163
  preparation/agreement, 162–164
  process, 165
self-awareness success, 171
self-management, 14–15
  success, 171
senior manager
  concerns, 219
  report, 2
sitting CEO, impact, 140
stakeholders, perspective, 25
stepping down, 223
strategy, 169–170
subordinate, interaction, 159–160
succession, complexity, 23–24
successors
  designation, 62
  origin, 110–111
  possibilities, 109–110
  reporting, 144–145
successors, relationship (failure), 173
survival, 204
taking-hold plan, 149–150
tasks, 98, 224–225
tenures, 36
time, 173
  allotment, 52
  conservation, 76
titles, 226
  relinquishment, 28
  usage, 157
transition, 126, 162–166
  board complexity, increase, 29
  challenge, 157
  director job, 156–157
  duration, 64
  process, 165

Chief Executive Officer (CEO)
(*Continued*)
RASI chart, production, 108
role, flowchart, 158f
Chief Financial Officer (CFO)
first-round interview, 42
functional capability, 53–54
hiring, organization preparedness,
52–53
IT reporting, 37–38, 53
leadership style, 40–41
needs/style, 55–56
position, acceptance, 48–49, 231
presence, 202
promotion, 48
path change, 131–132
retirement, 231
Chief Human Resources Officer (CHRO)
adjustments, 8, 29–32
advisory role, 15–17
assistance
failure, 59–60
provision, 61
behavior, 60
characteristics, 246
communication improvement,
207–208
competency, 209–210
connecting, 201–203
director, interaction, 140–141
feedback, 140
information, 228
collection, 248
internal advisor, 188
role, 15–16
interviews, research, 30
journal, creation, 209
operation, 24
opportunity, 182–183, 187
perseverance, 75
perspective, 125
planning, absence, 60
position, 183–184
role, 186
priority, 52
problem solving, 76

propositions/prescriptions, 190
questions, 75
recruitment, 30
responsibility, 113, 191
review, first draft, 110f
role, 10, 16–18, 180, 186
search contact, 75–76
style assessment, impact, 61
support responsibility, 199
tasks, 98
top-level transition, 199
transition
coordination, 185
role, flowchart, 184f
steps, 190
Chief human resources officer (CHRO),
search process coordination, 1–2
Chief Learning Officer (CLO), 111
Chief-of-staff position, 74
Chief Operating Officer (COO)
experience, 166
hiring, 37, 204
impact, 27–28
leadership, impact, 225
role, 33
tension, 63–64
Chief Technology Officer (CTO)
position, creation, 59
CHRO. *See* Chief Human Resources
Officer
Clark, David, 210
Client, ability, 156
Coalition building
abilities, development, 246–247
leader action, 193, 196–198
learning/visioning, contrast,
196–197
Coalitions
blocking, 197
winning, 197
Commitment, capture, 198
Communication
company norm determinant,
103–104
formal lines, 97
forum, absence, 102

improvement
  mechanisms, CHRO usage, 207–208
  usefulness, 55–56
miscommunication, avoidance,
    119–120
plan, usage, 170
problem, 141
Communicator, role, 31
Companies
  assumptions, problems, 67
  balance sheet, strength, 86
  board objective, culture preparation,
    35–36
  candidate style/personality assessment,
    70–71
  capabilities, knowledge, 88
  components, absence, 132
  cultural norms, leadership
      understanding, 78
  directors, assumptions, 62
  examination, 50
  execution error, 10
  failures, reasons, 88–89
  fortunes, growth, 215
  handoff, smoothness, 170
  improvement, 60
  inherited structure, problems, 37
  innovation, reputation (stagnation), 86
  joining, transition myth, 58–62
  norms, determinants, 103–104
  operational infrastructure, 36–38
  operation, leader learning, 97–98
  performance, culture (impact),
    100–101
  personnel, self-awareness, 76
  political environment, 70
  political structure, leadership
      understanding, 77
  political system, CHRO advisor, 15
  products/services, life cycles, 111
  public-company experience, 51
  reorganization, plans (finalization), 66
  resources, control, 27
  running, 147, 169
  structure, resistance, 54
  success, change (requirements), 89

term, meaning, 6
well-being, long-term benefits, 39
Compensation Committee,
    recommendation, 168
Competitiveness, impact, 81
Complexity, 21, 25
  elements, 32–33
Connecting, 201–203
Conservative traditionalist,
    self-description, 81
Consultants, financial analysis, 66
Cooperation
  ability, 247–248
  company norm determinant,
    103–104
Coordinator, role, 31
Core beliefs, 41–42
Core concepts (understanding), education
    programs (usage), 208
Corporate cultures, reaction, 153–154
Corporate decision-making style,
    179–180
Corporate leader, authority (example),
    154
Corporation
  resurgence, 69
  transitions
    failure, 24
    management, 21–22
Counselor
  personality/skills, 161
  role, 155
Coworkers, 360-degree appraisal, 60
Cross-functional design/development
    teams, impact, 107
Crossroads, 250–252
Cultural attention, 148–150
Cultural challenges, 149
Cultural factors, importance, 106
Cultural knowledge, usage, 148
Cultural landscape, directorial
    management, 148
Cultural norms, leadership
    understanding, 78
Cultural pyramid, 42f
Cultural systemic adjustments, 41–45

Culture
    attention, 13
    change, 42–43
    creation, 128–129
    difference, 82
    impact, 100–101
    influence, 104
    mastery. *See* Organization.
    nature, understanding, 148
    power structure, relationship, 98–104
    study, 105
Curiosity, impact, 250
Curricula developer, 161
Customers
    relationships, impact, 94
    visits, usage, 40

D

Decision-making. *See* One-alone way
        decision-making
    authority, 108
Decision-making style, 159
    caution, 70
    corporate decision-making style,
        179–180
    diagnosis. *See* Leadership.
    discussion, 44
Decisions, communication, 38
Department cooperation, necessity,
        102
Derivative defections, 84–85, 93–96
    possibility, 95
    syndrome, 94
        impact/damage, 94–95
Destructive myths, 47
Digital media, usage, 210
Directors
    assumptions, 62
    balance, absence, 142
    CHRO, interaction, 140–141
    experience/skills, 142
    impact, rationale, 118
    involvement, range, 120
    players, status, 121–127
    questions, 138

Direct reports, 51–52
    impact, 218
Discussions, 44
    facilitation, 147
    one-on-one discussions, 155
    sessions, 238
    tension, 87
Distribution center, same-store
        sales/financing, 215
District managers, problems, 205
Distrust, mutual respect (contrast), 138
Dividends, payment, 148
Division
    president, naming/retention, 68
    revenue/cost targets, failure, 68
    support staff, migration, 72

E

Education programs, usage, 208
Emotional legacy, 175
Empathy, 141
    absence, 71–73, 142
Empowerment, concept, 216
Endorsement, 22–23
Engagement
    rules, 141
    senior manager rules, 219
Engineering, head (retirement), 102
Enron (scandal), 136
Enterprise resource planning (ERP)
        system, analysis, 47–48
Entrepreneurial competitors, emergence,
        130
Environment, collaboration, 104–105
EVP. *See* Executive vice president
Execution
    errors, 9–11, 81, 84
        CHRO responsibility, 113
    execution-related work, 29
    leader contact, 30
Executives
    chairs, nonexecutive chairs (impact),
        137–138
    conference meeting, 224
    control, 217–218

effects, 79
entry, 59
hiring rationale, 95–96
meeting, 161
next-in-line executives, hiring, 5
pressures/needs, understanding,
112–113
psychologist interviews, 133–134
reporting, 217
responsibility chart, 32
search firm, location, 22
senior-level executive, hiring, 109–110
skills, 245
acquisition, 95
strategic paths, 89–90
win-win outcome, 88
Executives, transition, 21
Executive vice president (EVP), 230
opinion, importance, 168
promotion, 232
Expectations, 146–148
clarification, 146
defining, inadequacy, 106
layer, understanding, 42
list, 147

F
Failure
reasons, 20f
roots, 7–20
Fasolo, Peter, 184
Feedback, 124, 140
Finance department, problems, 55
Finance organization
competency, 49
solidity, 53
Financial package, shaping, 112
Financial performance, analysis, 236
Formal style/personality assessments,
57–58

G
General Electric, Immelt (CEO), 94
Gerstner, Lou (IBM control), 34–35

Glass Door (media site), 98
Goal, achievement (satisfaction),
233–234
Gorsky, Alex, 185
Governance pressure points, 154
Great Companies Deserve Great Boards
(Behan), 147
Growth expectations, meeting, 35

H
Hands-on experience, impact, 51
Harvard Business School, 99
Heidrick & Struggles, executive search
survey, 85
Heroic mission, 174
Heroic stature, 174
Hero's Farewell, The (Sonnenfeld), 174
Hewlett Packard (Whitman arrival),
34–35
High-level managers, changes
(implementation), 216
Hiring decisions, 183–184
Home Depot (Nardelli CEO), 94
Humana, 30, 189
Broussard, hiring, 179
traditions/values, 181–182
Humana, interviews (focus), 57
Huval, Tim, 180–181, 189
hiring, 182

I
IBM (Gerstner arrival), 34–35
Immelt, Jeff (Welch replacement),
94
Incumbent
board, relationship (dynamics),
138
successor, relationship, 85–90
In-depth conversations, usage, 55–56
Inferential data, interpretation, 41
Influence
manifestation, 105
power, relationship, 104–106
skills, 246–247

Information
  collection, 248
  infrastructure system, 36–38
  organization/interpretation, absence,
      96–106
  requirement, miscalculation, 84
  sessions, 238
Information technology (IT), 130
  centralization, 167–168
  department, report, 37–38
Infrastructure, systems, 36–38
Initial Public Offering (IPO), 170, 240
Innovation, increase, 101–102
In-process programs, documentation, 50
Institutional investors, growth, 136
Institutional knowledge, usage, 94
Insubordination, term (usage), 168
Interim CEO, installation, 132–133,
      215–216
Interpersonal factors, 209
Interpersonal skills, 155–156,
      246–247
Interpreter, role, 31
Interviews, 149
  focus, 57
  preparation, 96
Involvement, company norm
      determinant, 103–104
IPO. *See* Initial Public Offering
ITW, 30

J
Japan, production systems, 100
Job, completion myth, 58, 62–65
Johnson & Johnson (J&J), 30, 184–185
Joly, Hubert, 101
Journals, usage, 209
Just-in-Time (JIT) delivery, 114
Just-in-Time (JIT) programs,
      development, 99–100

K
Kanban (JIT process), 100
Know, term (emphasis), 65–66

L
Leadership
  actions, 193
  arrival, preparation, 227–228
  assistance, 193
  board, relationship, 135
    formation, 12–13
  capabilities, 88
  CEO-designate, naming, 119
  challenges, 120
  changes, implementation, 38, 40, 189
  continuity, 62
  control/establishment process, 77–78
  crisis, factors, 83
  decision-making style, diagnosis, 38
  decisions, 133
    communication, 38
  departure, 84, 90–93
  direction, change, 69
  direct reports, 218
  distance, maintenance, 176
  due diligence, 96–97
  educational program, 236
  entry, preparation, 90
  experience, 247
  handoff, 125
    elements, placement, 13
  information, input (process), 38
  isolation, 176
  onboarding, mishandling, 109–114
  personality/style, 166
  philosophy
    focus, 238
    understanding, 43
  predecessor, impact, 39–40
  profile (determination), cultural
      knowledge (usage), 148
  question responses, 146–147
  reorganization, 37
  self-image, exploration, 174
  situation, complexity, 23–24
  specifications, 223
  strategy, grafting, 76–77
  strengths/weaknesses, 74–75
  style, 236

style/priorities, adaptation, 18–19
success, 191
    difficulty, 65
successor spot, 144
transitions, 26
    complexity, 7–8, 25
    problems, 47
    term, meaning, 6
    vision, blocks, 195–196
Lean program, 61
    launching, 54
    responsibility, 49
Learning
    absence, 73–74
    blocking, 193–194
    CEO initiative, 74
    coalition building, contrast, 196–197
    curve, 235–236
    factors, 248–251
    image, shaping, 195
    initiation, 73
    leader action, 193–194
    programs, suggestion, 109–110
Learning and people development
    (L&PD) department, 161
Lecturing, avoidance, 207
Legacy
    categories, 175
    evidence, 176
    term, usage, 175
Listening, 203
    active listening, 203–204, 207
    aggressive listening, 203
    passive listening, 203
    types, 203
Litwin, George, 99
Livingstone, Catherine, 124–125
Lloyd's of London, 123–124
L&PD. See Learning and people
    development

M

Make-sure list, 237
Management
    development efforts, change, 95–96

scrutiny, increase, 137
self-management, 154, 171–177
style, effects, 129
team, components, 50–51
training programs, delivery, 111
Managers
    change, 75
    departures, 93–94
    district managers, problems, 205
    high-level managers, changes
        (implementation), 216
    industry leaders, 50
    loyalty, 39–40
    power, 232–233
    sounding board, 31
    transitions, problems, 47
Marketplace, response, 37
Market share
    capture, 70
    gaining, failure, 68
Market tours, usages, 40
Mayer, Marissa (Yahoo control),
    34–35
Mayo, Elton (Western Electric projects),
    99
McCallister, Mike, 179–180
McClelland, David, 188
McKinsey & Co., 103
McMillon, Doug, 134
McNerney, James (3M CEO), 94
Measurement (infrastructure system),
    36–38
    merging/conversion, 36
Meetings
    importance, CHRO understanding,
        202
    information/discussion sessions, 238
    make-sure list, usage, 237
    one-on-one meetings, 201
    senior managers, 239
Mega-division, running, 68
Moore School of Business study, 183
Moralizing, avoidance, 207
Motivational style, impact, 81
Murray, Jim, 179–180
Mutual respect, distrust (contrast), 138

N

Nardelli, Robert, 94
Negative emotions, senior manager
        origin, 230
Negotiations, 149–150
New York Stock Exchange rules, 136–137
Next-generation CEOs, 133
Non-executive chairman, interactions,
        139
Nonexecutive chairs, impact, 137–138
Notebooks, construction, 236, 239–240

O

Onboarding
    effort, problems (reasons), 112–113
    experience, 112
    mismanagement, 113
    programs, 114
        preparation, 240
One-alone way decision-making, 43
One-on-one discussions, 155
One-on-one meetings, 201
Operating divisions, responses, 55
Operational changes, impact, 221
Operational factors, assessment, 163–164
Operational momentum, maintenance,
        77
Operational review, 89
Operational systemic adjustments, 36–38
Opinion, shaping, 19–20
Organization
    central nervous system, formation,
        97–98
    CEO impact, 42–43
    change
        management, 198
        readiness/capacity, CHRO
            understanding, 188–189
        senior manager perspective, 221
    culture, mastery, 101
    day-to-day work, 228
    determination, director knowledge, 123
    development consultants, impact, 99
    external forces, 98
    image, impact, 195

leader
    entry, 246–247
    impact, 40
    opinion, shaping, 220, 227
    preparation, 32–33, 150
    preparedness, absence, 52–53
    state, optimum, 167
    structure, 96
Organizational change, challenges, 2
Ownership patterns, change, 136–137

P

Partnerships, 12
Passive-aggressive behavior, 228–229
Passive listening, 203
Passivity, 72
Pension funds, usage, 136
Performance
    adequacy, 144
    improvement, CEO impatience, 59
    judgment, 143–146
    review, 183–184
        mechanics, 143
Personality
    assessments, usage, 111, 238
    style, 236
Pioneer simplicity, 181
Planned transition, 7
Plants, capabilities (understanding),
        231
Players
    impact, 249
    status, 121–127
    transition understanding, 250
Policy decisions, making, 154
Political attention, 148–150
Political environment, 70
    understanding, plan, 55–56
Political factors, 209
Political landscape, senior leader
        interpretation, 182
Political skills, impact, 105
Political structure, leadership
        understanding, 77
Political support, absence, 72

Political systemic adjustments, 39–41
Politics layer, understanding, 42
Power
  influence, relationship, 104–106
  manifestation, 105
  social need/drive, 188
  structure, 148
    advantage, 143
    CHRO understanding, 197–198
    culture, relationship, 98–104
  topic, 187
Preproduction manufacturing, 102
Prescriptions, avoidance, 207
Presentation skills, impact, 81
President
  job offer/acceptance, 67–68
  naming/retention. *See* Division.
Private equity firm partners,
    235–236
Private-equity investors, executive hiring,
    21–22
Problem resolution, absence, 89
Productive thinking, transition myths
    (impact), 71–76
Productivity, decline, 226
Products
  cross-functional design/development
    teams, impact, 107
  development, revitalization, 82
  innovation, 101–102
  life cycle, 111
Profit, elusiveness, 83
Progress, feedback, 100
Projects, time pressure, 107–108
Promotion, theoretical paths, 97
Prototype manufacturing, 102
Psychologist interviews, 133–134

Q

Qualitative success, quantitative success
    (contrast), 143
Qualitative targets, board measurement,
    145
Questioning, absence, 74–76
Questions, variety, 165

R

RASI. *See* Responsibility, authority,
    support, inform
Rational legacy, 175
Readiness, myth, 58, 65–71
Reassurance, avoidance, 207
Recruiter, selection, 149
Recruitment process, importance, 57
Relationships
  building, 234
  establishment/nurturing, board
    consideration, 135–136
  expectations, 118
  impact, 140–141
  management, 134, 147–148
  methods/mechanisms, 198
  types, 200f
Resources, control, 233
Responsibility
  agreement, clarification, 108
  chart, 32
  charting, 106–107, 184, 209–210
    origin, 106–107
  failure, 137
Responsibility, authority, support,
    inform (RASI) chart, 106,
    107f, 209
  production, 108
  written chart, 109
Retention bonus, 68
Retirement. *See* Engineering
  date, agreement. *See* Chief Executive
    Officer.
  enjoyment, 216
  mandatoriness, 139–140
Reward and recognition system, usage,
    103
Rewards (infrastructure system),
    36–38
  merging/conversion, 36
Risk management functions, 130
Rituals layer, understanding, 42
Rock Center for Corporate Governance,
    executive search survey, 85
Rodgers, Carl, 207

Roles
  assignments, formulation
  clarity, 106
  types, 200f

S

Sales meetings, usage, 40
Sales plan, progress (relationship), 40
Same-store sales, 215
Sarbanes-Oxley legislation, 136–137
Self-awareness, 171–177
  CEO success, 171
Self-confidence, impact, 81
Self-management, 154, 171–177
  CEO success, 171
Senior leaders
  advocacy/resource, 182
  success, 6
Senior-level executive, hiring, 109–110
Senior-level managers, leader conviction,
    237–238
Senior-level people, onboarding
    (mismanagement), 113
Senior management team, misnomer, 153
Senior managers, 18–19
  adjustments, 32–34
  attention, 32
  candidate, formal style/personality
      assessments, 57–58
  capabilities/potential, 95
  CEO encouragement, 229
  CHRO dependence, 191
  competition, 229
  defining, 33
  demoralization, 229
  departures, 93–94
  education, absence, 170–171
  effort, problem, 94
  emotions, increase, 32
  engagement/protocol rules, 219
  expectations, 235
  growth plans, 130–131
  imperatives, 19–20
  knowledgeability, 246
  leaders, entry, 33–34

meetings, 239
  negative emotions, origin, 230
  plans/systems/processes, adaptation,
      218–219
  position
    complexity, 218
    occupying, 228
  presentation, 240
  role, 18, 215
    flowchart, 220f
  tasks, 98
Senior positions, turnover, 4–5
Senior post, ability, 58, 65–71
Senior staff
  functions, 37
  support, 185–192
Senior team
  meetings, training programs, 217
  term, problem, 216
Services, life cycle, 111
Share of mind, 219
Shuttle diplomacy, 29
Six Sigma program, 61
  launch, 54
  responsibility, 49
Small-cap companies, CEO departures, 4
Social needs/drives, impact, 188
Sonnenfeld, Jeffrey, 174
Stakeholders, impact, 82–83
Stalk, George, 99
Steering committee, reinstitution, 103
Strategic factors, assessment, 163–164
Strategic opportunities, 120
Strategic paths, 89–90
Strategic priorities, 218
Strategic review, 89
Strategic systemic adjustments, 34–36
  balance, 35
Strengths/shortcomings, prediction, 149
Style assessment, 238
  impact, 61
  usage, 111
Success
  factors, 156, 247–251
  roles, 11–16
Succession, director involvement, 87–88

Successors
   CEO relationship, failure, 173
   coaching, 119
   designation, 144–145
   execution, 35
   handoff, blockage, 69
   hiring, 2–3
   incumbent, relationship, 85–90
   management, CEO right, 63
   relationship, 22–23
   spot, designation, 144
   transition, CEO understanding, 156
Success rates, improvement (problem),
       5–6
Success roles, 11–18
Superstructure, description, 51
Suppliers, predictability, 25
Supply chain, 49
   creation, 82
Support
   delivery, 227
   forms, 200
   provision, 108
Systemic adjustments, 34–45

T

Taking-hold plan, review, 149–150
Tasks
   difficulty, 155
   list, formulation, 154
Teams, approaches, 108
Teamwork, 141
   ensuring, 141
   requirement, 248
   training programs, 217
Telstra, 30
   board, involvement, 124–125
Tenures
   duration, 53
   obtaining, 44
   talent, growth, 94
Thinking, 209–210
   clarity, absence, 47
   errors, 8–9
Thodey, David, 124–125

3M, McNerney (CEO), 94
Thrive together principle, 181
Top-level handoffs,
       complexities/dynamics, 246
Top-level transition, 8–9
Total Quality programs, development,
       99–100
Traditions layer, understanding, 42
Training programs, 208
Transaction-based connection, 134–135
Transition myths, 9
   destructiveness, 78
   embracing, 72
   impact, 56, 71–76
   learning, absence, 73–74
   questioning, absence, 74–76
   types, 58
Transitions
   addressing, delay, 126
   attention, nonrequirement, 58–59
   board work, 125
   CEO role, flowchart, 158f
   challenge, 3–7
   challenge, CEO success, 157
   CHRO coordination, 185
   completion, 62
   complexity, 7–8, 31, 121
   continuation, 162–163
   coordination, 186–187
   core concepts (understanding),
       education programs (usage), 208
   crossroads, recognition, 250–251
   description, 240
   direction, CEO role, 153
   director
       job, 156–157
       responsibility, 160
   duration, 64
   empathy, absence, 71–73
   failure, 24, 87–88, 122
       reasons, 88
       risk, calculation, 131
   failure, cost, 4
   images, clarity, 160
   implementation, mastery, 190
   learning, 249–250

Transitions (*Continued*)
  management, 23
    CHRO initiative, 202–203
    example, 21–22
    preparation, 84
  oversight, 127–134
  pace, control, 157
  phases, 163f
  plan, 158–159, 174, 183, 234–235
  planned transition, 7
  political systemic adjustments, impact,
    39–40
  preparation, 90
  problems, 47
  process, 165
    compromise, 63
    image, formation, 165–166
    implementation, CHRO mastery,
      191–192
    mismanagement, 10–11, 84, 96, 106
  requirement, 69
  risk, calculation, 131
  role, flowchart, 127f, 184f
  senior manager role, 18
  steps, control, 157
  success, 76–77
    barriers, 57
    framework, 20f
  support, 201
  thinking, inadequacy, 57–58
  top-level transition, 8–9
  types, 6–7
True partnerships, 12
Tunnel vision, 10

U
U.S. Securities and Exchange
    Commission (SEC), federal
    prosecutor role, 205

V
Vetting process, 70–71
Vice president, performance (impact),
    67–68
Visioning
  coalition building, contrast,
    196–197
  leader action, 193, 194–196
  mental process, 195

W
Walmart, 30
  global trends, outlook, 133
  inside promotions, 134
Watkins, Michael, 114
Welch, Jack, 94
Weldon, Bill, 185
Western Electric (Mayo projects), 99
Western Nigeria Civil Service, 106
Whitepapers, 208–209
Whitman, Meg (Hewlett Packard
    control), 34–35
Working relationship, creation, 88
WorldCom (scandal), 136

Y
Yahoo (Mayer arrival), 34–35